Praise for *The Faith of Donald J. Trump*

"David Brody has real insight into a question on many people's minds: What is Donald Trump's faith and how does it relate to the presidency? A longtime D.C. reporter, Brody has access to insider accounts from those closest to Donald Trump. Brody's decades on the political beat of D.C. lay a foundation to help unravel the intriguing man that is Donald Trump and the faith that motivates him. You'll be glad you took the time to read David Brody's important book."

—Michele Bachmann

"If you're looking to fully understand Donald Trump's unique relationship with evangelicals, you've found the right book. David Brody is one of the few journalists in America who not only has gotten to know Trump very well but also has firsthand knowledge of his relationships inside evangelical circles. Combine that with Scott Lamb's vast comprehension of the history of evangelical Christianity in America, and what you have is a must-read piece of history that will serve as the definitive chapter on the association between Donald Trump and the evangelicals who propelled him to the White House."

—Ralph Reed, founder of the Faith and
Freedom Coalition

"Why do evangelicals have unprecedented access to this president? What explains the high number of Christian cabinet members and appointees in this White House? Read *The Faith of Donald J. Trump* to find out. Brody and Lamb reveal new material drawn from exclusive interviews with President Trump and evangelical leaders. The result is fascinating and important."

—Dr. Jerry A Johnson, president and CEO,
National Religious Broadcasters

"David Brody and Scott Lamb hit the mark as they take you inside Donald Trump's spiritual journey, dating back from his childhood and all the way to the White House. President Trump's desire to 'Make America Great Again' is rooted in his fervent belief in the Judeo-Christian history of our country. Brody and Lamb provide the crucial link that gives clarity to one of the most transformational figures in American history."

—Pastor Robert Jeffress, First Baptist Church, Dallas

The Faith of DONALD J. TRUMP

The Faith of
DONALD J. TRUMP

A SPIRITUAL BIOGRAPHY

DAVID BRODY AND
SCOTT LAMB

HARPER

An Imprint of HarperCollins*Publishers*
www.harpercollins.com

HarperCollins books may be purchased for educational, business, or sales promotional use. For information, please email the Special Markets Department at SPsales@harpercollins.com.

FIRST EDITION

Library of Congress Cataloging-in-Publication Data

Names: Brody, David, 1965- author.
Title: The faith of Donald J. Trump : a spiritual biography /
   David Philip Brody.
Description: FIRST EDITION. | New York, NY : Broadside Books, 2018. |
   Includes bibliographical references and index.
Identifiers: LCCN 2017048086 (print) | LCCN 2017052778 (ebook) |
   ISBN 9780062749598 (ebk) | ISBN 9780062749581 (hc : alk. paper) |
   ISBN 9780062749604 (pb : alk. paper)
Subjects: LCSH: Trump, Donald, 1946—Religion. | Presidents—United
   States—Biography.
Classification: LCC E913.3 (ebook) | LCC E913.3 .B76 2018 (print) |
   DDC 973.933092 [B]—dc23
LC record available at https://lccn.loc.gov/2017048086

18 19 20 21 22   DIX/LSC   10 9 8 7 6 5 4 3 2 1

David: To my exquisite wife Lisette, the smartest woman I know, with an enduring spirit who allows me to pursue my passions.

Scott: Dedicated to Walter and Rexanna Lamb, a father and mother who helped me to see the beauty of Jesus Christ. And by hauling me around to see historical places as a child, gave me a love for our God-blessed nation. When I read the Bible verse, "To whom much has been given"—I immediately thank God for having you as my parents.

CONTENTS

Foreword

When my friend David Brody told me he was writing a book titled *The Faith of Donald J. Trump*, I was tempted to laugh. But I didn't.

The reason I didn't laugh was because I know that David Brody is an extraordinary journalist and a real man of faith, so if anyone could tackle this very difficult and thorny subject seriously, he could, and with his coauthor Scott Lamb, he has done just that. In fact, what they have produced in this volume is downright impressive, and on several levels, too. The scope of their research is nothing less than extraordinary; you will learn things in this book that I am sure you will never read anywhere else. By the way, this is what journalists are supposed to, but these days rarely, do—so my heartiest congratulations to these authors for taking the hoary path that was once the mainstay of all journalism: digging for facts.

But I must say it once more, that at first, I really was tempted to giggle. Because if anyone besides Brody and Lamb had used a title like *The Faith of Donald J. Trump*, I would have sworn it was one of those political gag books you see every now and again. Remember *The Wit and Wisdom of Sarah Palin*? Or *Reasons to Vote for a Democrat*? And of course the big goofball joke is that when you open it up, you see nothing but blank pages. Ha ha ha. Don't forget to slap your knee.

So this is not that sort of book at all, but the dissonance most people feel when they think of the subject of Trump and faith must be acknowledged. I guess this would be a good time for me to confess that a year before the election—before I dreamed that it would eventually come down to a Battle of Armageddon showdown between

Donald Trump and Hillary Clinton—I had some fun with the subject of Trump and faith myself when I wrote a humor piece for the *New Yorker* titled "A Few More #TrumpBible Verses." The made-up "bible verses" were of course in the form of Trumpian tweets. Here are a few you might remember:

> In the beginning was the Word, and the Word was TERRIFIC. And also HUUUUGE. #TrumpBible

> Nathan said to David, "You are the man!" And David said, "No, YOU are the man!" And they high-fived each other. It was fabulous. #TrumpBible

> Among whom was Mary Magdalene, Mary the mother of Jesus, and the mother of James & John. Three classy ladies. TREMENDOUS class. #TrumpBible

Enough? Well, the point of quoting these dumb jokes here is to say that I actually think it's good to laugh sometimes—especially when something dissonant presents itself. And as I have already said, what could be more dissonant than the subjects of Donald Trump and faith?

Which is precisely what makes this book so bold and so extraordinary.

Because the simple fact—and an indigestible conundrum to so many—is that Donald Trump has demonstrated two things that typically don't go together at all. On the one hand, he has been tremendously popular with evangelical Christians and outspoken in his defense of faith in public life; on the other hand, he has evinced a startling lack of familiarity with the Bible and has even admitted being unable to recall ever asking for God's forgiveness. Nor need we mention that his personal life before running for president and his tweets before, during, and—alas!—after have been less than what one might expect of someone advocating for many of the issues dear to the hearts of those for whom faith is paramount.

But the terrifically stubborn fact is that Donald Trump has been embraced by many serious Christians, and this has caused many Christians and non-Christians alike to seethe with fury at the seeming hypocrisy of the whole arrangement. One vital clue to solving this thorny riddle has to do with what may well be the most fundamental dissonance and misunderstanding in the history of the world. I'm talking about the difference between moral behavior on the one hand and grace and faith in the God of the Bible on the other.

Martin Luther rightly clarified this for all time five centuries ago, but even some of the most devout Christians have confused the two ever since. So to be clear, the God of the Bible does not ask us to be morally perfect so that He will accept us. He asks us to admit that we cannot be morally perfect, to see that only He can be morally perfect, and to understand that if we have any hope in being accepted by Him, it lies in our acceptance and confession of these facts.

People who understand this therefore understand the concept of grace and are willing to give grace to those who—as they—are morally imperfect. But those for whom God is a moralistic taskmaster (some will call them Pharisees) do not understand this and predictably rage against it. The elder brother in the parable of the Good Samaritan is an infamous example of that extremely sad ilk.

All the more reason then to robustly commend Messrs. Brody and Lamb for doughtily wading into these roiling waters. In the process, they have plumbed such astounding depths of this president's biography that we will all learn many, many things—and are therefore all in their debt. *Soli Deo Gloria.*

Eric Metaxas

New York City

November 2017

Introduction: This Trump Is Your Trump

I heard footsteps and turned my head to see Donald J. Trump dressed in a neatly pressed white shirt and silver tie strutting boldly toward me at a brisk pace. He had something in his hand—a paper of some sort. Maybe it was a contract to sign before the interview? Is that what these rich businessmen do? Surely not.

On a sunny spring day in 2011, I sat twenty-five floors above the streets of midtown Manhattan, soaking in the beautiful skyline of my hometown from the window of Trump Tower. With my Christian Broadcasting Network (CBN) crew at my side, I was geared up for my first interview with the mega-billionaire who owned the building.

He walked into the room, shook my hand, and gave me the item. "Here you go," Trump said matter-of-factly. "I thought you might be able to use this for the interview." It was a black-and-white picture of his June 1959 Christian confirmation class, taken at First Presbyterian Church in Jamaica, Queens, New York. As we moved to our seats, I could tell how proud he was of that picture showing a young, just-turned-thirteen Donald standing alongside his fellow confirmation graduates.

Looking back, the process for getting that interview turned out to be simple. I sent an email to Michael Cohen, his lawyer and part of his public relations team—and one of the first people to seriously push the idea of Trump running for president. Trump had flirted with this idea a few times before, but in 2011 the conversation seemed to be more serious. I would later learn that Trump had been making calls to friends—Christian friends—to ask for their prayers as he made the decision. I kept my pitch to Cohen simple: If Trump runs for president, he would need to start winning over evangelicals immediately—and what better way to begin than to sit down with CBN?

I knew I'd have to ask about everything: his relationship with God, his marriages, public policy positions, including his new pro-life stance—everything. But what I found remarkable is that I never received any pre-interview inquiries from his staff, poking into the specific interview topics. No Trump people reached out with "suggested questions" or "off-the-table topics." Nothing was off-limits, including matters of faith. In essence, Trump would just show up and be, well, Trump. He wasn't being handled, nor did he ask for a list of talking points that would be good for a Christian audience to hear. That's not Trump's style. He is who he is, and ultimately, even his detractors admit that the "let Trump be Trump" philosophy of being authentic helped propel him into the presidency.

Our wide-ranging interview was vintage Trump, as he launched into familiar lines of attack against China, the trade imbalance and how "the United States is getting ripped off," and how the world looks upon us as a "laughingstock." But it was something Trump said about "church attendance" that caught me off guard. "I go as much as I can. Always on Christmas. Always on Easter. Always when there's a major occasion. . . . And during Sundays. I'm a Sunday church person. I'll go when I can." The answer provided a valuable piece of information about Donald Trump: He was never going to pretend to be something he's not. Even talking to the Christian Broadcasting Network, he wouldn't pretend to be a born-again altar boy who has seen the light. Trump knew that game, but he wasn't going to play it, because what you say in Iowa should match what you say in New Hampshire. He grew up in the 1950s in a home that respected religion, the church, and the clergy—and part of that means you shouldn't invent piety to pander to a crowd.

. . .

Before we go any further, we should explain our use of "I" and "we" throughout the remainder of this book. The "we" refers to the fact that David Brody and Scott Lamb coauthored *The Faith of Donald J. Trump*. But whenever you see "I" it is Brody's firsthand reporting or personal narrative. David flew all over the nation covering the 2016 election, interviewing politicians on camera as the chief political correspondent for CBN. Scott attended dozens of campaign events across many states, but we felt the best way to create an enjoyable book was to have the "boots on the ground" reporting always be in David's voice. That said, each of us stands fully behind the entirety of the book.

One of the joys of writing this book together has been to test the theory that evangelicals who swim in different theological streams can work together on a joint venture—even one loaded with significance like a spiritual biography of a sitting president. In the endless conversations we have had since becoming friends, we are amazed at how our mutual evangelical friends don't talk to each other very much—and in many cases don't even know each other. We're referring to people who will enter eternity on the same side of the truth of John 3:16. So up front, we should tell you a little bit of our own background—not because this book is about us, but because an author's worldview invariably shapes a text written to explain "the faith" of another person.

David grew up in a Jewish household in Manhattan, though neither of his parents was very religious. Scott grew up in a Southern Baptist home in Missouri and was in church every time the door was open. David began coming to faith in Christ in college, through the influence of his girlfriend (now wife) Lisette—especially when she invited him to come with her to a charismatic church that had just gotten started—Times Square Church. Scott doesn't recall ever once being in a Pentecostal church growing up; individual Baptist churches didn't get fussy about it, but generally, there was a "we're not charismatic" approach within the Southern Baptist Convention (SBC).

David: In 1988, I professed faith in Christ as a newlywed living in Colorado. I was earning my stripes in broadcasting, originally on the producer's side of the camera but later transitioning to the on-camera side of the news. After sixteen years of reporting and winning an Emmy in the Rocky Mountain state, I went to work for CBN in 2003—one of the very first Christian television networks in America, brought into existence by Pat Robertson in 1961, four years before my birth.

Scott: In 1980, I professed faith in Christ as a kindergartner and was baptized by my dad, a bi-vocational SBC pastor who walked around singing "What can wash away my sin? Nothing but the blood of Jesus" and Johnny Cash's "A Boy Named Sue." I also became a bi-vocational pastor and served in Baptist churches for sixteen years while teaching and writing. In 2008, I went to work for Albert Mohler, the president of my seminary alma mater, as his researcher and editor. In 2012, I started Calliope Media in service to Christian authors and institutions. Now, as this book goes to press, I am moving across state lines and beginning new work as a vice president of Liberty University.

All that to say, though we have *not* spent a lifetime swimming in the same evangelical streams, we are united by our faith in and commitment to the Lord Jesus Christ. And as we look out at American evangelicalism and pray for the future of the church, we hope to see fewer silos being built and more breaking of bread together. This book itself has been a project built on that prayer.

So, what do we mean when we write "the faith" of Donald Trump? First, we are not primarily speaking about his "religious piety" (or the lack thereof if you listen to his critics). This book isn't about his external actions of spirituality, though such discussion is sprinkled throughout. Instead, we are mostly concerned to explain the worldview of the man—his framework and philosophy for understanding the world, himself, life, and eternity. Everybody has a worldview, though some people may not consciously examine or speak consistently about their system of beliefs. Like Muzak in an elevator or a fish in water, people have a personal worldview that surrounds them even when it goes unarticulated. We have written this book to explain the worldview background of Donald J. Trump (Part I) and how his structure of beliefs played out on the stage of the 2016 campaign and the first months of his administration (Part II).

Trump is most certainly *not* a secularist—someone who lives his life apart from religious belief or practice. As one who, for years, did not fight the label "billionaire playboy," Trump could be described as a pleasure-seeker or a materialist (values material things more than the spiritual). But Trump has not lived apart from religion. In this regard, he is very American. Though the demographics are shifting rapidly, for most of the country's history, a majority of American citizens would not have stated "none" when asked about their religious preference. Baby boomers like Trump practiced their religion in fits and spurts and sometimes not at all. They dropped out of denominational and theological commitments with the same ease that they divorced and lost trust in government institutions. But in the end, eight of ten baby boomers report an affiliation with religion.

Trump is the product of American culture, not an anomaly to it. To explain this, we'll tell stories from US history—including pop culture, as his pre–White House fame came through celebrity culture channels. Like Ronald Reagan's life before entering politics, people know Trump for the same reason they know Katy Perry or Perry Como. Our apologies to the reader if we drop a cultural reference point that makes no sense—it just means you need to ask your grandkids or your grandparents for help, whichever the case may be. But there's a second reason to toss pop culture into the chapters. We're a couple of conservative Christians who believe that politics is downstream from culture. To understand the current state of politics, it is important to understand the culture that gave birth to it.

Further, Trump is not an anomaly to either American religion in general or even American evangelicalism. He was born into the Mainline church that suffered the loss of two things during the twentieth century: biblical theology, and the vast majority of its membership. If Donald Trump, as a Presbyterian, can't recite the Westminster Confession or the books of the Bible, one might ask Presbyterian denominations why they stopped teaching the catechism long before Trump's birth.

And evangelicals (that's us) aren't off the hook, as one poll after another shows our biblical literacy rates are falling, our divorce rates are rising, and our commitment to live for Christ in our daily life is too often neither hot nor cold. We're not here to preach a sermon to anyone, but we do hope to promote some self-evaluation among evangelicals. Jesus talked about removing the log in our own eye first before we try and help remove dust in the eyes of others. We would agree with the evangelical scholar who wrote the following words a decade ago: "Voters don't just send a candidate to Washington; they send a message about what's important to them. When you identify with a candidate in a fundamental way, voting for the candidate is, in a sense, voting for yourself." Since eight of ten white evangelicals voted for Donald Trump for president—and during the GOP primary the "Bible Belt" states voted for him too— then what does that say about evangelicalism? We won't attempt to answer that huge question, but we do hope to add to the discussion.

When you are in the process of writing a book, your friends email you questions about the subject. One of the most often asked queries went something like this: "Is Trump a Christian?" Within the evangelical context that means "Is he born again?" or "Is he headed for heaven?" or "Is his name written in the Lamb's book of life?"

Okay, so just up front: We're not answering that question. We both have an opinion on that subject, and both of our opinions have shifted over the past two years. Instead, we've labored to let the voices of other people speak on this issue. Like when we interviewed Vice President Mike Pence for this book: "President Donald Trump is a believer. I say that with great conviction." Or again, "I think his faith in God and his faith in the American people are the foundation of his life and his service." Or, when we interviewed President Trump in the Oval Office: "I would say that the faith is that I am a believer. I believe. And when you believe, many good things can happen. And hopefully, those good things will happen for the nation."

Also, this is a "spiritual biography" but not a "definitive biography." We neither gloss over nor magnify the shortcomings of Trump. There have been a dozen biographies written about him over the past twenty years, and they spend a collective thousand pages or more on his financial challenges and marital infidelities. We've read them all for the facts of the stories. But regurgitating all that material is not the premise or promise of this book.

Okay, the man has flaws. So does the Christian faith have anything to say about flawed humanity? (That's sarcasm.) James Robison, who has become a spiritual counselor and friend to the President, nearly shouted into the phone with excitement when he made this point to us: "God uses imperfect people to accomplish his perfect will. He always has and always will."

One major theme of Part II of this book will be that Donald Trump seems to be on a spiritual voyage that has accelerated greatly in the past few years as he has regularly interacted with evangelicals. That was the consensus of a great number of Christians who we interviewed. When Trump described to us his interaction with evangelicals—"I've been exposed to people that I would have never been exposed to"—he was repeating what sources like Mike Huckabee told us: "There is a deep, abiding respect that he has, not just for God, but for people who truly follow God. I think he's intrigued by it. I think it almost is something that he just finds amazing and fascinating. He has real respect for people of faith." And Trump used journey-esque language when I asked his thoughts on growing older and his own mortality (always an awkward question to ask, even more so when the interviewee sits behind the Resolute desk in the Oval Office): "I think as you grow older, you do think about that more and more. And maybe you want to do a better and better job with your life because of that."

As we interviewed a hundred people, read a thousand articles about "the faith of Donald J. Trump," and then wrote this book, we have done so with eternity in mind. As Christians, we know that there is only one eternal kingdom, and the One who sits on the throne of that kingdom has nail prints on his hands and feet. We pray this book honors that king, even as we obey his command to "pray for rulers and those who are in authority over us" (1 Timothy 2:2).

As president of the United States, Donald Trump has been put in a position of authority by Almighty God, which makes the narrative about his faith even more vital to understanding the man who promises to "Make America Great Again."

PART

I

1

Luck and Pluck

Donald Trump stood before twenty thousand people at the Quicken Loans Arena in Cleveland, Ohio, and 35 million people watching live on TV. At its peak, *The Apprentice* drew 20 million viewers, so this was the largest ever number of eyes on him—the biggest stage of his life.

"My dad, Fred Trump, was the smartest and hardest-working man I ever knew. I sometimes wonder what he'd say if he were here to see this tonight." Donald wanted the world to know that Fred was a man of great accomplishment and character. Fred had put it into his heart that life is about competition and developing skills needed to succeed in the world. Donald knew that whatever success had come his way, the legacy of his father and grandfather had made that possible. And so, he wanted the viewers to hear about the glory of the Trump family name. After all, this is the heart of the Fifth Commandment—to make your father's name great by honoring him in word and deed.

Trump also used this same language about another man's father when he addressed fifty thousand people at Liberty University's 2017 graduation. He said, "When I think about the visionary founder of this great institution, Reverend Jerry Falwell Senior, I can only imagine how excited he would be if he could see all of this and all of you today, and how proud he would be of his son and of his family." Generally speaking, Trump and Falwell Jr. both followed in their father's businesses and expanded that work many times over. Neither son began his work from scratch. In the case of Trump, both his father *and* grandfather built up a foundation of resources (construction skills, capital, and contacts) for the multigenerational success of a family business focused on real estate development. These family patriarchs, though far from perfect, accomplished these works through hard work, frugality, calculated risk-taking, savings, and delayed gratification.

Scholars debate where the most influential source of the Protestant work ethic originates. Was it the Lutheran theological stream that arrived on the shores of America with wave after wave of German immigrants? Or was it the Calvinist theology of the Presbyterian Puritans and Pilgrims, coming to the New World from the Netherlands, England, and Scotland?

Either way, Donald Trump is covered. Donald's parents brought to America a worldview steeped in the two leading branches of the Protestant Reformation. His Presbyterian mother emigrated to America from Scotland in 1930 at the age of eighteen. And his father came to America while in the womb of Donald's grandmother, as she and her entrepreneurial husband emigrated from Martin Luther's Germany.

Frederick Trump, Donald Trump's grandfather, came to New York City in 1885 as a sixteen-year-old, leaving his parents and hometown of Kallstadt, Germany. When he arrived on the Lower East Side of Manhattan (also known as Little Germany) to live with his married sister, he immediately found work as a barber. He stayed there for six years before moving out to Seattle (population less than fifteen thousand) with his life savings of a few hundred dollars.

For the next decade, Frederick built hotels and restaurants where miners could eat, sleep, gamble, and spend some time in his "rooms for ladies." During this time, he also became a citizen of the United States and voted in the 1896 election. In a rapid succession of moves from one mining town to the next in Oregon, Alaska, and the Yukon, he built lodging establishments from scratch and turned them into boom-time successes—before selling them fortuitously just ahead of the inevitable downturns.

Frederick moved back to Germany and met Elizabeth Christ, a blond, blue-eyed beauty eleven years his junior, who had grown up across the street. Frederick's mother wanted her now-wealthy son to marry higher up on the socioeconomic ladder. But he opted for Elizabeth, a woman with conservative ideals and a physical constitution of steel.

They moved to New York City, and then back to Germany again when Elizabeth became homesick. However, the Bavarian authorities accused him of intentionally skipping out of the mandatory years of service in the German army of Kaiser Wilhelm II. Frederick filed appeal papers and worked with the local magistrates but to no avail. They told him he was no longer welcome to be a citizen of Germany and would have to leave the country.

So, in 1905, he and Elizabeth—now pregnant with Donald Trump's father, Fred—packed up their belongings and their baby daughter and headed back to America. This would be the third and final emigration for Frederick and one that he had worked hard to keep from making.

In addition to Fred's older sister (also named Elizabeth), Frederick and Elizabeth added another son, John, who would go on to become one of America's leading physicists. He taught electrical engineering at MIT for forty years, and he helped defeat Germany during World War II through his pioneering work in radar technologies. President Harry Truman and King George VI of England—and later, President Ronald Reagan—decorated him for his service. When you take together the lifelong accomplishments of just John and Fred, one must consider placing the Trumps in the pantheon of great American families.

• • •

In the spring of 1918, Frederick and twelve-year-old Fred walked along Jamaica Avenue toward their home in Woodhaven, Queens. By this time, Frederick owned their house, several empty lots, stocks, savings, and other investments. But most importantly, he was still young enough, at forty-nine, to have big plans for buying and developing real estate in the rapidly expanding borough. But he felt ill that afternoon and lay down in bed, never to get up again. He died the next day, an early victim of what became known as the Spanish flu outbreak that killed tens of millions of people world-wide. "Just like that," Fred recalled later. "It seemed so sudden. It just didn't seem real."

Frederick's death widowed Elizabeth with three children still in the home. Fred was already inclined to follow in his father's real estate development work, but since he was a minor and unable to sign contracts, he formed a business with his mother: E. Trump & Son. This was the beginning of the company we now know as The Trump Organization. Fred—with the early help of his mother, who lived until 1966—became one of the great real estate developers of the twentieth century. When he died at the age of ninety-three in 1999, his obituary in the *New York Times* was titled "Postwar Master Builder of Housing for Middle Class," a title he earned by having built and managed twenty-seven thousand apartments and houses in Brooklyn and Queens.

In the 1920s and 1930s, Fred mastered the art and business of constructing quality single-family houses. During World War II, he built barracks and apartments for the army and the navy. And when millions of soldiers returned home and needed affordable, quality housing, Fred built countless more homes and immense apartment complexes. The financial backing for much of this work came about through the newly created Federal Housing Authority (FHA) pro-gram. That said, Fred wasn't the only developer who stood in line for the funding and the work. The competition was often fierce, and the profit margins didn't allow for sloppy and inefficient oversight. You could make a lot of money in such projects—and Fred did, leaving an estate worth $250 to $300 million when he died. But these earnings only came with gritty determination and endless sweat equity poured out over five decades.

2

Making Augsburg Great Again

How did Fred Trump's Lutheran worldview shape his son Donald's life and worldview? Ever since the Protestant Reformation began five hundred years ago, you can't talk about modern Germany without referencing Martin Luther. This Roman Catholic monk turned the world upside down when he studied the Bible and came to understand that what the Apostle Paul taught about justification (being right with God) did not equate with the official teaching of the church. Paul taught that God justifies people based only on their faith (*sola fide*) in Christ alone (*solo Christo*), and that God does this work entirely on the basis of grace (*sola gratia*). That is, a person's good works cannot produce merit and right standing before God. Good works are the fruit of justification, not the basis of it.

Luther's journey began with his "95 Theses," a blistering criticism of the church's practice of selling indulgences. At the time, a rich person could repent, pay the church, and supposedly be forgiven by God through the office of the pope. Luther didn't intend to break from the church. He wanted to reform the church using reasoned debate and discussion—a protest that would lead to reform (hence, "Protestant Reformation"). But the Pope didn't take kindly to Luther's critique and summoned him to a meeting in the city of Augsburg, where he was to recant his teaching.

The meeting was held at the immense new home of Jakob Fugger, who most historians rank as the third-richest man in the modern era, behind only John D. Rockefeller and Andrew Carnegie. A recent biographer described Fugger as "the most influential businessman of all time."

> He had character flaws like anyone else. He was headstrong, selfish, deceitful and sometimes cruel. . . . But he turned at least one of those flaws—a tendency to trumpet his own achievements—into an asset. His boasts were good advertising; by letting visitors know what he paid for a diamond or how much he could conjure for a loan, he broadcast his ability to do more for clients than other bankers. He chased the biggest opportunities. He won favors from politicians. He used his money to rewrite the rules to his advantage. He surrounded himself with lawyers and accountants. He fed on information. . . . He was the first to pursue wealth for its own sake and without fear of damnation.

Before he died, Fugger even wrote his own epitaph: "Second to none in the acquisition of extraordinary wealth, in liberality, in purity of life, and in the greatness of soul, as he was comparable to none in life, so after death is not to be numbered among the mortal." Fugger was rich in many things—humility not being one of them.

Fugger had loaned the Pope vast sums of money to finance the building of St. Peter's Basilica. To recoup that money, the Pope had sent out men who would sell indulgences. One of the Pope's best salesmen in Germany was Johann Tetzel, with his slick advertising jingles: "As soon as the coin in the coffer rings, the soul from purgatory springs."

Martin Luther couldn't stand Fugger—nor the encroachments upon the soul that all this buying and borrowing and banking was having on the people. Luther published "An Open Letter to the Christian Nobility" declaring, "We must put a bit in the mouth of the Fuggers and similar corporations."

It wasn't that Luther was opposed to a person being rich, but he thought the better way to accumulate wealth was through craftsmanship and agriculture—not through lending money at interest and the other mechanisms of banking and finance. Luther wanted his German countrymen to till the ground, raise crops, plant orchards, make inventions, learn crafts—to take dominion over the earth.

Luther's protest set the world on fire and directly led to the "Modern Age"—with all its strengths and weaknesses: freedom of religion, individualism, globalization, technological innovation, the scientific revolution, the secularization of politics, and the rise of nation-states. And in 1530, a group of Luther's friends turned Augsburg into a word that will forever be linked with Lutheranism. They traveled to the city and presented Emperor Charles V a written explanation of their doctrinal beliefs: The Augsburg Confession.

Fred Trump grew up in the home of first-generation immigrants who embodied the culture and worldview of Luther's Germany: Hard work is the duty of those who walk with God, rather than good work being the path *to* God. In true "melting pot" fashion, Elizabeth and her children had Americanized their cultural inheritance and passed it along to their children. But what do we make of that "cultural inheritance"?

First, all the Trumps—living and dead, blue collar and white— are known for being hard workers. That is an undisputed fact. The Trumps incarnate the abstract "Protestant work ethic" concept. Donald's own statement about his father—"the hardest-working man I ever knew"—is supported by thousands of people who worked alongside Fred or who lived in his buildings. You don't build tens of thousands of middle-income residential units without knowing how to put in a hard day's work. Fred knew (as does Donald) "how to read a blueprint, frame a building, and lay bricks; he knew how to retar a roof and how to lay a plumb line."

Luther wrote the following words against lazy preachers—but they apply to any Christian in any profession: "Truly, this evil, shameful time is not the season for being lazy, for sleeping and snoring. Use the gift that has been entrusted to you, and reveal the mystery of Christ." In other words, there's no place for laziness in the life of a Christian.

Also, Luther taught that all honest vocations have equal merit and worth in the eyes of God. People who build literal houses are doing so in service to God just as much as pastors who build up the spiritual house of God. The Augsburg Confession affirmed the righteousness of everyday (non-clergy) vocations: "The Gospel does not overthrow civil authority, the state, and marriage but requires that all these be kept as true orders of God and that everyone, each according to his own calling, manifest Christian love and genuine good works in his station of life."

Such a conviction not only frees us to pursue a vocation that society may deem "beneath your status," but it also frees us to treat others with dignity no matter what their vocation. Donald Trump said this about Fred: "It's because of him that I learned, from my youngest age, to respect the dignity of work and the dignity of working people. He was a guy most comfortable in the company of bricklayers, carpenters, and electricians—and I have a lot of that in me also."

Nowadays, men like Mike Rowe remind us that "dirty jobs" have intrinsic worth, that blue-collar jobs and manual labor provide more than a paycheck. There is a source of pride and joy that comes from working hard and going home tired. And such jobs may or may not require a college degree.

Fred Trump lived out this ideal. He went to work at the age of thirteen while finishing his high school studies. He didn't get involved in extracurricular activities, opting instead to earn money and learn construction-related skills. He also performed beast-of-burden labor, assisting horses in pulling lumber up a hill—or when the unpaved roads were too muddy for the horses, pulling it up himself.

And remember, Fred's father did not leave his family destitute. Fred could have finished high school without simultaneously starting a construction business. There was enough money on hand for Fred to have gone to college or to have pursued leisure activities. But delayed adolescence wasn't the future Fred charted for himself, because a lack of money isn't the only motivation for work. Fred wanted to build buildings—literally, to build them—not just finance the construction crews and then show up to cut a ribbon on opening day.

Fred's children remember him working twelve-hour days, even on Saturdays. Maryanne Trump Barry said that her father didn't have any hobbies. "He never thought about anything but work and family." They recall being with him a lot, even if it was driving around to check in on his properties. "What else would he do on a Saturday, hang around the house?" Robert Trump asked.

"I don't consider it work," Fred once told a reporter, while sitting in his trailer-office on the construction site of a seventy-million-dollar housing project ($550 million in today's dollars). "There are irritations and disappointments. But generally speaking, I call it a hobby." In like manner, I remember how in my very first interview with Trump, I asked him, "What do you do for a vacation?" His reply: "I work."

Further, people who believe in the importance of having a strong work ethic also hope to pass this on to their children—even if their children are born into wealth. Like Trump, Kentucky governor Matt Bevin was a businessman—a manufacturer of big bells—before he entered politics. He didn't grow up with a silver spoon in his mouth, and the bell business had many setbacks before success—most people would have called it quits. We asked Bevin his assessment of Donald Trump, having been around him numerous times. Bevin said:

> Look at the work ethic he has instilled in his children. It is remarkable. His children have a work ethic and a focus and an appreciation for work that is truly impressive—and not just for intellectual and theoretical work, but physical, manual labor. The things that he has exposed them to, the things he has taught them to do, and the opportunities he has put before them are amazing. If every father in America had done what he has done, we wouldn't have nearly the issues we have with this most current generation and their sometimes questionable work ethic.

From Frederick to Fred to Donald to his grown children—the Protestant work ethic has been passed down the family line.

Donald often talks about how making bad choices in personal matters can diminish the chances of success: "The world is so tough and competitive. . . . If you don't drink and you don't do drugs, your children are going to have a tremendously enhanced chance of really being successful and having a good life." There's a biblical principle (not a promise) that points to a cause-and-effect mechanism present in the world.

- "Lazy hands make for poverty, but diligent hands bring wealth." Proverbs 10:4
- "All hard work brings a profit, but mere talk leads only to poverty." Proverbs 14:23
- "If anyone is not willing to work, let him not eat." 2 Thessalonians 3:10

Fred believed that people should discover what they enjoy doing and then learn the skills of that work. "You must like what you do," he said. "You must pick out the right business or profession. You must learn all about it. . . . Nine out of 10 people don't like what they do. And in not liking what they do, they lose."

Even after he had millions in the bank, Fred Trump never retired. He had wealth, but not flash and glitz. We can agree that such a statement is relative. Until his death in 1999, Fred lived in the home that he built in the 1950s. It had dozens of rooms but was not fancy. He never traded up and never left the upper-middle-class neighborhood where he had raised his kids. As biographer Gwenda Blair said about the house: "It was the home of a man who made his money himself and had not tried to distance himself from that fact."

There was a humility to his work despite the very public nature of these projects. His brand was the buildings themselves, not his name on top of them. Only two of Fred's projects used his last name: Trump Market, a grocery store he built and quickly sold in 1933, and the Trump Village apartment complex he built in 1963 on Coney Island. "It took a long time to sell me the idea," Trump told a reporter, explaining his reluctance at the naming. "They told me it would be a monument to me and most monuments I know are granite or marble." The son of one of his partners recalls that though Fred was wealthy, "he wasn't flashy. He never tried to impress anybody with his wealth. He didn't seem to care if anybody had ever heard of him." In the end, Fred conceded to the name because it would be "something to remember the name Trump by."

There are dozens of stories about Fred's frugality. He would pick up nails off the ground at a job site and give them back to the workers the next day, both to save the pennies and to set an example to the carpenters. He had chemists figure out the formula for the floor disinfectant he bought in mass quantities, then had them mix up batches at a fraction of the cost he had been paying. He tried to eliminate waste wherever possible, "turning off lights and getting up on a stepladder to remove any bulbs he deemed unnecessary." In other words, he lived by the "Waste not. Want not" maxim of American frugality flowing from the tradition of Benjamin Franklin's *Poor Richard's Almanac.*

When asked for the key to success in real estate development, Fred once said, "You have to follow up and follow up and follow up." Whatever that answer lacks in sophistication it makes up for in real-world wisdom. Grit—that combination of discipline, consistency, and a determination to get the job done right—defined Fred's career.

There's a profound backstory to Martin Luther's figuring out what it really took to know that God the Father was pleased with him. His own earthly father had grown up as the son of a farmer. This being the tail end of the Medieval period, there wasn't much chance (or expectation) of moving upward financially from one generation to the next. But Martin's dad decided he'd at least try, so he moved to another town where he could get involved in mining for copper. Sure enough, by the time Martin had come of age, his dad's hard work and ambition had created surplus funds, and he intended to invest some of that capital by putting Martin through university and law school. Such an investment would bring even more financial uplift to the entire family.

But Martin got caught out in a field during a lightning storm. Afraid of dying and facing the wrath of God, he made an oath to God that he would become a monk. Nevertheless, Martin Luther's father was furious that his son would waste the opportunity to pursue a lucrative career in law for a life of poverty in service to the church.

But if Luther's father being displeased caused him grief, that was nothing compared to his own tormented conscience about his sinfulness. In the monastery, he would confess his sin constantly, to the point that his confessor told him not to come back until he had really done something worth confessing. Luther would sleep on cold stone floors and flagellate himself—all in an attempt to feel a sense of right standing before God the Father. But then, through his study of Galatians and Romans, Luther realized that though a holy God must judge sin, he had already provided a substitute who took the punishment for sin on his behalf: Jesus Christ. And it was by faith in Jesus' death on the cross that a person has right standing with the Father (John 3:16). Call it "evangelical" or "Lutheran" or "Protestant" or "Billy Graham's message"—but that is the Christian Gospel in a nutshell.

It is probably fair to say that "saved by works" is the default way that most people think about eternal salvation. We believe in the merit system and earning pay for doing what the boss says. Besides, doesn't the Bible say that "God helps those who help themselves"? Actually, it doesn't, though 75 percent of all Americans and even 68 percent of self-identifying "born again" Christians think that concept comes from the Bible.

Pulling yourself up by your own bootstraps is a wonderful mindset for economic achievement, but it makes for a lousy theology of salvation. *Sola bootstrapsis* is not in the Bible and runs counter to the heart of the Gospel.

When people think they are earning merit for their soul every time they do something good, then eventually they'll want to get paid. But the heart of Luther's gospel is that good works are only good when they flow from a heart of faith in and gratitude to God for what he first gave in Christ. And a Christian's earthly labors can be an aspect of worship and service to God—a means of bringing him glory. As the Apostle Paul told Christians: "whatever you do, do all to the glory of God" and "whatever you do, work heartily, as for the Lord . . . You are serving the Lord Christ."

Johann Sebastian Bach, the great German Lutheran composer, wrote "S.D.G." at the bottom of his works. Those initials mean *Soli Deo Gloria*—"to God be all the glory."

Two anecdotes—one about Donald and one about Fred—serve well to close out this chapter.

First, in the early 1970s when Donald wasn't yet thirty, he was working on an ambitious deal—far beyond what most people his age would attempt to do. It would require endless insider conversations to go just right, and for that Trump enlisted the help of a man named Ned Eichler, who saw firsthand the relationship that Fred and Donald had with each other. "Many very successful fathers, self-made men . . . are rather ambivalent about their sons at a very young age becoming big figures and successful. But it seemed clear to me that this was a very unusual relationship, that his father seemed totally supportive that this was Donald's project."

Eichler admits having "never at any time liked Donald personally," but thought he was insanely focused and skilled at what they were hoping to accomplish. It was all business. "You didn't talk about any of the ordinary things, like movies or books," Eichler said. "With Donald, there was no small talk."

Eichler observed Trump, trying to figure out what motivated him—because it didn't seem to be about the money. Blair writes that one day at lunch, Trump gave Eichler a peek on the inside: "Trump supplied a clue in an uncharacteristically reflective moment. He told Eichler that he assumed he would not marry and would be dead before he was forty."

Second, Blair relates a story about Fred and Donald from the spring of 1991. Fred was sitting in the back of a packed room in New York's City Hall while Donald was at the front of the room with Mayor David Dinkins. Donald talked expressively about a great new real estate project that he and civic leaders were agreeing to launch—"one of the greatest developments anywhere," he said.

"When asked about his own career," Blair writes, Fred "declined to comment. 'I like to keep low and not have a lot of attention,' he said. 'Other people can have it, I don't need it.' He paused, then added, 'As Shakespeare said, Work is what you do while you're waiting to die.' " As he spoke these words, Fred was in the final decade of his life; Donald was about to turn forty-five. His earlier prophecy about his own mortality (and matrimony) had proved to be wrong.

Nobody lives forever. Faced with his potential death in a lightning storm, Martin Luther turned to God and ended up changing the church and the world. How would Donald's prediction about an early death propel him in his own vocation?

3

Mother Mary Comes to Queens

"Who wants to live forever?" That was Queen's melodramatic love anthem for the soundtrack to the 1986 movie that has become a cult classic: *The Highlander*. Set in Donald Trump's New York City (no, he didn't have a cameo), this action fantasy film featured sword-wielding warriors who live forever—or at least until they lose their head to another immortal.

Of course, there's no such thing as immortal warriors, but here's where art imitates life. The main character in the movie is an immortal from the Highlands of Scotland (hence the title of the movie) whose name is *Connor MacLeod*. And in real life, Donald Trump's mother came from a part of Scotland even more rustic than the Highlands. And her maiden name was *Mary Anne MacLeod*.

These real-life MacLeods got their start from a patriarch named Leod ("Mac" means "son of") who lived in the thirteenth century, with a MacLeod line of succession that continues to this day. Family history records that Tormod MacLeod was an incredible soldier and fought the English at the Battle of Bannockburn (depicted as the final scene of Mel Gibson's *Braveheart*). But the specific line of MacLeod chieftains on the Isle of Lewis, where Trump's mother was born, ended in the seventeenth century. Even so, modern DNA testing of people with the surname of "MacLeod" (or who had a mother who was a MacLeod) from the Isle of Lewis reveals that "almost 10,000 people alive today are all descended from this man"— the original MacLeod patriarch.

But even more fascinating, the genes also show that these

MacLeods descend from "a Norse aristocrat called Ljot, a relative of Olaf, King of Man." In other words, from time to time the Vikings would show up and cause havoc, including the siring of offspring.

All that to say there's a good chance that Donald Trump, being a "son of Leod," has Viking blood running through his veins.

Mary Anne MacLeod, the tenth of ten children born to Malcolm MacLeod and Mary MacLeod, entered this world on May 10, 1912—three weeks after the sinking of the *Titanic*. The MacLeods lived in a tiny, one-lane village called Tong, about four miles north of Stornoway, the biggest city on the island of ten thousand. Lewis is part of a series of islands known as the Outer Hebrides of Scotland. Though not without natural beauty, the geography and culture of this land was rough and primitive.

During Mary Anne's childhood, World War I took the lives of 1,150 of the young men of Lewis—mostly in the trenches of France. An additional 181 soldiers died in 1919 on their way home, killed in a shipwreck just off the coast of Lewis. Even with their Christian fortitude and work ethic propelling them, the economic realities on the island gave little hope for a sustainable life. And for young women who longed to marry and have a family, the loss of life during the "War to End All Wars" dimmed their hopes nearly altogether. For all these reasons, the promise of a new life had pulled Scotland's sons and daughters across the Atlantic for a century. Several of Mary Anne's older siblings had already emigrated, and in the spring of 1930, the almost eighteen-year-old mother of Donald Trump said good-bye to Scotland and boarded a steamship for New York City.

To live in Scotland is to be surrounded by Presbyterian churches. This is the land of John Knox, the man who brought the Protestant Reformation to Scotland directly from John Calvin's Geneva.

Knox was ordained in 1536—the same year that William Tyndale was executed for translating the Bible into English and for speaking out against the marriage plans of King Henry VIII. Tyndale's final words were "Lord, open the King of England's eyes." Likewise, Knox did not live in fear of imprisonment or execution, saying that "One man with God is always in the majority." He spoke plainly and boldly to royalty, without fear of the consequences. In modern parlance, Knox "spoke truth to power," telling kings and queens that they were not the ultimate authority. Such ideas were considered treasonous, of course, but Knox persisted, preached, and prayed. And from exile, he also pamphleteered, spreading his ideas throughout England and Scotland.

Knox and Tyndale worked out a system for ordering the churches they established throughout the land. Instead of a pope and bishops, they would convene annually for big decision-making and discussions; but they would also have more localized church governance using districts: presbyteries. Knox had pleaded with God in prayer—"Give me Scotland, or I die."—desiring the Gospel to take root among his Scottish countrymen. God answered his prayers, and Scotland became a stronghold of vibrant Protestant faith. But his influence brought him into conversation and conflict with the newly installed Mary, Queen of Scots—a Roman Catholic who said, "I fear the prayers of John Knox more than all the assembled armies of Europe." In one of their discussions, the Queen asked Knox, "Think ye that subjects, having the power, may resist their princes?" Knox replied: "If their princes exceed their bounds, Madam, no doubt they may be resisted, even by power."

Knox's ideas echoed all the way across two centuries and the Atlantic Ocean, impacting American colonials who questioned whether they had a God-given right to rebel against King George. As British historian Jasper Ridley wrote, "The theory of the justification of revolution is Knox's special contribution to theological and political thought." And this theory wasn't written in an ivory tower or published under a pseudonym. Knox stood in front of the queen when he spoke these words. Which is to say, Knox embodied something that Scottish people are known for: straight talk.

In 2016, Derick Mackenzie, a resident of the Isle of Lewis, set up a pro-Trump Facebook page. He explained to CNN that Trump's style and tone were characteristic of someone who hailed from the island. "There is an expression you hear: Lewis straight talking. It's a kind of honesty," Mackenzie said. "This kind of not being concerned with what people think. They will give it to you between the eyes." Not all Scots agreed with Mackenzie's assessment. Another Scot wrote an online response to that idea, with unintended irony: "As for 'Lewis straight talking'—[there's] no such thing, except for the fact that there are [a] few loud-mouthed idiots in every village. Donald Trump couldn't have less in common with Lewis if he'd been raised on Saturn."

Let's consider five specific ways in which Scottish Presbyterianism impacted either the history of the United States or the life of Mary Anne McLeod.

First, Sabbatarianism—the belief that Sunday was to be set aside for worship and that most work, travel, and entertainment was to be curtailed—was practiced throughout Scotland since the time of John Knox. And Sabbatarian practice was more than a voluntary practice; laws in England, Scotland, Denmark, and the United States prohibited merchant activity on Sunday. These "Blue Laws" were still on the books at the end of the twentieth century—though in many places they were ignored. During Mary Anne's childhood, however, strict Sabbatarianism was still practiced on the island of Lewis. Even today, nearly all shops and gas stations are closed on Sunday. In fact, it wasn't until 2009 that local ordinances allowed for the ferry to run back and forth between the Isle and the mainland. As two current citizens explain, "God wants us to have a break from our work outside the home and inside the home. We eat light meals, so there is not too much kitchen work. It gives us time to spend with our children and focus on their souls as well as our own."

Though Mary Anne did not practice Sabbatarianism as a mother in America, the Trumps were regularly in attendance at Sunday worship while raising their family. German-Lutherans in America, such as Fred Trump's upbringing was, envisioned a different way to keep the Sabbath. After attending worship, Lutherans believed they had Christian freedom to spend Sundays in recreational pursuits—and in that way they saw the day as "holy" (meaning, "set apart") because they were working hard the other six days of the week.

Second, Presbyterians emphasized using the Sabbath day for the spiritual training of the children. This practice, known as catechizing, became the norm throughout Scotland and was still practiced by the churches on Lewis during Mary Anne's childhood. The very idea of having a catechism flows from the idea that the Christian faith goes beyond a personal experience of faith. Rather, there is a body of doctrine that needs to be understood, taught, and believed—the "faith once delivered to the saints" (Jude 3). The early Presbyterians thought their churches were made up of people bound together by more than a shared cultural experience or geography. The church shares Christ—and that means believing in a shared understanding of Christ and the Gospel and "the whole counsel of God" (Acts 20:27).

A century after Knox, the Presbyterians (or "Puritans") gathered in London for two years and wrote the Westminster Confession of Faith and the Westminster Shorter Catechism. And to our point, this was the theology heard by Mary Anne MacLeod on the Isle of Lewis. The Church of Scotland had the Westminster documents translated into Gaelic for use in the Highlands and the Western

Hebrides. Given that Mary Anne's native tongue was Gaelic, this would have been the 107-question catechism she was taught. But since most of us don't know Gaelic, we'll stick to English in stating the famous first question of the catechism: "Q: What is the chief end of man? A: Man's chief end is to glorify God, and to enjoy him forever." Some Scottish churches would reward a young person with a Bible if he or she could recite the answers correctly to the entire catechism. We will revisit this topic in chapter four when we look at Donald's catechismal training at his Presbyterian church in Jamaica, Queens.

Third, Presbyterians placed great emphasis on the importance of both family worship and active participation in the local congregation. At present, there is no way of knowing exactly what depth of spiritual instruction took place in the MacLeod home. But we do know the children were baptized into the Stornoway High Church—a congregation affiliated at that time with the Church of Scotland. The mission house in Tong is part of the ministry of the Free Church in Back. The MacLeods could have worshipped there in Tong or walked four miles north to Back. Instead, they chose the third option and walked four miles south to Stornoway for worship.

All the Presbyterian churches around Mary Anne were theologically and culturally conservative. Ask the locals today what they think about the famous son of Mary Anne and strong opinions can be heard: "Donald Trump's lifestyle would not be compatible with his background on the island," Reverend James MacIver, who is a "friend of the family," told a reporter. "It's not that he has made it big in financial terms—it's how he has done it. It's the kind of devil-may-care attitude. It doesn't matter what happens to people as long as he gets what he wants. That doesn't sit well with the mentality on the island." Another local, Kenny MacIver, said that Trump would be a total misfit: "People here are modest in terms of their achievements, leaving the boasting to others. That's the way we are, I suppose it's the Presbyterian ethics. Not only is [boasting] not encouraged, it is positively discouraged." But the fellow who started the Facebook page differed in his assessment, telling the *Irish Times* that Trump "supports the Bible. The reason our world is in moral and economic ruin today is because we in the West have over time thrown the Bible away. This is fatal." So, from one side of the Atlantic Ocean to the other, "the faith of Donald Trump" proves to be a point of debate and division.

Fourth, Scottish Presbyterians directly influenced the colonies in the buildup to the American Revolutionary War. In 1955, Billy Graham came and preached for six weeks in what was called the "All Scotland Crusade." Graham's Scottish ancestors had settled in North Carolina, and in 1775 they even signed the Mecklenburg Declaration of Independence—the first such declaration made in the colonies. As Graham told a group of clergy and press, in explaining his rationale for coming to Scotland: "Among the Puritans which came to America between 1620 and 1640, one-fifth of them were of Scottish Presbyterian persuasion. These virile Scots were possessors of a vital faith which helped to pour the foundations of the American way of life. Every American owes a debt he can never repay to Scotland. This little country, with only five million population, has long had a mighty influence on the United States."

John Witherspoon, a Presbyterian minister from Scotland, came to the colonies in 1768 to lead the College of New Jersey (Princeton) in its primary mission of training pastors. Witherspoon preached sermons that included such zingers as, "Rebellion to tyrants is obedience to God" and "There is not a single instance in history in which civil liberty was lost, and religious liberty preserved entire." Thus, many of Witherspoon's students joined Washington's army and gave their lives on the battlefield to secure our independence. "Call this war by whatever name you may, only call it not an American rebellion," a German Hessian mercenary wrote during the war.

"It is nothing more or less than a Scotch Irish Presbyterian rebellion."

And Witherspoon's greatest impact on our nation came from his tutelage of James Madison—the "Father of the Constitution." As Church historian Donald Fortson wrote: "Witherspoon had taught his students about a balanced political structure where misuse of power may be corrected. Madison had apparently also imbibed from Witherspoon the old Calvinist doctrine of total depravity and man's natural inclination to vice and political corruption." Belief in the need for checks and balances as a means of resisting tyranny flowed from Calvin to Knox to Samuel Rutherford (another Scottish Presbyterian minister, and the author of *Lex Rex*) to Witherspoon to Madison.

Fifth, the emergence of a politically engaged evangelicalism in the 1970s was aided by evangelical Presbyterian pastors and authors like Peter Marshall Jr., D. James Kennedy, and Francis Schaeffer. And since it was the evangelical voting bloc that sent Donald Trump into the White House, this is something worth taking note of. A significant intellectual precursor to the Christian Right was Schaeffer's book (1976) and film series (1977) *How Should We Then Live?* Schaeffer then followed up with his book against abortion, *Whatever Happened to the Human Race* (1979), coauthored by Reagan's future surgeon general, C. Everett Koop, an evangelical Presbyterian.

Schaeffer's 1981 book, *A Christian Manifesto*, laid out a theological and philosophical basis for Christians to practice civil disobedience. The book sold 300,000 copies in its first year alone. It remains in print today and continues to spark a lively discussion among the Christian Right. And Schaeffer dedicated the book to Rutherford, calling him "an important trail marker for our day"—a guide for Christians who believe their government is unresponsive to the people who it should be serving.

It follows from Rutherford's thesis that citizens have a *moral* obligation to resist unjust and tyrannical government. While we must always be subject to the office of the magistrate, we are not to be subject to the man in that office who commands that which is contrary to the Bible. . . . That is exactly what we are facing today. The whole structure of our society is being attacked and destroyed. It is being given an entirely opposite base which gives exactly opposite results. The reversal is much more total and destructive than that which Rutherford or any of the Reformers faced today.

It is impossible to read "we are not to be subject to the man . . . who commands that which is contrary to the Bible" without thinking of news stories from the past four years that evangelicals followed closely: Little Sisters of the Poor and the Health and Human Services (HHS) Mandate; florist Barronelle Stutzman; Kentucky county clerk Kim Davis; Sweet Cakes by Melissa; Hobby Lobby and abortifacient birth control; high school coach Joe Kennedy's termination for on-field prayers; Houston's mayor issuing a subpoena for the sermons of area pastors.

Schaeffer wrote *A Christian Manifesto* in the immediate aftermath of Ronald Reagan's 1980 victory, which he described as "a unique window open in the United States"—a period of opportunity to overturn tyrannies before they do irreparable harm to the nation.

Likewise, six months after the 2016 election, Robert Jeffress—pastor of First Baptist, Dallas—hosted Trump for an Independence Day celebration that provoked either red-faced cursing on Twitter or tweets of "Amen." Jeffress said:

It is also an indisputable fact that in recent years there had been those who tried to separate our nation from its spiritual foundation. And that reality has caused many of us, many Christians to despair and to wonder, "Is God finished with America? Are our best days over? Has God removed his hands of blessing from us?" But in the midst of that despair came November the 8th, 2016. . . .

Millions of Americans believed the election of President Trump represented God giving us another chance. Perhaps our last chance to truly make America great again. And how grateful we are. We thank God every day that he gave us a leader like President Trump.

American evangelical politics continues to be shaped by Scottish Presbyterians like Knox and Rutherford. When yet another high school valedictorian gets a written warning against mentioning God or quoting Scripture, evangelicals sense that there really is something at stake for our nation in this season.

Former Ohio congressman Bob McEwen (a Scots-Irish name if ever there was one) was elected to office in 1980 with the Moral Majority–fueled Reagan Revolution. We asked him to compare that election with what happened in 2016. McEwen said that to make a change in the direction of the country takes at least three presidential terms, maybe four—and that there have only been three presidencies when the country fundamentally made a permanent turn: Andrew Jackson, Abraham Lincoln, and FDR. "And so, I believe that had Hillary gotten eight years on top of Obama's two terms, then the America that you and I know would not have existed at the end of those eight years. I firmly believe it."

When Donald Trump visited the Isle of Lewis in 2008, a gaggle of reporters followed him around. After touring the modest home in Tong where Mary Anne grew up, he stood for some pictures with his cousins who live there. Donald's sister Maryanne, who has a deep relationship to her mother's homeland, was with Donald also, and even sported a yellow-and-black-patterned scarf—the official MacLeod tartan. Donald turned to the media and made a few remarks: "I like it. I feel very comfortable here. It's very interesting when your mother, who was such a terrific woman, comes from a specific location—you tend to like that location. I think I do feel Scottish."

Maryanne (Donald's sister) has visited dozens of times and even donated a quarter million dollars to a nursing home in Stornoway. Her generosity came to her by the example of her mother, as Mary Anne always brought a round of gifts to Scotland with her, for family and neighbors alike. "She was a philanthropist with a genuine interest in helping people," Reverend MacIver said. "Her own background would have [led] her to do that—growing up in poverty."

Mary Anne (Donald's mother) returned to Scotland on numerous occasions, visiting her dad, who lived until 1954, and her mom, who died in 1963. "She never, ever forgot her roots," Reverend Calum MacLeod said. "Folks speak of her as kind and considerate—and someone who never forgot who she was. She never forgot the island that nurtured her before she took off to the States."

When Mary Anne came back home, she would worship at the church of her youth. People there still remember her visits, and not simply because she was a stately and glamorous guest—though that factored in. She would walk around the church, talking to everyone in her native Gaelic tongue and singing heartily—just like things were back in the day, with one motorized exception. Unlike her childhood experiences, Mary Anne didn't have to walk the four miles to church because Fred would pay to have a car shipped overseas with her so she could get around the island. Mary, Queen of Scots, had her royal carriage; Mary Anne Trump, Scot from Queens, had her Cadillac.

In some of those trips, Mary Anne might have heard local reports about an experience of revival that came to the Hebridean churches in the years 1949–1953. Hundreds of people on the island turned to Christianity in a short period, and there was a season of spiritual awakening even among seasoned Christians. As small as the island is, Mary Anne may have even known some of the people who personally took part in these meetings and experiences.

She certainly would have watched or listened with interest to those Billy Graham Crusades that came to her homeland in 1955. American TV and radio broadcasted sermons and highlights from the Crusades, as Graham pleaded with the people of Scotland—the neighbors of Mary Anne's youth—to come to Christ:

> You who are listening throughout many parts of the British empire, and other parts of the world, of all races, let's join hands at the throne of grace, praying daily that something will begin in these rugged hills that could change the entire Western world at this desperate hour. Pray that the spiritual fires which blazed mightily in the sixteenth century shall blaze again and that the spiritual heat from this fire may be felt around the world for the glory of God.

Sociologists and historians conducted statistical research after the 1955 Crusade to see what effects these mass evangelistic events had on the nation. A few years afterward, the church attendance in Scotland was still higher than it had been in the years leading up to Graham's preaching. Unfortunately, the winds of modernity and a postwar focus on the material world led Scots to leave the Christian faith in unprecedented numbers. In 1956, the Church of Scotland had an active membership of around 1.3 million people. Today, active membership runs about 380,000.

"Go into your pulpits and preach a gospel message. Then ask for decisions and rededications," Graham had told Scotland's ministers. He knew that humanly speaking, the long-term spiritual impact of the Crusades would come only if the ministers caught a vision for the spread of the Gospel in their own church.

4

Back to the Future Presbyterians

Since Fred and Mary Anne Trump met in the mid-1930s to the present, there are three churches that the family has been a part of—and the first may have only served as the place of matrimony. Two of the churches that young Donald Trump attended can claim to be "the oldest" in North America—one is the oldest continuously existent *Protestant* church in North America, and the other is the oldest continuously existent *Presbyterian* church. To put the age of these churches in perspective, the King James Version of the Bible was still "the newest in Bible translations" when these churches were being formed in the New World.

It's quite fascinating how the Trump family has sat under the ministry of churches and pastors whose names are found in American church history books. Keep in mind that in the mid-twentieth century when Donald was born, there would have been about 250,000 to 300,000 houses of worship in the United States. Which is to say, 99 percent of Americans did *not* worship at a church that had reason to be mentioned in a history textbook. By contrast, the Trump family have been involved with three such churches.

In January 1936, German-Lutheran Fred Trump walked the matrimonial aisle with his Scottish-Presbyterian fiancée. Only "death would them part"—as they remained together for sixty-three years, until Fred died in 1999 (Mary Anne followed in death one year later). And those six decades of marriage all began under the roof of the Madison Avenue Presbyterian Church (MAPC).

Madison Avenue. That very name conveys with it the very heartbeat of commercialism, especially in 1937—as this had been the world epicenter of the modern advertising industry since the 1920s. And, of course, New York City serves as the national center for banking, finance, and the stock markets. But the Madison Avenue church building wasn't simply located within the city of wealth; many of the wealthy of the city were located within the church.

When Scottish-American Andrew Carnegie gave his only daughter's hand in marriage, two very famous clergy married the young couple at Carnegie's mansion: William P. Merrill, the pastor of Brick Presbyterian, and Henry Sloane Coffin, the pastor of Madison Avenue Presbyterian.

Coffin, himself an heir to a fortune from the furniture company W. and J. Sloane & Co., graduated first from Yale, then Union Theological Seminary in the city. In 1910, he took the pastorate of MAPC for a yearly salary of one dollar, with the provision that the church followed his leadership into what was becoming known as the Social Gospel. Coffin preached to pews filled with the very wealthy, but he wanted MAPC to extend a hand to all members of the city. Many upper-class churches like MAPC had traditionally sponsored church work in the lower-class neighborhoods, but did not want the unwashed masses coming through the door of their own house of worship. Like his evangelical friend, the Chicago-based evangelist Dwight L. Moody, Coffin reminded wealthy parishioners of Jesus' words about how the rich will find it hard to enter the kingdom of heaven. But unlike Moody, Coffin had abandoned older, orthodox ideas about the Bible and the Gospel. He and Moody were still using a shared theological vocabulary, but they were using different dictionaries.

As America prepared to turn the page on the nineteenth century, the theologians in many of the nation's Protestant seminaries were teaching the young men (and yes, it was only men) a much different message than they had just one hundred years earlier. The rise of Charles Darwin's message in the mid-1800s, combined with skeptical "higher criticism" approaches to the Scripture, stripped away confidence in the Bible. But most Protestants in the pews had not yet shifted their theology, so the theologians and denominational leaders began to use doublespeak. Of course, people aren't stupid, and they began to ask questions, especially when they gathered for their national meetings.

Presbyterian laity wanted accountability for what was being taught. Were the young pastors being drilled on the Westminster Confession? Are we still Calvinists? Do we still believe what our grandparents believed about the Bible? In 1904, the Presbyterians in their General Assembly (the national meeting) accepted some changes to the Westminster. Something was afoot.

Then, in 1909, the New York Presbytery couldn't agree whether to ordain as pastors three men who wouldn't affirm the virgin birth of Jesus—a miraculous conception brought about by the Holy Spirit. The problem wasn't that the Scripture lacked clarity on the subject, but that since a "virgin birth" is one of those pesky Christian teachings with a miracle (a supernatural event) it had become an embarrassment. The new theologies wanted everything to be explainable scientifically. The issue went to the General Assembly, which accepted the men into ministry but instructed a committee to work up some basic doctrinal guidelines for future ordinations. Obviously, the Westminster wasn't the standard now, the argument went, but you needed to have some sort of benchmark, right?

So the General Assembly passed the "Doctrinal Deliverance of 1910," stating that there were five "necessary and essential" doctrines that must be held to:

1. The inspiration and inerrancy of the Bible
2. The virgin birth of Christ

3. Christ's death as an atonement for sin
4. Christ's resurrection was bodily in nature; he truly came back to life
5. The historicity of events in the Bible

These five planks hardly represented the whole of the Christian faith, nor did they convey any Presbyterian-specific doctrines. Even so, the "Deliverance" became controversial.

Over the next five years, a captain of the California oil industry by the name of Lyman Stewart—a staunch Presbyterian— anonymously paid to have a series of ninety essays published and distributed free of charge to pastors and missionaries: *The Fundamentals: A Testimony to the Truth*. Many of the authors were leading scholars of their time, and none of the explained doctrines were of the sectarian sort—only the major doctrines of the Christian faith were defended. Over time, people self-identified as "Fundamentalists" as a way of identifying themselves and supporting the movement. People on the other side became known as "Modernists."

In 1915, Coffin published a book with the opposite agenda, titled *Some Christian Convictions: A Practical Restatement in Terms of Present-Day Thinking*. Coffin called for "a readjustment of our view of the Bible, which frankly recognizes that its scientific ideas are those of the ages in which its various writers lived, and cannot be authoritative for us today." Modern science, he argued, should change our confidence in the Bible's authority. Coffin was pushing the line back against the fundamentalists, and his Madison Avenue congregation, being one of the wealthiest and full of culture-influencing parishioners, exerted an outsized influence on all Presbyterians.

J. Gresham Machen, a highly esteemed Princeton theologian, gave an address in 1921 titled "Liberalism or Christianity?" He argued that the Fundamentalists and Modernists were two very different religions altogether. This is a key point, not just for understanding

Presbyterianism in general, but for comprehending where we are at today in the United States religious landscape. When we talk about "Mainline" and "Evangelical," these arise from the older "Modernist vs. Fundamentalist" labels. The division that began in the 1920s never reversed itself.

In 1922, Harry Emerson Fosdick responded by preaching a historic sermon titled "Shall the Fundamentalists Win?"—seeking to rouse the Modernist side to lusty battle and victory. As a result, he was almost brought up on heresy charges by the Presbyterian Synod. Machen said of Fosdick, "The question is not whether Mr. Fosdick is winning men, but whether the thing to which he is winning them is Christianity."

Fosdick, a Baptist, pastored the First Presbyterian Church of Manhattan. He wasn't particularly committed to being a Baptist; they weren't particularly committed to being Presbyterian. It was a good match, but the son of oil magnate John D. Rockefeller wooed Fosdick to come pastor his special ecclesiastical creation: Riverside Church. Fosdick didn't seem eager to go, telling Junior it was because "you are too wealthy and I do not want to be known as the pastor of the richest man in the country." By that time, Fosdick was already being described as a heretic by Conservatives—but "to become a pastor to rich people" was something that troubled him. Laughing, Junior poked right back: "I like your frankness, but do you think that more people will criticize you on account of my wealth than will criticize me on account of your theology?"

Rockefeller biographer Ron Chernow described the Riverside Church building as "an ecumenical shrine that seemed to bridge both the spiritual and temporal worlds. Instead of saintly statues lining the chancel screen, one found . . . Louis Pasteur, Hippocrates, Florence Nightingale, and Abraham Lincoln. Statues of Confucius, Buddha, Muhammad, and Moses stared down from archivolts above the main portal, while Darwin and Einstein occupied honored niches." Riverside formally opened in 1931, the year after Donald Trump's mother passed through Ellis Island from Scotland, where the iconoclastic Presbyterianism she grew up in would not have allowed even a statue of the Apostle Paul to be in the church— let alone Buddha.

Coffin helped write the "Auburn Affirmation," a protest document signed by over twelve hundred pastors to say, in essence, "Quit telling us we have to affirm what you want us to affirm. We won't." The document denied the inerrancy of Scripture, the right of the General Assembly to govern the doctrine of the Presbyteries, and refuted the 1910 "fundamentals" as a test of ordination. The approval of the Auburn Affirmation was a pivotal moment in American Presbyterianism—and really in American Christianity as a whole because of all branches of Protestantism, the Presbyterians had always been the most creedal by tradition. When doctrinal aberrations surfaced fifty years earlier, heresy charges were brought and a trial commenced. Now the doctrinal redefiners had turned the table, saying not only were they changing the content of the faith, but they were also stripping away the governing body's right to censure. If you don't like it, you can leave.

Protestants under the "Fundamentalist" label did just that in one denomination after another, as similar conversations were being held about theological boundaries. The Southern Baptist Convention wrote their first denomination-wide statement of faith—The Baptist Faith and Message—in 1925, the same year that the Scopes Trial seemed to give Conservatives a black eye in the minds of people throughout the country. The Modernists were in the ascendancy; the Fundamentalists were in retreat. And Coffin was on his way to the presidency of his alma mater, Union Theological Seminary— the academic epicenter of Liberal Christianity in America.

TIME magazine celebrated his move to the seminary with a

front-cover spread for its November 15, 1926, issue. That day also happens to be the birthdate for NBC (or more specifically, NBC Radio)—an irony not lost on anyone who recalls Modern theologian Rudolf Bultmann's famous quote about Christianity: "It is impossible to use electrical light and the wireless and to avail ourselves of modern medical and surgical discoveries, and at the same time to believe in the New Testament world of spirits and miracles . . . to do so is to make the Christian faith unintelligible and unacceptable to the modern world."

Fred and Mary Anne were married in January 1936 by Coffin's like-minded replacement, the Reverend George Buttrick, who had already become a nationally known minister himself and had delivered Yale University's Lyman Beecher Lectures on Preaching in 1931—arguably the most prestigious such lectures in the world at the time. And by the end of the 1930s, Buttrick served as the president of the ecumenical Federal Council of Churches. In that capacity, he even had private correspondence with President Roosevelt, expressing a "separation of church and state" concern over the President's plan to send a personal representative to the Vatican. Roosevelt ignored Buttrick and countless other Protestants on the issue, but it wouldn't be until Ronald Reagan in 1984 that the "personal representative" position turned into "ambassador."

At century's end, *Preaching* magazine editor Michael Duduit compiled a list of "The Ten Greatest Preachers of the Twentieth Century," with the criteria being "the influence that preacher had on the church and on the wider society"—regardless of their theological stripe. The top five: (1) James Stewart, (2) Billy Graham, (3) George Buttrick, (4) Martin Luther King, and (5) Harry Emerson Fosdick. To be put at the top of such a list—and sandwiched in between Graham and King—shows just how influential Buttrick was as a preacher and as a teacher of preaching.

At this point in time, the paper trail cannot establish a precise date for when Fred and Mary Anne came to be at MAPC. And it is possible that the couple were married by Buttrick without being members—Fred was, after all, a wealthy New Yorker by that time. Having become engaged to the Presbyterian Mary Anne, he may have simply picked MAPC as the logical choice for an up-and-coming businessman like himself.

If you recall the basic facts from the previous chapter, Mary Anne MacLeod was born on May 10, 1912, in the hamlet of Tong just north of Stornoway (population: 8,000), Scotland, on the Isle of Lewis (population: 18,000). When searching for the New York marriage certificate of Mary Anne MacLeod and Fred Trump, we came up empty. That doesn't mean there isn't one—we just couldn't find one. But what we did discover was a 1942 "Petition for Naturalization" for a Mr. James Drysdale. Who?

Now pay attention because this is where it gets interesting. Mr. Drysdale—born in 1905, the same year as Fred Trump—came to America from Dunfermline, Scotland (the birthplace of Andrew Carnegie), in the 1930s. His name is on several ship manifests during that time. Then, on his 1942 application for citizenship, Drysdale stated that he was married to "Mary MacLeod" who was born in 1912 at Stornoway, Scotland. And the application states that he and MacLeod got married in 1933. What? Did Mary MacLeod have a pre-Fred, first marriage to a fellow Scot? After all, how many Mary MacLeods could have been born in Stornoway in 1912? We checked.

Nine. In 1912, in a parish with only about ten thousand people, nine baby girls were born into "MacLeod" families and given the name "Mary." And most of the parents' names were similar too— lots of "Donald" and "Malcolm" and even the awesome "Murdo."

So we dug into the ship manifests and found that in a five-year period (1929 to 1934), a "Mary MacLeod" who was born in 1912 in Stornoway made five cross-Atlantic trips. When comparing additional data in the manifests, we found that there were three different Mary MacLeod women, all from Stornoway, all born in 1912, who cumulatively made those five trips in that five-year span of time. But Donald's mother (the Mary born on May 10, to Mary and Malcolm MacLeod) was *not* the Mary who married Mr. Drysdale in New York in 1933. There was no "pre-Fred" first marriage. Phew! Glad we got that cleared up.

But wait, there was just one more fascinating item we discovered about this Mr. Drysdale and his wife Mary MacLeod—they worked at the same location where they lived. He was a butler and valet; she was "domestic help." And where did they work? Andrew Carnegie's Manhattan mansion. Of course, Mr. Carnegie had been dead for over a decade by this time (he died four months after marrying off his daughter), but his widow, Mrs. Louise Carnegie, still maintained the house and employed a large staff—including Drysdale and MacLeod. They both list Carnegie as their employer and the mansion as their place of residence. The 1930 census puts the value of the Carnegie residence at $4 million ($56 million in today's dollars). Talk about an upgrade from a small Scottish dwelling.

We believe these facts serve to support a hypothesis for solving the puzzling question of why Mary Anne MacLeod—a Conservative, Free Church Presbyterian, would so quickly end up getting married in one of the most affluent churches in America and one that was on the Modernist side of Presbyterianism. With dozens of Presbyterian churches in New York from which to choose, how did she find her way to MAPC?

One theory we have is that Donald's mom knew and kept up with the other Mary MacLeod. Wouldn't you? Imagine if you grew up four miles away from someone just two months younger than you—and you even shared names. And then you both left your tiny villages, independent of one another but within one year, to sail across the ocean and plant roots in the most electrifying city on earth. Wouldn't you keep up with each other? Especially if your friend is "domestic help" for Andrew Carnegie's widow, and her husband is the butler? And when Donald's mom asked her friend about the church, it is likely that the second Mary told her about MAPC.

A second theory, however, and one that will have to wait for future biographers of President Trump to tackle, is that Mary Anne knew about MAPC because of her older sister Mary Joan (MacLeod) Pauley. At the time that Fred and Mary Anne met, Mary Joan lived and worked with her husband, Victor, as domestic helpers to a wealthy family—and that residence was only a few blocks south of MAPC.

And it gets even better. The family that Victor and Mary Joan served were of no small consequence, as the name of the patriarch—Richard M. Hurd (1865–1941)—carried weight in his time. Hurd was a pioneering real estate economist, a member of Yale's Skull and Bones society, and a close friend of President Theodore Roosevelt. But of most interest to us is that in 1903 Hurd authored a groundbreaking and influential book titled *Principles of City Land Values* that taught real estate developers the importance of calculating how much money a piece of land could earn out during the lifetime of the building—and then build accordingly, so as to increase wealth with the best use of the land. And Hurd was no academic, as he led the mortgage division and later was president of one of the biggest mortgage companies in the city.

When Frederick Trump landed permanently in New York with his wife and children in 1905, he rented an office in lower Manhattan—one block away from Hurd's mortgage firm—and started a barbershop to earn a living while he planned his next moves—in real estate development. Did Frederick and Richard ever meet? We don't know. But Richard had five children, including a son—Clement, who was about Fred Trump's age. Clement studied architecture at

Yale, but used his drawing talent instead to become a world-famous illustrator of children's books—the best known being *The Runaway Bunny* (1942) and *Goodnight Moon* (1947). And the author of those books, Margaret Wise Brown, was an alumna of the prep school that Donald Trump would attend decades later.

Meanwhile, back at Richard's magnificent home in Manhattan—the one just blocks south of MAPC—Victor and Mary Joan worked throughout the early 1930s. Then Mary Joan's baby sister Mary Anne came to America too. And at some point around 1935, she met Fred and was married a year later. The fact that Mary Anne's sister kept house for one of the most influential mortgage executives who also pioneered real estate development theories—both areas of great interest to Fred—seems to be too great of a coincidence.

In case you're wondering whether the Hurds went to MAPC, they didn't—they were Episcopalian. At some point after Hurd died in 1941, Donald's aunt and uncle went to work for the family of W. R. Reynolds, another extremely wealthy businessman. The Pauleys followed them out of Manhattan when the Reynolds moved into a mansion in Palm Beach, two miles south of the Mar-a-Lago mansion now owned by Donald Trump. And Mr. Reynolds was active as a vestryman in his local Episcopal church a few blocks away—Bethesda by the Sea—the church where Donald and Melania were married in 2005 and where they attend for worship when they are in Florida.

With all those Mary MacLeods sailing from Scotland in a short span of time, it's little wonder that some of the stories about Donald Trump's mom that came out during the 2016 election would jumble and mix up the Marys. For example, *The New Yorker* ran a piece, "Donald Trump's Immigrant Mother," that opened with the lines:

In November of 1929, a seventeen-year-old Scotswoman, Mary Anne MacLeod, boarded the S.S. *Transylvania* in Glasgow, bound for New York City. . . . On at least two ship manifests and in the 1930 census, her occupation is listed as "maid" or "domestic."

Not exactly. The "November of 1929" MacLeod is the eighteen-year-old who got off the boat and went to work for Louise Carnegie—and then later married James Drysdale. Which makes *The New Yorker* mistake even more amusing, because if you viewed those 1929 travel logs and actually thought you were looking at Donald Trump's mom, then your story should lead with "Donald Trump's Immigrant Mother Went Straight to Work at the Carnegie Estate." Oh well, that ship has sailed.

In reality, Donald's mom doesn't show up on the 1930 census because her feet didn't land on US soil soon enough to be counted that year. She received her immigration papers on February 17, 1930, and then sailed out of Glasgow on the *Transylvania* on May 2, 1930. Mary Anne arrived in the port of New York City on Sunday, May 11, one day after celebrating her eighteenth birthday while on board a ship full of strangers all heading to their own destiny in America—the City on a Hill.

5

City on a Jamaican Hill

In 1630, William Laud, the Archbishop of Canterbury, and King Charles I of England punished a Presbyterian medical doctor, Alexander Leighton, for publishing a pamphlet that criticized the Anglican church. Leighton was put in leg irons and thrown in solitary confinement in an open-air cell where he was exposed to the elements for nearly four months. After that came the real punishment. Leighton was "tied to a stake and received thirty-six stripes with a heavy cord upon his naked back; he was placed in the pillory for two hours in November's frost and snow; he was branded in the face, had his nose split and his ears cut off, and was condemned to life imprisonment."

As any student of American history knows, a large portion of the people who left England in the seventeenth century, braving the three-month voyage across the Atlantic, did so not because they dreamed of gold, but because they pursued religious freedom. The church where Donald Trump grew up, First Presbyterian Church of Jamaica, Queens, sits just south of Jamaica Hills and to the west of Jamaica Hills Estates (where the Trumps lived). This congregation, the oldest continuously active Presbyterian church in the Western Hemisphere, was founded by such men and women.

Facing increased persecution, Puritans intensified their immigration to the New World. In the summer of 1630, John Winthrop led a fleet of ships full of Puritans across the sea as part of the Massachusetts Bay Colony. Before they landed, Winthrop stood on the deck of the *Arbella* and delivered one of the most significant sermons in history—"A Model of Christian Charity"—otherwise known as the "City Upon a Hill" sermon.

> We shall find that the God of Israel is among us, when ten of us shall be able to resist a thousand of our enemies; when He shall make us a praise and glory that men shall say of succeeding plantations, "may the Lord make it like that of New England." For we must consider that we shall be as a city upon a hill. The eyes of all people are upon us. So that if we shall deal falsely with our God in this work we have undertaken, and so cause Him to withdraw His present help from us, we shall be made a story and a by-word through the world.

Without using the phrase "American exceptionalism," Winthrop established that theme, and it still guides the consciousness of Winthrop's heirs today. Scots-Presbyterian Peter Marshall Jr.'s book *The Light and the Glory* is essentially a book-length explanation of how Winthrop's vision had been carried out in the United States. It sold millions of copies during the patriotic fervor of the mid-1970s and provided the nascent Religious Right with a sense of historical rootedness.

Even non-evangelical leaders have been drawn to Winthrop's message for inspiration. Two weeks before his inauguration, President-elect John F. Kennedy quoted from it in a speech to the Legislature of Massachusetts:

> . . . I have been guided by the standard John Winthrop set before his shipmates on the flagship *Arbella* three hundred and thirty-one years ago, as they, too, faced the task of building a new government on a perilous frontier. "We must always consider," he said, "that we shall be as a city upon

a hill—the eyes of all people are upon us." Today the eyes of all people are truly upon us—and our governments, in every branch, at every level, national, state and local, must be as a city upon a hill—constructed and inhabited by men aware of their great trust and their great responsibilities. For we are setting out upon a voyage in 1961 no less hazardous than that undertaken by the *Arbella* in 1630. We are committing ourselves to tasks of statecraft no less awesome than that of governing the Massachusetts Bay Colony, beset as it was then by terror without and disorder within.

Three decades later, President Ronald Reagan referred to the speech in his televised farewell address to the nation as he departed the White House. From behind the big oak Resolute desk in the Oval Office, Reagan said:

And that's about all I have to say tonight, except for one thing. The past few days when I've been at that window upstairs, I've thought a bit of the "shining city upon a hill." The phrase comes from John Winthrop, who wrote it to describe the America he imagined. What he imagined was important because he was an early Pilgrim, an early freedom man. He journeyed here on what today we'd call a little wooden boat; and like the other Pilgrims, he was looking for a home that would be free.

I've spoken of the shining city all my political life, but I don't know if I ever quite communicated what I saw when I said it. But in my mind it was a tall, proud city built on rocks stronger than oceans, windswept, God-blessed, and teeming with people of all kinds living in harmony and peace; a city with free ports that hummed with commerce and creativity. And if there had to be city walls, the walls had doors and the doors were open to anyone with the will and the heart to get here. That's how I saw it, and see it still.

And how stands the city on this winter night? More prosperous, more secure, and happier than it was 8 years ago. But more than that: After 200 years, two centuries, she still stands strong and true on the granite ridge, and her glow has held steady no matter what storm. And she's still a beacon, still a magnet for all who must have freedom, for all the pilgrims from all the lost places who are hurtling through the darkness, toward home.

In 1634, two years after Winthrop landed in Massachusetts, Puritan Robert Coe also brought his family over, joining in with the Massachusetts Bay Colony. Coe, who some say is an ancestor of former first lady Barbara Bush, would establish many settlements on Long Island, including Jamaica. From 1658 to 1664, Coe served as the magistrate for Jamaica; in 1662 he helped to establish First Presbyterian Church of Jamaica.

The debate over whether "America is a Christian nation" will forever reference Winthrop's thesis. And the debate gets fierce, even among evangelicals. But one thing that unites all evangelicals is the desire to defend and even expand religious liberty. As Baptists in London wrote in 1640, at a time when they enjoyed precious few religious liberties: "all other liberties will not be worth the naming, much less enjoying."

Given that the Trump campaign, and now the Trump administration, made religious liberty such a central issue, the fact that he grew up in a church birthed by fresh-off-the-boat, religious-liberty-seeking Puritans is something worth taking note of. Without a doubt, to be a member of FPC is to know the history of the congregation. After all, that history is well documented by the church and has often been told—especially every fifty years when the church celebrated milestone anniversaries. In 1943, when the Trumps were members of the church, FPC published 600 copies of a 250-page hardback, *First Presbyterian Church of Jamaica, New York*—building on several earlier works. If young Donald Trump picked this volume up off the shelf of his church library, then he would have opened to the first chapter, "Why Presbyterians Left England and What They Found in Jamaica"—with its gruesome anecdote about the torture of Leighton, printed on the first pages of the book.

Three decades before the Revolutionary War and then about three decades after, the colonies experienced the "First Great Awakening" and "Second Great Awakening" periods of protracted interest in and conversion to Christianity. These times of religious renewal greatly affected the course of history for our nation, so it is fascinating to discover direct points of connection between key preachers from these events and First Presbyterian Church.

For example, Gilbert Tennent, the son of the man who founded the forerunner of Princeton University, preached at FPC in 1740 during the First Awakening. And David Brainerd, a missionary to the native Americans whose short life was chronicled by the eminent Jonathan Edwards—America's greatest theologian—had dealings with FPC as they shared support and recommendations of ministers. George Whitfield, the Billy Graham of his day, came to Jamaica twice, once in 1740 and again in 1764. The second time he came, he "attracted such crowds" that "there was no building large enough to accommodate his hearers, so he preached to them under an apple tree not far from the Stone Church."

During the Second Awakening, Presbyterian Asahel Nettleton's preaching and individual counseling "led directly to the conversion of 30,000 people at a time when the entire nation's population was only nine million." He traveled throughout New England, preaching in churches that asked for him, or had an empty pulpit that needed to be filled, that's where Nettleton intersects with our story, because for nine months in 1826, Nettleton preached at FPC. The church had lost its pastor the year before due to "some dissatisfaction arising in the congregation," and Nettleton found the congregation to be "in a very divided and distracted state." Nettleton labored at preaching and counseling with this congregation. By the summer, "72 persons were added to the church on profession [of faith; conversion]; eighteen were baptized." In the short nine months that Nettleton was with this church, the "number of communicants" (members) increased from 197 to 263. And even after he left, the church continued to grow, reaching 400 members by the time of his death in 1844.

During the years just before the Revolutionary War, much of the New York leadership of the movement was known to come from the Presbyterian churches. After the Sons of Liberty dumped a boatload of English tea into New York Harbor in 1774, a resident of the city wrote to a friend in London to report that the Presbyterians "have been the chief and principal instruments in all these flaming measures, and they always do and ever will act against Government, from that restless and turbulent anti-monarchical spirit which has always distinguished them everywhere, whenever they had, or by any means could assume power."

Later that same year, when the town of Jamaica appointed a Committee of Correspondence and Observation that would coordinate communications and support with the First Continental Congress, five out of seven of the committee were members of the First Presbyterian Church. The Americans on Long Island were defeated early, on August 27, 1776, and the British occupied the whole of Jamaica for the remainder of the war.

Elias Baylis, an Elder at FPC and the chairman of the Committee of Correspondence, was captured by the British. Being blind and aged, a British officer questioned the soldiers as to why Baylis had been arrested. The answer: "He's blind, but he can talk." To that, Baylis let rip "a few words in vindication of the American cause"— and the officer was convinced, sending him to a prison ship where he remained until he became so sick that they released him, though he died while walking back to his home. It was said of Baylis that he "stood high in the community for uprightness and ability. He had a sweet voice, and could sing whole psalms and hymns from memory."

The town of Jamaica formed two companies of Minute Men, two-thirds of whom were Presbyterians, both led by members of FPC. Numerous men from the church gave their lives for the cause of American independence, including a man named Ephraim Marston who was killed in battle shortly after First Presbyterian recorded the baptism of his son, whom he had named patriotically: John Hancock Marston.

C. S. Lewis, the British author of the Chronicles of Narnia series, wrote about "men without chests"—people who have developed no internal "middle element" that connects their intellects with their appetites. Without this middle element—a "chest"—Lewis said that people either cannot or will not believe in the objective nature of truth and reality. But who wants to live in a society governed by such people? Lewis wrote: "We make men without chests and expect from them virtue and enterprise. We laugh at honor and are shocked to find traitors in our midst."

Tens of thousands of people left family and crossed the Atlantic yearning for religious freedom. Later, men died on the battlefield in a fight for the independence they would not live to experience— though they would pass it down as a heritage to their children. And old men died in prison for speaking up for the very freedoms we enjoy today. Such men and women had "chests"—and we take a step in the direction of having our own whenever we remember the actions they took and the motivations behind them.

Being born in a garage doesn't make you a car. And being raised in a church with a rich history of vibrant biblical Christianity and sacrificial love for America makes you neither a patriot nor a Christian. But the fact that, in centuries past, so many of these people worshipped God in the same congregation in which Donald Trump would spend his childhood and teen years means that he grew up in proximity to these stories of "men *with* chests."

And what's more, Christians in prayer often plead with God "for the future generations," asking God to call out and save the people who will one day inhabit the buildings and preach in the pulpits that they now enjoy. They pray for God to bless their posterity. James Dobson tells how his great-grandfather "prayed every morning from eleven to noon for his children and for future generations of his family" and that "toward the end of his life, he announced that God had made his ancestor a promise: Every member of four generations of his family would become Christians." When asked whether it is ridiculous to pray for future generations yet unborn—and who we will never meet—Billy Graham's organization answered:

> No, it isn't silly to pray for those who will follow us—even those who haven't been born yet. Repeatedly over the years, I've met men and women who had a godly grandmother or saintly great-grandfather whom they never met, but who prayed for them and for others who weren't yet born. These men and women were convinced that their own commitment to Christ was a result of those prayers, and I can't help but agree. This may have been what the Psalmist meant

when he prayed, "I will perpetuate your memory through all generations; therefore the nations will praise you for ever and ever." (Psalm 45:17)

Until eternity, most of us will not know if our ancestors were Christian and if they were praying for us. But if one grew up in a church with several hundred years of faithfulness to Christ, as did Donald Trump, then God only knows—literally—how many prayers were prayed to God on behalf of the future souls that would one day sit in the pews of FPC.

6

Hindenburg

We don't know exactly when Fred and Mary Anne joined the First Presbyterian in Jamaica (FPC), but the church is located within a couple of miles of every home Fred and Mary Anne ever lived in. They brought five babies into the world in their first twelve years of marriage, so one would be justified in assuming that they settled down at FPC Jamaica fairly quickly into their courtship or marriage simply as a matter of convenience.

In addition to the logistical considerations, however, they may have simply found the leadership to be to their liking. The pastor of the church at the time, Andrew Magill, had led the church since being called there and was well known and loved throughout the community. It was said of Magill that though he was foreign born (Irish), "he is more intensely loyal to his adopted country than many native-born Americans. His allegiances are to God and America."

In the history of Presbyterian schisms in America—of which there are many—the division that happened in 1936 at the General Assembly of the Presbyterian Church ranks high on the list as being one of the most historic—and permanent. And if we understand the battle to have been between two competing sides—the Fundamentalists and the Modernists—then it seems that FPC ended up leaning in favor of the denomination and the Modernists. Since this was the church that Donald Trump spent his entire childhood and teen years attending, and since he continues to identify himself as "Protestant, Christian, Presbyterian"—though he has not been a member at a Presbyterian church since he left FPC, then it is important to quickly tell the story of this battle for the soul of the denomination to which FPC belonged.

In 1929, Princeton Seminary's Conservative professors resigned in protest at the theological drift and unaccountability of the institution. They immediately formed Westminster Theological Seminary—a name that left no doubt as to their position about whether "ancient creeds" should serve as a standard for theological fidelity. The next few years saw a response and counterresponse between the Conservatives and Liberals in the denomination as a whole. Now, remember, we're not talking about some small group of religious people having private squabbles. This was THE Presbyterian Church in America (stylized as PCUSA)—the Presbyterian denomination that operated most of the colleges, seminaries, churches, mission boards, and finances bearing the label "Presbyterian."

Tension escalated quickly when Pearl S. Buck, Pulitzer Prize–winning novelist (*The Good Earth*) and daughter of PCUSA missionaries to China, wrote a series of articles praising a 1932 denominational report called "Re-Thinking Missions." Funded by John D. Rockefeller (another example of a wealthy captain of industry trying to "fix" the church), the "rethinking" that Buck and the Modernists desired was for foreign missions to evolve: no more evangelizing non-Christians to get them "saved"—no more "hell" or "wrath of God" stuff.

Modernists refused to counter Buck, so the Conservatives formed an independent mission board. In 1935, a denominational court responded by declaring Machen guilty of "acts contrary to the government and discipline of the Presbyterian Church in the U.S.A." In other words, they moved to defrock the leader of the Conservatives—to take away his ordination. This made front-page news all around the nation: "Possibility of Presbyterian Rift Is Seen as Dr. J. G. Machen Discusses Controversy" (*The Cincinnati Enquirer*).

Machen appealed the ruling to the 1936 General Assembly, but they upheld it and Machen was expelled from the PCUSA. So, the next week the Conservatives formed their own denomination, the Orthodox Presbyterian Church. The remainder of the twentieth-century history of Presbyterianism in America are footnotes to what happened in this altercation. As much as the 1925 Scopes Trial, where evolutionary theory was debated in a court of law by William Jennings Bryan and Clarence Darrow, Machen's 1935–1936 battle with the Modernists was seen as a national referendum on the future of biblical theology within the Mainline churches.

From the vantage point of eighty years, what can an outsider ascertain about FPC's thoughts on the theological battle? The defrocking was mentioned in the June 2, 1936, edition of the *Brooklyn Eagle* newspaper, mentioning an elder from FPC Jamaica, Frank Donaldson, who had served as a delegate to the General Assembly:

> Elder Frank Donaldson of Hollis . . . became conspicuous by being the only voice raised against most of the decisions. The decisions had to do with the controversy between the Fundamentalist and Modernist groups. . . . Mr. Donaldson arose twice to have his vote officially recorded and was supported by only a few stray votes. The decisions were all against the group headed by Dr. J. Gresham Machen.

In other words, Mr. Donaldson stood up for Machen and the Conservatives. Four days later, the Saturday edition of the *Brooklyn Eagle* printed the following notice:

> Elder Frank Donaldson, who attended the Presbyterian General Assembly at Syracuse as a delegate, will speak tomorrow evening at Jamaica Presbyterian Church on the problems facing the Presbyterian Church, especially the break between the Fundamentalist and Modernist groups,

in which he took an active part at the Assembly, voting against the ousting of the Fundamentalist group.

One person alone does not speak for an entire church body, so here are two counterfactual pieces of data that reveal more about the theological trajectory of the church.

First, in the church's own published history—published in 1943, just after these events—they make no mention of them whatsoever. But when describing the Reverend Lewis Lampman—their pastor before World War I—they tipped their hand for the reader to know where they stood on the Modernist vs. Fundamentalist debates (emphasis mine):

> Lewis Lampman was more than an efficient pastor and a lovable man. He was forward-looking and realized that a simpler statement of its beliefs was imperative in order to insure the future prosperity of the American Presbyterian Church. Fortunately, he and his successors in the pastorate of the Jamaica church, Mr. Hobbs, Mr. Dickhaut, *and Mr. Magill, have been liberal.*

The history then describes how "less than one hundred years ago" the session (i.e., pastors) of this church had found that some people who wanted to join the church didn't believe that souls went to hell—they believed in "annihilationism." The pastors of that past age did not think such people—those who did not believe in the doctrine of a literal hell—should be admitted into the church. But the 1943 history book censured these long-deceased pastors for that rigid biblicism:

> Too often has the insistence on subscription to non-essentials become an insurmountable barrier to church fellowship!

Happily, so far as the Jamaica church is concerned, that practice was abandoned long ago. Today, it is the established policy . . . that in the Presbyterian Church no acceptance of the doctrines of the Church is required of any communicant, beyond a personal faith in Jesus Christ as Son of God and Savior of the world, and a sincere acceptance of Him as Lord and Master. In the movement for this liberal attitude, which was intended to induce people who were already followers of Christ to become members of the church, Lewis Lampman was a leader.

So, as a simple matter of factual record, FPC leaned toward the Modernist side of the theological debate. They didn't mind stating this publicly in their published history, even to the point of publicly declaring their nineteenth-century forefathers to have been mistaken in their rigidness.

Second, in the same month (April 1937) that Donald Trump's oldest sibling, Maryanne, was born, FPC held a series of special events to commemorate the 275th anniversary of the founding of the church, including a catered banquet for 600 people, on the evening of April 28. The newspaper recorded: "It was an occasion particularly enjoyed and notable on account of the presence of Dr. Robert E. Speer, Secretary of the Board of Foreign Missions, as the principal speaker of the evening."

Though Speer had earlier written articles for *The Fundamentals*, as things shook out he sided with the Modernists and helped lead the charge against Machen. The two men even famously debated "Modernism" in 1933. When the Liberals put Speer's name forth to be moderator of the 1924 General Assembly, *TIME* magazine wrote of him: "Dr. Speer is a conservative. There is no weak-spot in his armor of orthodoxy. He could stand up with the best Fundamentalist before the judgment seats of John Calvin and John Knox. But he is not a Fundamentalist. He believes that Christianity is greater than theology."

When Speer addressed the banqueting members of FPC on a spring evening in Jamaica, Machen's defrocking had taken place less than a year earlier. With many conservatives leaving the denomination now clearly led by Modernists, one could only guess as to the future direction and stability of Presbyterianism in America.

One week after the banquet, New Yorkers looked skyward at the spectacular sight of the German airship *Hindenburg* making its way south to dock at nearby Lakehurst, New Jersey. Hours later, the *Hindenburg* caught fire and crashed to the ground. The photographs and newsreel of that event became iconic, considered to be some of the first image-driven "breaking news" items in the history of journalism. A radio announcer on the ground who saw passengers falling to their death exclaimed over the airwaves: "It is bursting into flames. . . . This is terrible. This is one of the worst catastrophes in the world. . . . Oh, the humanity!"

Modernity was ushering in a new world with each passing year. Those born in 1662—the year FPC was founded—would have had more in common with Moses than they would have had with someone born in 1900. But with the rapid advancements of modernity, people wondered if the ancient Christian faith would survive. Would Christian Truth still be viable in a world now structured by scientific truths? And if Christianity crashed, what would be the result?

As did nearly all churches in the postwar years, First Presbyterian Church would continue to grow into the 1950s and then begin to recede in the 1960s and 1970s. Certainly "white flight" played its part as the neighborhood experienced demographic shifts. Even so, across the nation, the Mainline Presbyterian churches (PCUS and UPCUSA) have plummeted from 4.1 million members in 1960 to 1.6 million in 2015. At the same time, however, the Conservative Presbyterian denominations have seen steady and continuous growth over the decades. The Mainline Presbyterians fought and won the right to "rethink" missions, evangelism, and the Gospel—and the results speak for themselves.

When CNN ran a piece about the faith of Donald Trump, they told an anecdote from a pre-Inauguration prayer meeting that Trump had with two Presbyterian pastors: Reverends Patrick O'Connor, senior pastor at FPC Jamaica, and Scott Black Johnston of Fifth Avenue in Manhattan.

> It was clear that Trump was still preoccupied with his November victory, and pleased with his performance with one constituency in particular.
>
> "I did very, very well with evangelicals in the polls," Trump interjected in the middle of the conversation—previously unreported comments that were described to me by both pastors.
>
> They gently reminded Trump that neither of them was an evangelical.
>
> "Well, what are you then?" Trump asked.
>
> They explained they were mainline Protestants, the same Christian tradition in which Trump, a self-described Presbyterian, was raised and claims membership. Like many mainline pastors, they told the President-elect, they lead diverse congregations.
>
> Trump nodded along, then posed another question to the two men: "But you're all Christians?"
>
> Yes, we're all Christians.

The *Huffington Post* then piggybacked off CNN with their own piece, titled "Donald Trump Apparently Doesn't Know Which Christians Are Evangelicals." There's no denying that Trump got muddled by the Mainliners' denominating of their denomination, but it seems a bit pedantic to criticize a layman for not knowing the difference between one Presbyterian group and another. The First Church of the Flying Spaghetti Monster (that's a real denomination, look it up) can claim creativity in brand-naming; Presbyterians—not so much.

Furthermore, as we have attempted to show, most Presbyterian groups have been an object-in-motion theologically. The whole program of being "not an Evangelical" is something new to Presbyterianism within Trump's own lifetime. Liberal Presbyterian churches are clearly not evangelical now, though they once were. And others who were once Liberal have now apostatized beyond the pale of even the most minimal definition of Christianity.

From a distance, one could argue that the FPC Jamaica of Donald Trump's experience (c. 1946–1970) was evangelical-ish in orientation; not Liberal, though in a denomination drifting to the Left. The evangelical voice within the PCUSA has now almost entirely left the denomination—but that wholesale flight only came after the past few General Assembly meetings, when the denomination gave its blessing to same-sex marriage for laymen and clergy alike. But again, those decisions came about over three decades after the Trumps last held membership in a PCUSA church.

So, what is FPC Jamaica like today? For starters, FPC is almost entirely a congregation of color, reflecting the demographics of the neighborhood and an ability to match up with those demographics regarding effective outreach. That's a fancy way of saying that the church is reaching its neighborhood—a community that has changed much in the past fifty years.

During the 2016 election, journalists flocked to FPC to catch a peek into Trump's childhood house of worship. When they saw and heard all the minority congregants (over thirty nations are represented in the current membership), many journalists took the easy-bake story based on the externals, stating how ironic they thought the situation was because, you know, Trump and the GOP don't like such people—so the argument goes.

But the fact-based reality about denominations paints a different picture. First, the racial diversity and growth of FPC Jamaica make it an anomaly within its own denomination, the PCUSA—the largest and most liberal Presbyterian denomination in America. As Emma Green of *The Atlantic* noted:

> First Church's congregation of immigrants may be saving it from the fate of other churches in Presbyterian Church USA, a mainline group that has been declining for years. Between 2011 and 2014, the number of churches in the denomination shrank by more than 600. Members are getting older, and few young people are joining; as of 2014, nearly 70 percent were over age 50, according to Pew Research Center.

You can find a Mainline church in any city you visit. But if you visit, you won't find many minorities. Membership in the three large Mainline denominations (PCUSA, Evangelical Lutheran Church of American, United Methodist Church) is lily-white: 88 to 96 percent Caucasian. Evangelicals like the Southern Baptist Convention (85 percent) and the Presbyterian Church in America (80 percent) are only slightly more blended. By contrast, the Assemblies of God (66 percent) and Roman Catholics (59 percent) have strong racial diversity.

Race and religion in America is an immense and complicated topic beyond the scope of this book. But clearly, FPC Jamaica shifted with the changing demographics of the neighborhood to the point that it now looks the exact reverse of its own denomination. If they had not done so, the church Donald Trump grew up in may have closed. From a peak attendance of over one thousand in the early 1950s, FPC dwindled down to less than one hundred in 1975 and considered turning out the lights. Instead, a new pastor came in during the 1970s—once the Trumps had moved their membership into Manhattan—and led the remaining members to focus on reaching the neighborhood as it currently was, not as it was at the turn of the century. And that's what they began to do. Forty years later, the church is full during worship and seems to have a clear vision and resources for living out the gospel in their community. And yes, it is full of minorities and immigrants, starting with the pastor who was born in the other Jamaica—the island nation in the Caribbean.

Though FPC is a member congregation of the liberal PCUSA, their website talks about their ministries being "purpose driven"— the language of evangelical mega-church pastor Rick Warren. In 2015, the church went through a "spiritual journey called 40 Days of Purpose." Again, that is Warren material, literally a best-selling book written by the best-known baby boomer evangelical on the planet.

And under the "Ministries" tab on their website, the top link leads you offsite to Right Now Media. When you click on the link, you see evangelical rock stars promoting the site: Francis Chan, David Platt, Tony Evans, Tim Tebow, and VeggieTales. "It's like the Netflix of Christian Bible Study," writes evangelical mega-church pastor Matt Chandler. Clearly, these resources don't come with a Henry Sloane Coffin or Harry Emerson Fosdick seal of approval. But the FPC website recommends them.

So, to return to the *Huffington Post*'s point—"Donald Trump Apparently Doesn't Know Which Christians Are Evangelicals"—we would wager that, like Trump, most Americans don't know which Christians are evangelicals. That is certainly one takeaway from the 2016 election. And, like Trump, most Americans could more easily distinguish between varieties of apples in the produce aisle of their neighborhood grocer than they could distinguish between varieties of Presbyterianism in their neighborhood.

7

We Have Confirmation

When ground was broken in 1922 for what would become the new Jamaica Hospital, the invocation was given by FPC's Reverend Magill, who the newspaper said "represented all the Protestant denominations." His church had been an early financial supporter of the hospital, dating back to the nineteenth century. Later, Fred Trump would make contributions and sit on the board of the hospital; Mary Anne volunteered her time there for decades. The hospital now boasts a Trump Pavilion for Nursing and Rehabilitation—built in 1975 with funds from the Trumps and named in honor of Mary Anne. And on June 14, 1946, this was the location of Donald Trump's birth—entering the world in a hospital that his family and church family had helped to build.

In the modern world, where families often have to pick up and move from one place to another, Donald's family was more "Old School"—establishing roots and raising their children in this one civic and church community. If Donald were to take you down memory lane of his pre-adolescent years, nearly everything happened within these few square miles. Two of those memories involve his religious experiences and, though he would not have been aware of this, both experiences were impacted by the theological skirmishes that have been discussed in the last chapter.

First, Trump was given a Bible by Mary Anne when he was eight years old, on June 12, 1955—the Sunday he graduated from Sunday Church Primary School at FPC. Church officials signed their names on the inside cover, and his name is imprinted on the front cover.

Giving a child a Bible at this age is not a sacramental act, but more a matter of practicality—younger children haven't developed the responsibility to care for a nice Bible or even the reading comprehension to make it worth the expense.

Donald Trump has been given hundreds of Bibles by well-wishers over the years. During our first interview, he told me how he keeps them in a very nice place inside Trump Tower. "There's no way I would ever . . . do anything negative to a Bible. . . . I would have a fear of doing something other than very positive." But the copy given to him by his mother is the one he counts most special. This was one of the two Bibles on which Trump placed his hand when he took the oath of office as president in January 2017, the other being a Bible belonging to Abraham Lincoln. Both Bibles are common editions. The "Lincoln Bible" was simply a Bible that the clerk of the United States Supreme Court grabbed for the occasion because Lincoln's personal belongings had not yet arrived at the capital. The Bible was an 1853 Oxford University Press edition of the King James Bible that, apart from it being connected to Lincoln, would sell at an antique bookstore for less than fifty dollars. Trump's Bible was the brand new, best-selling Revised Standard Version (RSV) of 1952—published by Thomas Nelson & Sons.

When "best-selling" is used as a label for the Bible, that normally signifies the sales status of all Bible translations put together. But this RSV translation became a best seller all on its own: It ranked number one for nonfiction in 1952, 1953, and 1954. Advertisements in 1952 for the Bible declared it the "Greatest Bible in 341 Years" (referring to the 1611 publication date for the KJV) and included endorsements from Norman Vincent Peale and Harry Emerson Fosdick.

Evangelicals, however, were suspicious of the Bible due to the liberal commitments of the translators—and having Fosdick endorse the product certainly didn't help. The ecumenical National Council of Churches sponsored the Bible, and a Yale Divinity School scholar named Luther Weigle led the committee. Conservatives perceived the RSV wasn't merely giving the reader "easier to read" English, but was changing the text to suit the Modernist theology. The Virgin Birth was once again at the center of the controversy, when Isaiah 7:14 was read and compared to the KJV:

(KJV) Therefore the Lord himself shall give you a sign; Behold, a virgin shall conceive, and bear a son, and shall call his name Immanuel.

(RSV) Therefore the Lord himself will give you a sign. Behold, a young woman shall conceive and bear a son, and shall call his name Immanuel.

The controversy resulted in Protestantism being further split— now they wouldn't even be reading from the same translation on Sunday mornings. No evangelical pastor in 1955 would have preached from the RSV; no liberal preacher would have presented a young person with a Bible in the archaic language of the KJV. This may all seem quaint now, given that there are so many translations from which to choose, but in 1955 that wasn't the case. It wasn't until 1971 that evangelicals produced their own "easy to read" version, the perennially best-selling New International Version (NIV).

It was also during the 1950s that the battle to maintain Bible reading in public schools was being fought in the courts. In 1962's *Engel v. Vitale* and then, in 1963, *Abington School District v. Schempp*, the Supreme Court ruled 8–1 that:

[N]o state law or school board may require that passages from the Bible be read or that the Lord's Prayer be recited in the public schools of a State at the beginning of each school day—even if individual students may be excused from attending or participating in such exercises upon written request of their parents.

This ruling is considered by evangelicals to be a day that went down in infamy, when "prayer and Bible reading were taken out of schools" and naked secularism began its reign as the state religion of America. In 1984, Reagan quoted from Justice Potter Stewart (the lone dissenting vote in the case) during a time when the Senate debated "prayer in schools" legislation. Stewart had written:

> . . . if religious exercises are held to be an impermissible activity in schools, religion is placed at an artificial and state-created disadvantage. . . . And a refusal to permit religious exercises thus is seen, not as the realization of state neutrality, but rather as the establishment of a religion of secularism, or at least, as governmental support of the beliefs of those who think that religious exercises should be conducted only in private.

This is not dusty history, however, for the 1963 decision continues to be interwoven into the campaign speeches of conservatives whenever the topic of religious liberty comes up. Weigle, the RSV scholar, himself testified in court, arguing in favor of Scripture in schools:

> The First Amendment to the Constitution has two clauses dealing with religion. . . . Most of the discussion in these recent years has centered about the first of these clauses, quaintly disguised as the erection of a wall. It is time to center our thought and action about the second clause; it is time for believers in God to claim and to justify their full religious freedom.

Weigle's defense of Bible reading in public schools is a fascinating example of the fluctuations in political and theological alliances that have taken place during the lifetime of Donald Trump.

The second religious experience from childhood that Trump recalls is when he received confirmation into the First Presbyterian Church, made famous during the 2016 campaign by the Confirmation photo he frequently showed people. The picture is dated "June 1959"—the month he turned thirteen. It shows him on the back of three rows, the first two lined up with twelve young girls in white dresses and flowers and the back row with seven young men in mostly dark suits—Trump being the tallest.

Now, for hundreds of years of Presbyterian history, a confirmation class would have been structured around the memorization of the Westminster Shorter Catechism. As has already been established, the Presbyterian denominations moved away from the Westminster as a standard for membership, so it is not a surprise that the confirmation class that Donald Trump went through used other materials. Unlike independent churches that choose their curriculum based on the preferences of their own leadership, FPC would have utilized the confirmation preparation material produced by the PCUSA denomination itself. Even now, it is easy to acquire a used copy of the exact booklet, called "This Is My Church" (1957 edition), that young Donald would have gone through in preparation for confirmation. Compared to the Westminster documents, this booklet has the theological weight of a preschooler's picture book. On the other hand, compared to the extremely low bar for church membership that many evangelicals have today, the book is surprisingly meaty.

At the end of the process, the students would sign a "Certificate of Church Membership." This document certified that the individual "has publicly confessed Jesus Christ as Lord and Savior and has been received into the communicant membership" of the local church. There would be a service held to establish and pronounce that the individuals were ready "for admission to the Lord's Supper." Publicly, they would be asked to confess, confirm, and promise the following:

> Do you confess your faith in God the Father Almighty, Maker of heaven and earth, and in Jesus Christ his only Son our Lord, and do you promise with the aid of the Holy Spirit to be Christ's faithful disciple to your life's end?
>
> Do you confirm the vows taken for you in baptism, and with a humble and contrite heart put your whole trust in the mercy of God which is in Christ Jesus our Lord?
>
> Do you promise to make diligent use of the means of grace, to share faithfully in the worship and service of the church, to give of your substance as the Lord may prosper you, to give your whole heart to the service of Christ and his Kingdom throughout the world, and to continue in the peace and fellowship of the people of God?

Then the minister would give this charge to the communicants:

> And now, as a member of Christ's church, go forth into the world in peace; be of good courage; hold fast that which is good; render to no man evil for evil; strengthen the fainthearted; support the weak; heal the afflicted; honor all men; love and serve the Lord, rejoicing in the power of the Spirit.
>
> And the blessing of God Almighty, the Father, the Son, and the Holy Spirit, be upon you and remain with you forever.
>
> Amen.

8

The Church for Spock Babies

In one of those strange quirks of history, three future US presidents were born within ten weeks of each other in 1946: Donald Trump (June 14), George W. Bush (July 6), and Bill Clinton (August 19). Since Clinton defeated George H. W. Bush in 1992, five out of seven of our presidential elections have been won by a man born in the first summer after the end of World War II. Only President Obama (b. 1961) broke the pattern, and he did so by beating out Hillary Clinton (b. 1947) in the 2008 Democratic primary and then Mitt Romney (b. 1947) in 2012. For good measure, throw former vice president Al Gore into the mix too (b. 1947).

By sharp contrast, not one person born in the 1930s ever became president or even served as vice president—John McCain (b. 1936) and Michael Dukakis (b. 1933) came the closest. Ron Paul (b. 1932), Ted Kennedy (b. 1932), Gary Hart (b. 1936), and Pat Buchanan (b. 1938) all failed too. Likewise, nobody born in the 1950s has yet won even their party's nomination—Mike Huckabee came in second while winning eight states in 2008; John Kasich won his home state of Ohio in 2016; Tim Kaine (b. 1958) was put on Clinton's 2016 ticket. So, the current vice president, Mike Pence (b. 1959), is the closest anyone born in the 1950s has gotten to the presidency.

Seriously? Nobody from the 1930s and only one from the 1950s— but *three men from the summer of 1946*? That's just odd. Eventually, a sociologist or psychiatrist will make a career out of exploring the relationship between Oval Office achievement and this 1946–1947 birth-year phenomenon. Was there something in the water? Was the school curriculum different? Was it their watching *Howdy Doody* (1947–1960)? Was it the Russian launch of Sputnik in 1957, sending the US into buckle-down-against-Communism mode? Was it the *Pax Eisenhower* stability and financial boom of the 1950s? Was it because Elvis Presley broke out in song and gyrating hips just as they finished elementary school? Or was it because the Beatles brought the "British invasion" just as they finished high school? (As an aside, when the Beatles famously landed at an airport in NYC, don't forget two facts: That airport had just been renamed "JFK" two months earlier in honor of the slain president, and that airport is in Jamaica, Queens—four miles from the Trump home.) Was it the sense of mortality—having witnessed the assassinations of JFK, MLK, and RFK—all coming before this group turned twenty-five? Was it the escalation of Vietnam? Was it Watergate?

Yes, pretty much all the above. Baby boomers, like the rest of us, were molded by the history they lived through. At the peak of baby production, a boomer infant came into the world every eight seconds. The earliest of them were children in the 1950s, when Eisenhower sat in the White House and, for the first time, a TV sat in nearly every home (from 172,000 homes in 1948 to 15.3 million in 1952). Childhood playmates recall the Trump family having the first color TV in the neighborhood. These boomers entered adulthood under the shadow of the same dramatic events—Vietnam, student protests, and assassinations. They embraced the sexual revolution of the sixties and the drug culture of the seventies, mainstreaming them both into the middle class. They watched Watergate explode, ushering in an anti-institutional shadow of cynicism that has yet to leave our public discourse. They got married and started their families in the 1970s. Finally, they hit their vocational stride in the "material world" of the 1980s, and they took over national offices in the 1990s and 2000s. Now, in the 2010s, they are beginning to retire and collect Social Security. Or, like Donald Trump, a few of them have started a new job in a new line of work.

Because one of the most significant influences on a person's character is the shaping that takes place by his or her parents, it is important to note that Donald Trump was born exactly one month before Spock's book tidal-waved over the landscape of American parenting.

Spock? The Vulcan science officer on *Star Trek*? No, we're talking about Dr. Benjamin Spock, the American pediatrician who wrote *The Common Sense Book of Baby and Child Care.* Released July 14, 1946, this book sold 750,000 copies in its first year alone and 50 million copies so far in its lifetime. Outside of the Bible, Spock's book ranks number two in the nonfiction category for most sales in the twentieth century. Any book that sells a million copies is a culture-shaping force to be reckoned with, but 50 million is ridiculous in terms of the effects it has on the culture. And even more so when it's an instruction manual for parents that takes a dramatic shift from the parenting methods of the past. Spock's name and his book were in every home—including the TV family of Lucy and Ricky Ricardo, who on several episodes were shown to be consulting the book to figure out how to parent young Ricky.

Spock's basic message was for parents to relax, to stop being stressed out about your child and start using your intuition. And what your intuition probably says is that most of you were raised too rigidly—too many rules, regulations, schedules, and spankings. Spock advocated "the so-called progressive ideal of child rearing," wrote historian Joshua Zeitz. "It counseled indulgence; it counseled understanding. It placed children and their happiness at the very center of the child-rearing project so that they were brought up in nurturing households that placed a lot of emphasis on their education and upbringing. . . . So, it was quite unlike anything that had come before."

Spock believed that the chief characteristic of his childhood, having been raised in Jonathan Edwards's Puritan New Haven, Connecticut, was the leftover aroma of staunch Calvinism: "I was brought up in a family with stern morals even by New England standards and acquired an oppressive conscience. I tried to free myself from these." Spock was guided in this regard by the writings of his first wife's great-grandfather, the Reverend Horace Bushnell, a leader in the decline of Puritan-Calvinism in the nineteenth century. Bushnell believed that kids aren't born "totally depraved" and in need of salvation—helped along by a parent's rod of discipline. Instead, they're blank slates that need positive reinforcement, affirmation, and affection.

Spock—the man and his message—has now become a Rorschach test of sorts in our culture. On the one hand, conservatives write pieces like "How Dr. Spock Destroyed America." On the other hand, *TIME* titled its gushing obituary of Spock "The Man Who Loved Children." Even parents who have never heard his name have probably engaged in debates over the question "Which parenting style is 'right'?" or "Are you growing your kids God's way?" There is an entire cottage industry within publishing devoted to affirming or rebuking Spock's ideas for how to parent.

The question remains: Were the Trump children raised by Spock parents? Was Donald Trump a Spock baby? In a word: No. Sure, a copy of the book might have found its way into the Trump household, but "newfangled parenting methods" is not the way anyone who knew Fred and Mary Anne describes their style of parenting. They were old school. Also, buying a book on parenting is more likely to be something that a first-time parent—or a young parent—

would do, but not so much for an established set of older parents with multiple kids already in the fold. For example, George H. W. Bush was twenty-two and Barbara Bush had just turned twenty-one when she gave birth to George, her firstborn. And Bill Clinton's mom was twenty-three and his father was twenty-eight when Bill entered the world as her firstborn.

By sharp contrast, however, by the time Donald arrived in the Trump family, his parents were neither young nor rookies at parenting. Mary Anne gave birth to Donald at the age of thirty-four; Fred was forty. And Donald wasn't the firstborn—he was the fourth of five. Donald came home from the hospital to a nine-year-old sister (Maryanne), a seven-year-old brother (Fred Jr.), and a four-year-old sister (Elizabeth). And after Donald's birth came the baby of the family, Robert, born in 1948. So Fred and Mary Anne were about as far removed from needing a book on parenting as any parent who gave birth during the baby boom.

Conservatives, including Donald Trump, view the 1950s as a Garden of Eden now lost and the 1980s as a glorious, temporary halting of culture's "slouching toward Gomorrah." But Fred and Mary Anne seem more like parents from the 1930s (think *The Waltons*) or even the grandparents' generation from that show. Which is to say, the Trump children were raised more by "Victorian" standards than anything resembling Spock.

In September 2016, I sat down with Michele Bachmann, who had recently joined the Evangelical Advisory Board for the campaign, to talk about Donald Trump. She made a statement that has stuck with me about how Donald Trump has "1950s sensibilities."

> What I really, really like about him is that he has 1950s sensibilities. By that I mean he really does believe in a strong America because he grew up being proud of the United States—"a John Wayne America."

Today, a lot of kids are taught, unfortunately, that the United States is an evil country and that somehow we've hurt the rest of the world. That's one of the biggest lies that young people have been told. We have been a force for good. No country's perfect, but we've been a force for good throughout time. God's blessed us, unlike any other nation, other than the Jewish state of Israel.

But Trump gets it. The Judeo-Christian underpinnings of this country, I think really came to the fore in the 1950s and were seen in the 1950s. Donald Trump is not ashamed of our Judeo-Christian underpinnings as a nation.

First, Trump believes in "strength" and a "strong America" that corresponds to traditional masculinity. The "John Wayne America" ideal man sits tall in the saddle; doesn't whine or complain; fights and dies for things that matter; exhibits courage in the face of danger; works hard—maybe even an unbalanced amount; provides for his family; builds things (institutions, buildings, businesses) that others inhabit; leaves the world a better place; may speak with machismo—but never effeminacy; and communicates hope even when it defies logic.

When you add up these qualities, they form a composite picture of his father, Fred Trump. And to understand Donald is to know just how much he wants to be like his dad. "He adores his father as kind of the icon of masculinity and what it means to be a businessman," says Robert Costa of the *Washington Post*. "In many ways, I think he's still thinking about his father. I'm not an armchair psychologist, but I think his father deeply influences him."

There are stories about Fred where he wore a suit and tie even to the beach. Does that reflect a man who couldn't leave work at the office or a man who believed society was better with proper formality—or both? In the early 1980s, Donald went down to Atlantic City to scout

out some properties along the Boardwalk. Trump biographer Blair wrote, "It was blisteringly hot, but the developer [Trump] wore his uniform of dark suit, dark shoes, and red tie." The man who assisted him "was wearing cutoff jeans and sneakers" and he "told Trump he was surprised that he wasn't dressed more informally." Trump replied: "I came down here for business, and in New York, this is the way we dress for business." Fault these men for being work-aholics if you want, but they accomplished a lot on the strength of their strong work ethic.

Another few examples of the "masculine" side of this "1950s sen-sibility" would be Trump's adoration of World War II generals Doug-las MacArthur and George S. Patton. The movie about Patton—that hard-fighting, impulsive, subordinate-slapping, always-victorious general—won seven Academy Awards when it came out in 1970. And an impressionable twenty-four-year-old Trump was perma-nently imprinted with it.

Second, Trump believes in a black-and-white world of right and wrong, good and evil. You always knew who the good guys and bad guys were in the movies. You believed that America was pointed toward righteousness and that the Communists intended evil. Later, President Reagan said as much, calling the Soviet Union the "Evil Empire."

Third, Trump is "not ashamed of our Judeo-Christian underpin-nings" which "came to the fore in the 1950s." It was in 1953 that the American Legion launched—with the help of President Eisenhower and Vice President Nixon—its "Back to God" campaign, promoting "regular church attendance, daily family prayer, and the religious training of children." And it was in 1955 that President Eisenhower signed into law that "In God We Trust" be put on US currency.

One of the most significant events in Donald Trump's biography during his adolescent years happened in the fall of 1959, when Fred ended Donald's education in the local private school and sent him off to the New York Military Academy (NYMA). Donald had apparently been a cut-up one too many times at home, at church, and in class. Fred was involved with huge building projects, and Mary Anne was running a house of five children and doing volunteer work with charities and local organizations. As the story goes, Donald had been hopping on the subway in Queens with a friend and going into the city to buy novelty items and fireworks. But they also took up collecting switchblade knives. When Fred found out about the excursion and the *West Side Story* wannabe knives, he decided his thirteen-year-old son needed more direct supervision and discipline than he would have time for, so he sent him to NYMA. During the next five school years, Donald would live at this boarding school located about an hour north of the city.

The man who oversaw young Trump, Ted Dobias, was a US Army veteran of World War II, and in his instruction at NYMA, he was a regular George Patton himself. Reading about Mr. Dobias's style of authority over these young men brings to mind the opening scenes of the movie *Full Metal Jacket*—where Gunnery Sergeant Hartman screams the raw Marine recruits at Parris Island into submission.

Dobias told biographer Michael D'Antonio that he wanted to instill in the boys tenets of manhood that included "Respect for authority. Set a good example in your appearance, your manners, and how you speak. Be proud of your family. Be proud of yourself."

Dobias said, "I coached baseball and football, and I taught them that winning wasn't everything, it was the only thing, Donald picked right up on this. He would tell his teammates, 'We're out here for a purpose. To win.' He always had to be number one, in everything. He was a conniver even then. A real pain in the ass. He would do anything to win."

And Dobias recalled that Fred was "really tough on the kid. He was very German. He came up on a lot of Sundays and would take the boy out to dinner. Not many did that. But he was very tough."

In an example of a movie unwittingly imitating life, *Dead Poets Society* sets its story in 1959 at an all-boys boarding school in New England—the exact year Fred shipped Donald off to NYMA. And the main plotline of the movie was how a young man committed suicide after ignoring the command of his stern father (i.e., the 1950s) and listening to the call of the free-spirited teacher (i.e., the 1960s), played by Robin Williams. The teacher, being a Ralph Waldo Emerson at heart, taught the boys a "Carpe Diem: Seize the Day" philosophy of life.

Ironically, Trump's story was the opposite. Before his years at NYMA, Trump had been living with a great amount of personal freedom (at least compared to what he would know at the academy). But when Fred intervened by cutting off his freedom and sending him to the Academy, Donald thrived: "He felt comfortable in uniform—spit-shined shoes and belt buckles polished with Brasso—and adjusted to mess-hall meals. Isolated in an all-male military environment, far from his mother and father and siblings, the boy quickly learned that 'life is about survival. It's always about survival.' A good but not stellar student, he became one of Dobias's favorites and absorbed the sense of superiority that was preached at NYMA with the consistency of a drumbeat."

For Donald, the sudden loss of personal freedom did not kill him—it led him to discover and develop personal discipline—dare we say, a "1950s sensibility"—that put the final nail in the coffin of his ever becoming a "Spock baby." Though Donald's instructor came packaged in army boots and was quite unlike Robin Williams's character, Trump left NYMA with a firm carpe diem resolve for accomplishing his life goal of succeeding in his father's business.

9

The Power of Positive Thinking

If all you know about Norman Vincent Peale are the things written about him since the day Donald J. Trump announced his run for president, then you probably have a caricature of the man who in his day was one of the most famous Christian ministers in the English-speaking world. Here are the three points of information that have been drilled into us since Trump's campaign began: (1) Peale was one of Trump's pastors, mentors, and friends. (2) The "self-help" aisle in your bookstore may not even exist without Peale pioneering that industry. (3) Peale was a theological simpleton at best, or worse—a theological fraud.

But there is more to the Peale-Trump story than that. Considering that the sitting President has been described as a "star pupil of Peale," there's a good reason to dig deeper. Who was Peale, what did he teach, and how much worldview impact did he have on Trump? While still only scratching the surface, this chapter aims to answer those questions.

Up front, it is important to note the paradox of Peale's importance. On the one hand, the *Washington Post* described him as "the man who may well be the '50s' most emblematic figure" and that "for a couple of decades he was, for better or worse, the nation's most influential minister." And yet, that article opened with the words "How soon we forget"—because this "Johnny Appleseed of positive thinking" was already (in 1992, the year before Peale died) in danger of being an unrecognizable name to most Americans at the end of the century that Peale dominated.

When *Church History*, a sister publication of *Christianity Today*, took a survey of its readers to ascertain which Christian ministers and authors from the past century had been influential—on a personal level or to the church—Peale barely made it onto any of the lists. Nor did his greatest spiritual descendant—Robert Schuler. Nevertheless, the grandchildren of his worldview—Joel Osteen, Oprah Winfrey, and Tony Robbins, to name just three—have profoundly impacted contemporary American spirituality. And though the *CT* reader poll did not evidence his influence, evangelical historians and chroniclers know the deeper reality: His legacy looms large over the entire American religious scene, including evangelicalism. As *CT* writer Tim Stafford wrote in 1992: "How one evaluates Peale is probably an index of how one evaluates modern American Christianity. Nearly every facet of Peale's work—his conservative politics; his individualistic, self-improving message; his concern for the power of the mind and its potential to transform life and health; his interest in modern communications and in numerical growth—has become dominant in the modern church."

The 1993 obituary of Peale in *Christianity Today* described him as "the patriarch of the twentieth-century self-help movement." When the eminent journalist George Vecsey wrote the *New York Times* obituary of Peale, he described him as "the first American clergyman to bring psychiatric practices into religion, preparing the way for thousands of professional, religious-based counselors. His later emphasis on 'positive thinking' predated the current flood of self-help books and movements." And every obituary took note of Peale's phenomenal best seller, *The Power of Positive Thinking*, a book that has sold close to 20 million copies; during the 1950s, only the newly Revised Standard Version of the Bible sold more among nonfiction titles.

And yet, for all his lifetime of influence, by the middle of the

2010s, the Peale name was nearly altogether forgotten. But Peale's growing postmortem obscurity turned into immediate infamy the moment Donald Trump descended on his Trump Tower escalator and announced his candidacy for president.

Many of the 2016 critiques of Peale took aim at the man and his message in the most superficial manner—essentially critiquing the man reflexively as a comment on Trump. Journalists even chased down Peale's closest living relative, his seventy-nine-year-old son John, who told the *Washington Post* that he "winces when Trump invokes his father's name. . . . 'I cringe . . . I don't respect Mr. Trump very much. I don't take him seriously. I regret the publicity of the connection. This is a problem for the Peale family. . . . I don't think the image of Norman Vincent Peale that comes through Donald Trump is any connection to the idea I have of him. He doesn't recognize the significant character of Dad's ministry, which is a sincere desire to help people.'"

But the son's biting comments about Trump don't square with the comments the famous preacher made about Trump, calling him "kindly and courteous," "ingenious," and "one of America's top positive thinkers and doers." Peale even said Trump had "a streak of honest humility"—which would be hard to hold on to with your pastor making predictions that you would become "the greatest builder of our time"—as Peale said of Trump. "He thought I was his greatest student of all time," Trump said, recalling his pastor's affections for him.

And what has Trump said about his famous pastor? Most of his public comments about Peale are in praise of the man's gift of oratory—Peale's ability to hold an audience spellbound, both live and across the radio and TV airwaves.

In September 2015, very early in the campaign, I asked Trump a question about the tension between standing in front of tens of thousands of people cheering you on while wearing your name on their clothing and the need to keep the ego in check. Trump immediately appealed to Peale as his inspiration for being able to enthrall large crowds.

Well, when I fill an arena like we did the American Airlines Center last night in Dallas—the people who are so enthusiastic, that it was easy to do. You know, I don't believe in teleprompters. If I would read my speech, it would be so much easier, and you never get in trouble, which is also good, right? But you read a speech, and you read it—and then you leave, and nobody goes crazy. I give it very much from the heart. You know, the greatest speaker I think I've ever witnessed was Dr. Norman Vincent Peale and he would speak the power of positive thinking. He would speak so much—and he'd bring it into modern-day life. He talked about success stories and people that were successful and became alcoholics, and then they conquered it. . . . He gave some of the greatest sermons ever, and just regardless of the sermon he was just a great speaker. But he wasn't reading anything—and I grew up watching that. He wasn't reading. I've [heard] plenty of pastors and ministers that read. It's not the same thing. Norman Vincent Peale would get up, and his arms would be flailing, and you hated to leave church because you wanted him to go on further. So, when I speak, even though you know you go into Mobile with thirty-one thousand or Dallas with twenty thousand people—and you don't have even literally notes in front of you, it's a little bit nerve-racking because you know, maybe who knows, right? But it's exciting, and the energy really does something to me that's incredible. You saw the crowds, you saw the response to standing ovations for five and ten minutes sometimes, so it's very exciting.

So, at least regarding the ability to hold the attention of an audience, Trump testifies to the influence that Peale had on him. But what about the content of the message itself? Well, before answering that question, there's Peale's backstory that must be told, because the Trumps didn't start attending Peale's church until the 1970s—when Peale was in his seventies and had been in ministry for five decades. So, lest we just grab the title of the 1952 best seller and simplistically describe Trump as a "positive thinker"—let's peel back the curtain on Peale a bit more.

The first thing to note about Peale is that given his long tenure in public ministry—from his ordination in 1922 until his death in 1993—he is best understood as having an early (1920s–mid-1940s), middle (1950s and 1960s), and late period (1970–1993) in his ministry. The Trumps came to Marble Collegiate in the early 1970s, when Peale's personal ministry and the worship attendance at the church was still in full bloom—though the flower had already been cut by the change in the culture's mood during the 1960s.

Early Peale was more doctrinal, having grown up as the pastor's kid of a Methodist minister in Ohio. If you dig deep and find early Peale writings, you'll read evangelical- and revivalist-inspired Methodism intertwined with a patriotic love for country. Peale attended Ohio Wesleyan and read plenty of his Methodist forefathers, but he also absorbed American originals like Ralph Waldo Emerson and William James. But in general, Peale did not appreciate abstract thought—or an aroma of intellectual elitism—a fact made apparent to him when he went to Boston University for seminary. He later described those days as being full of insecurity and lacking joy.

His Methodist credentials notwithstanding, Peale was called to the pastorate of the Marble Collegiate Church, a Dutch Reformed congregation. Founded in 1628—just six years after First Presbyterian of Jamaica—Marble Collegiate can boast of being the oldest continuously running congregation in North America. Trump biographer Michael D'Antonio described Collegiate during Trump's time there as a "celebrity church" whose members were "generally wealthy New Yorkers of the Protestant executive class. It was a place to see and be seen."

A nineteenth-century precursor to Peale and his status as a celebrity pastor from New York can be found in Brooklyn pastor Henry Ward Beecher—the brother of *Uncle Tom's Cabin* author Harriet Beecher Stowe. Peale considered Beecher a model for effective urban ministry, especially how Beecher was famous for his sermons—practical sermons preached without notes. Beecher preached a Gospel of wealth that assuaged the fears of the newly rich Americans who were troubled to know how their economic fortunes might influence their eternal status. He gave them assurances that all was well and they gave him national notoriety in return. At his height, he was the most famous preacher in America. But he gained the biggest publicity of his ministry for a sex scandal—an affair he allegedly had with the wife of one of his good friends. The matter went to court and filled the newspapers for six months. Though most everyone believed he was guilty (the wife had admitted as much), Beecher was acquitted. At any rate, the matter had no effect on his popularity or on his profession as a preacher. Beecher's original and lasting contribution to American religion was his embrace of celebrity, fame, and wealth—preaching about God almost exclusively with language about a "Gospel of love" and eschewing talk of judgment.

At the time of Peale's coming to Marble Collegiate, the church was flush with buildings and history but short on members or enthusiasm. Choosing a pastor from the Wesleyan-Methodist theological traditions was unusual for a Dutch Reformed congregation—as those theological streams don't usually mix. So, Peale's call to the MCC pulpit was yet another example of the lowering of the theological dividing lines that characterized this period. Peale remained at MCC for fifty-two years, attracting Sunday crowds numbering four to five thousand—in addition to the radio and TV audiences.

To give some idea of the flavor of Peale during the early days, here are a few snippets from the days when Donald was in diapers— before Peale's best-selling books made him a household name in the 1950s.

First, the December 15, 1948, edition of the *Christian Century* reported that "At a Thanksgiving Day service in the Marble Collegiate Church on Fifth Avenue, Norman Vincent Peale, pastor, lashed out at the 'desecration of the spirit of the day' by the staging that morning of the Macy Christmas parade, for which millions lined the streets. Dr. Peale pointed out that the President had designated the day for 'thanksgiving to God in your respective places of worship,' but that the parade was put on at exactly the time scheduled for services of worship throughout the city. He insisted that this was sacrilege and commercialization." One can hardly imagine any pastor of a major church today—conservative or liberal—decrying the timing of a popular cultural event.

Second, in a newspaper column published two weeks after Trump's birth, Peale called for citizens to be regular in their church attendance, connecting such piety with the health of the nation. Though Marble Collegiate was and is "Mainline," the language from Peale differs little from the so-called God and Country churches of the Religious Right today, those who are not shy in talking about "Christian America" or "the Christian foundations of our nation."

It is obvious to every thoughtful person that we have arrived at a crisis in American history. . . . This country is unique in that it is the first great nation in history to be established on a distinctly religious base. Our social and political institutions, as well as our religious life, were laid down by godly men who came here in the name of the Lord of Hosts. We are the descendants of a great breed of Christian forebears who, reading the Bible and having committed themselves to Jesus Christ, became free men, and established here a free state.

Peale continued, directly addressing Communism, the threat that loomed large to Americans as the Cold War began to heat up:

There are some small-minded people who have the idea that to be a Christian today, one must lean away over to the left or to the right: either to take Communism on the one hand, or something else on the other. For the life of me, I have never been able to understand how a man who regards himself as a leader of the Christian Church can attempt to so deprecate the teachings of Jesus as to try to get them into the thinking of Karl Marx or of some Fascist. Those puny little fellows, compared to the colossal mind of Jesus Christ, pale into mere insignificance.

Peale concludes with an appeal to the common man—be faithful attending church! Peale mentions the pew habits of presidents, ironically enough, as the two great Republicans (Peale was a lifelong Republican) who fought Communism—Eisenhower and Reagan—were not known for their church attendance. Nor is Donald Trump.

Who then shall save America? There was a time when I had some faith in the politicians and I still believe they can do a great deal, but there is just one person who can save America. He is the man who Sunday after Sunday sits in the pew of the Christian Church, absorbs the message and does his utmost to practice it in his daily life. One of the greatest institutions in America is the pew in the Christian Church. The most distinguished and honorable men in our history have sat in the pew and counted it an honor to do so. No man has ever been elected President of the United States who did not consider it a great privilege to sit in the pew. All of our great leaders have been men who have found their inspiration in the pew. . . . We Americans can save America by returning to the pew, there to gather strength and courage such as enabled our forefathers to build this great nation.

As for his political-religious activities, Peale gave ardent opposition to FDR and the New Deal from its inception. He also had been a firm Prohibitionist. When FDR ran for a third term, Peale published an open letter to clergy alerting them of the dire danger to our democracy, as he saw it, if such demagoguery was foisted on America by Roosevelt. When the American Legion inaugurated its "Back to God" campaign in the 1950s, Peale represented Protestantism on the national broadcasts.

As Billy Graham prepared to come to New York City in 1957 for what would become the longest evangelistic crusade of his ministry—and one of the most historic—he reflected on the unique opportunity awaiting him. Graham described the city as "the most strategic center in the world. We could have this many people in Louisville, Kentucky . . . Oklahoma City . . . even in Chicago . . . and it wouldn't mean as much as New York City. It becomes a stage on which we can do evangelism to the whole nation, to the whole world." After preaching to a full house at Madison Square Garden night after night, Graham ended the Crusade at Yankee Stadium, preaching to over 100,000 in the heat of the summer.

Vice President Richard Nixon addressed the attendees during the event. Over fifty thousand people made a commitment to Jesus Christ during one of the one hundred services. Even Peale had a spiritual experience under Graham's preaching: "I had the new birth experience before Billy Graham was born, but in his meetings here I received a second blessing. I believe that conversion may be a progressive experience. Under Billy, to whom I am devoted, I progressed, or went deeper."

Heading into the 1960 election, Peale and other Protestants and evangelicals organized to oppose JFK on the grounds of his being Roman Catholic—and by extension, to throw support behind Nixon. He received plenty of blowback from these efforts, even within his own congregation. After the JFK kerfuffle, he told his congregation that he had "never been too bright"—and they quickly forgave him. This event marked a turning point for Peale, making him less willing to broadcast such public political aims—though he still maintained his friendships with Republican officeholders. He served as a pastor to Nixon in the late 1960s and officiated the wedding of Nixon's daughter Julie to Eisenhower's grandson David.

Peale's national fame and influence burst forth during the "middle years," as Peale attempted, in the 1940s, to unite modern psychology with Christian pastoral practice. Then, beginning in the 1950s, he promoted the wildfire spread of these psycho-theological ideas through his books, tapes, radio, mailing lists, and his popular periodical of inspiring stories, *Guideposts.* Peale's ideas were mainstreamed into middle-class American homes of every religious background. Because of the sales and popularity, Peale began to receive harsh criticism from two sources: the professional psychiatric community, and the liberal, Mainline theologians.

All told, Peale authored forty-one books. But it was *The Power of Positive Thinking* that became something of a religious literature phenomenon. The book placed on national best-seller lists for three years and went on to sell 15 to 20 million copies. It opened with the first of ten principles: "Formulate and stamp indelibly on your mind a mental picture of yourself as succeeding. Hold this picture tenaciously. Never permit it to fade. Never think of yourself as failing." Peale taught the reader the secret formula for success: "Prayerize. Picturize. Actualize." And he poured into his books one true-life success story after another to illustrate how people got results by practicing "positive thinking" exercises—even people who lived in former times but were clued into these ideas ahead of Peale. He pulled in quotations from theologians, philosophers—and a hefty amount from successful business leaders, like Charles Schwab: "A man can accomplish almost anything provided he has unlimited enthusiasm."

Psychiatrists and the nascent Christian counseling movement became livid at Peale's armchair intrusion into their terrain. The psychiatrist's couch, after all, was to be covered solely in the sacred cow leather of Freud. Jesus-isms were unnecessary. The disapproving frown of the psychiatric establishment became so heated that Peale's early collaborator, a professional psychiatrist named Smiley Blanton, left the partnership and began disavowing Peale.

Liberal theologians heaped on their scorn too, faulting Peale for what they considered a low-brow approach to religion, a simplification of both theology and psychiatry that appealed to the masses—a populist preaching for the middle class. "The book, for all its success, was savaged by liberal theologians in a way that is almost incomprehensible today," Tim Stafford wrote. "They hurt Peale deeply. In many ways, he was following the liberal path, adapting the kerygma of the gospel to modern ways of thinking." Even Adlai Stevenson jumped into the fray, famously stating in 1952, "I find [Saint] Paul appealing and Peale appalling."

Ironically, given what Modernists had done to minimalize the doctrine of the Mainline, they critiqued Peale for the shortage of "God words" or teachings from Jesus. A few—key word "few"—conservative voices piped in with critique. Wayne Oates, a Southern Baptist professor of pastoral counseling, negatively reviewed *The Power of Positive Thinking*: "I personally find the material here sadly out of keeping with the prophetic religion of the Eighth Century Prophets and of Jesus, who gave their lives to demonstrate the shallowness of the success-religion of their contemporaries whose patterns of thought and action were Biblical examples of Peale." A Lutheran critic wrote, "The faith of which Peale speaks is more the message of Dale Carnegie, the *Reader's Digest*, and the modern American self-help movement than of the New Testament." On the other hand, Gaines "Mr. Sunday School" Dobbins wrote, "No preacher of discriminating intelligence will be hurt by reading this book, and many will be greatly helped."

Prompted by the critics coming from the right, Peale wrote the following words in *Guideposts*:

> I'm a conservative, and I will tell you exactly what I mean by that. I mean that I have accepted the Lord Jesus Christ as my personal Savior. I mean that I believe my sins are forgiven by the atoning work of grace on the cross. . . . Now I'll tell you something else. . . . I personally love and understand this way of stating the Christian gospel. But I am absolutely and thoroughly convinced that it is my mission never to use this language in trying to communicate with the audience that has been given me.

Of course, this was hardly a statement that would warm the theological toes of an evangelical or fundamentalist.

If Peale was self-critical of the thinness of his theological thought, he did not say as much in public or in his writings—except on one occasion in a 1978 interview with the *New York Times*.

> Looking back, Dr. Peale concedes that there are some aspects of the book he wishes he had done differently. For one, he argues that "I got false Criticism that I was trying to make people successful. . . . I would go through the book," he said, "and try to eliminate anything that might suggest this." He also acknowledged that some of his critics were correct in accusing the book of neglecting the traditional Christian emphasis on repentance. "It is an important aspect that ought to be thought through," Dr. Peale said, "because lives are being destroyed by sin. The need is to get sin out and bring the person to the point where he can know something better. In 1952, sin was generally recognized, and I didn't have to accentuate it. But I'm basically a very traditional Christian, and a sense of guilt is important. Too much guilt is unhealthy, though."

In a *Christianity Today* interview in 1992, the year before he died, Peale said, "I've got plenty of worst qualities. A good quality is I have always loved Jesus Christ and I think he's the greatest thing that ever happened to this world."

Despite all this, until Donald Trump decided to run for president on the Republican ticket, there was no sustained or substantial theological critique of Norman Vincent Peale from within evangelicalism. Quite the opposite. It is hard to conceive how one could argue that

Peale did not die a mainstream evangelical—as defined by 1993 and present-day definitions of the word. Evangelicals had mostly embraced, not critiqued, Peale since the 1960s. Undoubtedly, some of that goodwill came because of shared political interests— evangelicals liked Peale's politics.

> Political similarities rather than theological affinity finally allowed the NAE [National Association of Evangelicals] to regard Peale as one of them. Like Graham, Peale shared the NAE's conservative agenda on such issues as labor, anti-Communism, Red China, and containment. It was those Cold War issues that had first brought Peale and Pew together, with Pew serving as one of the important early contributors to *Guideposts*. It was also quietly reported that Pew was the financial backer of the NAE's publication, *Christianity Today*, which first appeared in 1956. An orthodox Presbyterian, Pew presumably would have little in common with Peale's theology as it was presented in *The Power of Positive Thinking*.

We are left to wonder why evangelical thinkers waited until Donald Trump ran for president to give such a robust critique of his late pastor, Peale. It seems that some evangelicals will remain silent about what they perceive to be aberrant theology, so long as the "heretics" (their term) don't mess around with the Republican Party.

In 1984 President Reagan awarded Peale the Presidential Medal of Freedom "for his contributions to the field of theology." Though Reagan was not a member of an evangelical church—he attended Bel Aire Church (PCUSA), the same denomination as Trump's childhood church, as well as that of Eisenhower once in office—he was a favorite of evangelicals and seemed to share in the "Bible and

Jesus" ethos of evangelicalism. Reagan said that Peale had become an "advocate of the joy of life, helping millions find new meaning in their lives."

The Trump-Peale-Reagan connection becomes even tighter when you consider that it was Peale who helped found the "Horatio Alger Association of Distinguished Americans" in 1947, "to honor the achievements of outstanding Americans who have succeeded in spite of adversity." Reagan won the Horatio Alger Award in 1969—very fitting considering his favorite fiction as a young man was the "Luck and Pluck" type of novels written by Mr. Alger. And Fred Trump won the award in 1985. His biography page on the group's website begins with one of Fred's maxims: "Always strive toward a new goal and use the power of positive thinking."

So how should we understand Norman Vincent Peale and what conclusions about "the faith of Donald Trump" can be drawn from that analysis? First, Peale was an American original, both in methods and message. Heeding the call of his intellectual forefather, Ralph Waldo Emerson, and his famous 1837 speech "The American Scholar," Peale broke out from both the liberalism of his Boston University training and the revivalist Methodism of his youth to create something unique and new—and what he built appealed to the masses. Likewise, in his own chosen vocation of real estate development, Trump took old buildings and pieces of land with hundreds of years of history—buildings that had come before. And he renovated, remodeled, or built from scratch works of architecture that have become landmarks on the Manhattan landscape.

Second, there is no doubt that Donald Trump's self-assurance and quest to win and succeed in life has a parallel with the message of Norman Vincent Peale. His longtime friend and lawyer Michael Cohen told me that he believes Trump "might possibly be mentally and emotionally the strongest human being I've ever met. The level of hatred by detractors, media pundits and others would totally overwhelm and cripple others. Not him. His convictions are so steadfast and purposeful that he dismisses the negativity so that he can create positive results for all Americans and deliver on his mantra to 'Make America Great Again.' . . . Norman Vincent Peale, his childhood spiritual mentor, would be proud of the values he instilled in a young Donald Trump." Roger Stone, another longtime friend and confidant, sees traces of Peale's teaching in Trump. "He's not a man who wears his religion on his sleeve. As regular churchgoers at Norman Vincent Peale's Marble Collegiate Church, it's a quiet form of solid Christianity, and kind of wrapped in that same 'Trumpian' style of confidence, service, positive thinking."

But then, three years later, Trump began to have a lot of "downside" during the years of the casino crisis, his divorce from Ivana, and a helicopter crash that killed three of his colleagues shortly after they left his side. If there was a season for despondency, this was it. In 2016, biographer Blair wrote that Trump credits the messaging from Peale as being influential in keeping his mindset positive:

> In 1990, after splurging on a third casino, an airline, the world's second-largest yacht and the Plaza Hotel, Trump found himself nearly a billion dollars in debt and the banks were threatening foreclosure. But after weeks of round-the-clock negotiations, he emerged relatively unscathed, and in a 2009 interview with *Psychology Today* he gave Peale's book credit for his survival. Citing his father's friendship with Peale and calling himself "a firm believer in the power of being positive," he said, "what helped is I refused to give in to the negative circumstances and never lost faith in myself. I didn't believe I was finished even when the newspapers were saying so."

But to put it bluntly, could you say the same thing about motivational posters, self-help literature, or the Oprah Winfrey show—that they all flow downstream from Peale and that Trump absorbed this messaging from the general culture? Yes, and he probably did. If two decades after the casino crisis Trump laid credit to Peale's teaching for keeping his hopes and spirits positive, then we are not going to argue with that. But it is interesting to note that even in discussing Peale with *Psychology Today*, Trump brought up Fred—"citing his father's friendship with Peale." In other words, Fred is the key—and literally, that is how it happened because it was Fred and Mary Anne who came to Marble Collegiate first, then Donald. Fred and Norman were of the same generation, only seven years apart in age. When Peale officiated Donald and Ivana's marriage in 1977, he was pushing eighty—and Fred was in his seventies. So, the "positive thinking" preacher came into Donald's orbit late, not early. Peale became another father figure to Donald, but was a supplemental source of the worldview Fred had already instilled in him.

So, in answer to the "which came first" riddle—did Peale produce Trump or was Trump already inclined this way due to his nature and nurture—we would make a strong case for the latter. Here's why: Fred Trump's way of being—driven, ambitious, self-assured—was already set in stone before he showed up at Peale's church. And nobody had a greater impact on Donald than Fred. Even Dobias, the commander-in-charge-of-producing-winners at the New York Military Academy, served only as a reinforcement to Fred's worldview. So, when you realize that Fred and Mary Anne didn't even become members at Marble until Donald was thirty—and that he followed them to Peale's pews—you may also draw the conclusion that Peale was less of an influence than either his dad or his "winning is everything" drill sergeant.

• • •

When we interviewed Jerry Falwell Jr., he said that he had talked with the President on the phone the night before—at the end of a week that had been filled with a lot of POTUS pressure—not that any week in the Oval Office is stress-free, but this one had been particularly hectic. Falwell related that he asked the President, "Is there anything I can do for you?" and he responded with an upbeat, "No, I think we're fine." Falwell analyzed that exchange: "He's always upbeat and positive—and my dad was always like that."

"Dad influences son" doesn't make for a clickbait headline quite like "How Norman Vincent Peale Taught Donald Trump to Worship Himself" does. But in Donald Trump's case, he just wanted to grow up to be like his dad. The fact that a famous pastor came into his adult life with a message that affirmed what Fred had taught him—then all the better.

Of that fact, we're positive.

10

Manhattan, Malaise, and Morning in America

Two of Donald Trump's great-aunts (Frederick's sisters)—Louise Trump Schuster and Katherine Trump Schuster—would often come over for a day of visiting and eating together with their sister-in-law Elizabeth and her son's families. One of them died before Donald was born and the other died when he was a toddler, so they had no direct influence on him. But their children were first cousins of Fred, and so they grew up together as children of Germans who had melted successfully into the pot of American culture. We've already seen how Fred moved from his ancestral Lutheranism into the Presbyterianism of his wife. Now, the fascinating thing about these two mid-Manhattan aunts of Fred's is that during prolonged years of widowhood they became dedicated to worship and service at the newly formed Glad Tidings Tabernacle—one of the very first Pentecostal churches in the city.

Glad Tidings was begun in 1907 by Marie Burgess, a twenty-six-year-old missionary from rural Illinois and the Moody Bible Institute. When still a teen, Burgess had a vision of Jesus asking her, "Will you forsake all and follow Me?" She answered, "Yes, Lord, all"—and that commitment led her to New York City's Hell's Kitchen neighborhood at a time when its poor and working-class citizens gave it the grittiness to equal such a name.

The church grew under her leadership, and then under shared leadership when she married Robert Brown. In 1914, the church moved into an existing church building about four hundred feet west of the current Madison Square Garden. And in that same year, the Browns gave leadership to the creation of the Assemblies of God denomination. Glad Tidings produced a weekly radio broadcast and was a leader in foreign missions giving within the denomination.

In 1927, Aimee Semple McPherson—arguably one of the best-known evangelists of the first half of the twentieth century—traveled from her nationally known church in Los Angeles to New York to "purge the city of some of its sin." Semple arrived on a Friday and proceeded directly to Glad Tidings, preaching twice that night to overflow crowds. Two thousand people listened inside the building and amplifiers were set up outside for the crowds who stood in the February cold to hear the message. McPherson made rounds of the nightclubs in the neighborhood that evening, including the dance and drink hall run by the world-famous hostess Texas Guinan. She invited all the dancers and patrons to come to Glad Tidings the next night—and Guinan did, taking a seat in the front row with a dozen ladies. With reporters and photographers in attendance and the Browns up on the platform, McPherson gave the Gospel from the Song of Solomon.

Though Pentecostal Christianity did not begin to enter the mainstream of evangelicalism until the 1970s, this church attended by Donald Trump's great-aunts was known in the city and throughout the nation for its vibrant Christian worship and witness. In a city that was full of every expression of Protestant Christianity in the first half of the twentieth century, Glad Tidings was altogether unique, both in its Pentecostalism and in its being led by a woman.

It is often said that one of Donald Trump's "closest spiritual advisers" is Pastor Paula White. But seventy years before Trump met White, his aunts sat under the ministry of the Paula White of early twentieth-century New York City—and in a day when there were only a handful of such figures in all of America.

. . .

In 1958, one year before Fred Trump discovered Donald's switch-blades and sent him to the military academy, an Assembly of God pastor in rural Pennsylvania read in *Life* magazine about seventeen gang members in New York who were going to trial for their crimes. The pastor, David Wilkerson, felt compassion and what he described as a prompting of the Holy Spirit to travel to the city and speak to the young men. The judge in the courtroom did not allow it to happen, but Wilkerson instead began a ministry to gang members and drug addicts on the streets of New York. He founded Teen Challenge in Brooklyn that year, an evangelical addiction-recovery program that still exists today.

One year later, a young Pat Robertson was celebrating his twenty-ninth birthday at the Reformed church where he was serving as an associate to Pastor Harald Bredesen. According to Robertson's autobiography, *Shout It From the Housetops*, the pastor began to speak in tongues. The next evening, Bredesen took Robertson with him to see Mrs. Norman Vincent Peale in her apartment on Fifth Avenue. Being of the same denomination, he had some church business he needed to attend to, and he was determined to tell her about the charismatic experience and message he had received. "We told of the outpouring of the Holy Spirit all over the nation," Robertson recounted, "and how hundreds of people were receiving the baptism in the Holy Spirit. . . . Mrs. Peale began to ask questions, interested questions. I felt an anointing of the Spirit and began to share something of my personal experiences . . . we began to pray, and under the unction of the Spirit, Harald spoke in tongues. [Fellow pastor] Dick Simmons gave the interpretation."

Robertson wrote that Mrs. Peale said, "This is difficult to believe, but I know it is of the Lord." She then had to leave for business at the *Guideposts* office. When she arrived, she told editor John Sherrill about what had just occurred. "Have you ever heard of 'speaking in tongues'?" Intrigued by what he heard, Sherrill said he wanted to meet Harald, thinking it might make for a good story for *Guideposts*. Sherrill wrote an entire book on the subject, *They Speak with Other Tongues*, which became "the first best-seller on the charismatic renewal" and was used to "introduce hundreds of thousands to the baptism of the Holy Spirit," according to Robertson.

Through Bredesen, Sherrill also met David Wilkerson and heard about his ministry to the gangs. Wilkerson, with the help of Sherrill and his wife, penned *The Cross and the Switchblade*, to tell the story of Wilkerson's ministry and the conversion of Nicky Cruz, who had been the leader of an infamous Puerto Rican gang. Published in 1962, more than 50 million copies of this book are in print in forty languages. In the summer of 1970, a film adaptation of the book was released, starring Pat Boone as Wilkerson and featuring the screen debut of Erik Estrada as Cruz. Fifty million people have seen the movie since that time—viewing its simple message that Jesus Christ can conquer the sin problems found in any heart or city—even those of the Big Apple.

A few months later, in October 1970, Boone and Bredesen joined hands with a few other evangelicals of Charismatic persuasion to pray with then California governor Ronald Reagan and his wife Nancy in the foyer of their Sacramento home. As businessman George Otis prayed, the group had a spiritual experience that moved them physically. "The Holy Spirit came upon me, and I knew it. In fact, I was embarrassed," Otis said. In his prayer, Otis's words "spoke specifically to Ronald Reagan and referred to him as 'My son.'" And then came a word of prophecy: "If you walk uprightly before Me, you will reside at 1600 Pennsylvania Avenue." Of course, this was six years before Reagan challenged Ford for the Republican nomination and ten years before Reagan won the presidency. As Reagan prepared to move into the White House in 1981, Boone asked his old friend if he recalled the prophecy made a decade earlier. Reagan did.

In 1971, Donald Trump decided the time had come for him to move out of Queens—the only place his father had ever lived—and move into Manhattan. Because Donald would commute back to the outer boroughs of Brooklyn and Queens each day for his work with Fred, the move was more symbolic than logistic. Queens had once been something akin to a Beverly Cleary novel—suburban safety wrapped in ethnic homogeneity. Manhattan, however, was the land of riskier and higher-stakes building projects.

Of course, the entire city was experiencing economic, social, and criminal duress that would get worse before it got better.

But as Trump later wrote in his 1987 best-seller *Trump: The Art of the Deal*: "I worried about the future of New York too, but I can't say it kept me up nights. I'm basically an optimist, and frankly, I saw the city's trouble as a great opportunity for me." Before you chalk those words up to Trumpian bluster, first consider that when compared to the bleak realities of New York City in the 1970s, Trump did defy those dystopian trends of the decade. He rebuilt the dilapidated Commodore Hotel into the Hyatt Regency, and he began work on Trump Tower—among other accomplishments and small successes one can credit to the rookie real estate developer. Trump continued, showing an instinctual confidence in the city itself: "Because I grew up in Queens, I believed, perhaps to an irrational degree, that Manhattan was always going to be the best place to live—the center of the world. Whatever troubles the city might be having in the short term, there was no doubt in my mind that things had to turn around ultimately. What other city was going to take New York's place?" And so, Trump moved his body to "the best place to live" and rented an apartment on the Upper East Side.

As he would later write, "Moving into that apartment was probably more exciting for me than moving, fifteen years later, into the top three floors of Trump Tower."

The same year that Donald moved out of Queens, the fictional family of Archie Bunker—living somewhere in Queens—began its long and revolutionary run on TV. Yes, "those were the days" when Norman Lear began creating sitcoms full of families that looked and talked more like real people—with all the problems, strengths, and shortcomings that one would find in the real world. Archie, as the main character and the head of the Bunker family, would make bigoted and stereotypical statements about all types of people not like him.

Ironically, a recurring couple on the show was the Bunkers' African-American neighbors, the Jeffersons, who came into some money and started a cleaning business that took off and made them wealthy. In a 1975 episode of *All in the Family,* the Jeffersons said good-bye to the Bunkers, loaded up their belongings, and left Queens for a "deluxe apartment in the sky." The next week, Lear's spin-off sitcom *The Jeffersons* began airing, with its opening theme song that paralleled young Donald Trump's own move on up to the East Side.

The first five years Trump lived in Manhattan were years he spent working with his dad and their thousands of apartments spread out over three boroughs. He was a young man with his own flair in clothing and getting his name in the newspapers. And he was a bachelor with an eye for pretty models—though friends remember him being intensely focused on work to the point that he talked about it continuously, rather than engaging in typical social banter or issues of the day.

And there were plenty of issues to talk about. The draft ended in January 1973, the same month as the Supreme Court's *Roe v. Wade* decision to legalize abortion. Watergate unfolded from 1972 through the resignation of President Nixon in August 1974. If anything could test the doctrine of positive thinking, becoming the first president to resign under threat of impeachment would do so. Even so, as Nixon's former pastor, Peale stood by his disgraced parishioner and offered him counsel and friendship throughout the ordeal.

It was during this same time that Fred and Mary Anne Trump left First Presbyterian of Jamaica—with its ever-shrinking attendance—and began worshipping at Marble Collegiate. Fred resonated with the optimism and pro-business message he was hearing from an accomplished man from his own generation. And the church continued to fill the pews every Sunday, including a large number of celebrities and famous leaders. Art Fleming, the host of the long-running game show *Jeopardy,* served as a deacon at the church, admiring the positive message of Peale. "You can be whatever you want to be," Fleming told a reporter. "I believe you are the master of your own fate."

By 1975, however, New York was not the master of its own fate, clinging to the hope that President Ford would offer a bailout, lest the city go bankrupt. Reluctantly, Ford authorized a two-billion-dollar federal loan, and the city kept the lights on. Well, the lights did go out in 1977—a blackout in the heat of the summer that gave opportunity for widespread looting and rioting. And film depictions of the city tended to be full of dark and despondent images too: the Death Wish series starring Charles Bronson that began in 1974, *Dog Day Afternoon* with Al Pacino (1975), *Taxi Driver* with Robert De Niro (1976), *King Kong* (1976), and *Escape from New York* (1981)—all placed the foreboding darkness of the city as the backdrop to their stories.

The doom-and-gloom prognostications may have had their feet on the ground of economic realism, but negative thinking was the exact opposite of what Peale was preaching and the Trumps were absorbing. Donald followed his parents to Marble Collegiate, though there is nothing to indicate that any kind of deep spiritual impact was made on him there. As we saw in the previous chapter, Trump gave high praise for Peale's oratorical abilities to hold the attention of the audience. And Peale rained praise down on his parishioner throughout the 1970s and 1980s for his real estate development prowess. But though Peale knew firsthand the "born again" language of evangelical Christianity, that "old-time Gospel" was not Peale's focus. Both Peale and the Trumps were products of their time, but they also helped shape their cultural moment, bringing shiny and hopeful updates to what they saw as dusty doctrines and buildings in disrepair.

Evangelicals in the mid-1970s held intense conversations about the relationship between personal faith and politics. In the 1976 and 1980 elections, they debated whether a candidate who came "from them" was the best person to vote into the Oval Office. Georgia governor Jimmy Carter, at the time a Sunday school teacher in a Southern Baptist church, described himself as "born again"—the language made common by Nixon's former aide Chuck Colson, who had a conversion experience before heading into prison. The press scoffed at Colson's conversion, thinking he was attempting to get a reduced sentence. But Colson was a sincerely changed man, and when his nine-month incarceration ended in 1976 he formed Prison Fellowship and spent the next thirty years taking the Gospel inside prisons.

As the Democratic candidate for president in 1976, Jimmy Carter was an honest and transparent man, telling *Playboy* magazine that he had sometimes had lust in his heart for other women—an admission that did not win him any points among evangelicals who could not fathom why a Christian would have even talked to a pornographic magazine.

In July 1976, the nation celebrated the bicentennial of the United States. For a few years leading up to the event, large numbers of citizens experienced a surge of interest in and appreciation for the Founders of the nation—their lives and their words experienced a renaissance as the nation remembered just how precious our experiment in liberty had been within world history.

That same month, I attended the Democratic National Convention at Madison Square Garden. I was only twelve, so I don't remember much—but I recall thinking that Jimmy Carter's accent didn't sound like the folks I grew up around as a Reformed Jew in Manhattan. But his words resonated with Watergate-weary people:

> There is a fear that our best years are behind us. But I say to you that our nation's best is still ahead. Our country has lived through a time of torment. It is now a time for healing. We want to have faith again. We want to be proud again. We just want the truth again.

The Democrats left town excited about their prospects against either Gerald Ford or Ronald Reagan (the RNC would be contested, with Reagan narrowly losing in his upset bid). A few weeks after the DNC, a young woman was murdered in the Bronx—the first of six killings perpetrated by the "Son of Sam"—a crime spree that put fear in the hearts of New Yorkers.

Amid that historic and eventful summer, Donald Trump met Ivana Marie Zelníčková. She had moved to New York as a model in support of the publicity for the Summer Olympics being held in Montreal. Ivana, then twenty-seven, had emigrated from Czechoslovakia after a youth spent in competitive skiing. She had been married twice before, though the second time was only for immigration purposes. She lived in Montreal, in a relationship with a man she had known since childhood. But Trump pursued her with roses, dinners, calls, and trips to see her. They were married on April 7, 1977, by Norman

Vincent Peale at Marble Collegiate Church. Donald talked about her bearing him three children: Donald John Jr. was born nine months after their wedding; Ivana "Ivanka" Marie was born in October 1981; Eric Fredrick came along in February 1984.

Jimmy Carter became president in November, aided by the newly organized voting bloc called evangelicals—a fact incarnated by *Newsweek* with their cover story calling 1976 "The Year of the Evangelical." But four short years later the evangelicals turned away from their Bible Belt POTUS and sent into the White House a divorced actor turned governor, who had spotty church attendance in his Mainline PCUSA denomination.

A hundred books have been written to explain the origins and motivations of these early evangelicals. But the basic impulse was found in a movie released the same month Carter won the election. *Network* was a satirical look at television and the influence of media in American culture. Its most famous scene comes when the fictional Howard Beale looks directly into the camera and gives a shouting diatribe on live television. He coaches America to go open their windows, lean out, and shout with him: "I'm as mad as hell, and I'm not going to take this anymore!"

Fresh from the thrill of political victory, the Christian Right began to organize and plan for even more success: Focus on the Family (1977), American Family Association (1977), Concerned Women for America (1979), Moral Majority (1979), Family Research Council (1981), and The Rutherford Institute (1982).

And in direct response to the rise of the Christian Right, Norman Lear founded his own organization in 1981—People for the American Way. As Lear explained the origins in his autobiography:

It had begun brewing in me years earlier with the proliferation of fundamentalist TV ministries that perverted the pulpit by mixing politics and religion. . . . What they were calling the Religious Right began with Pat Robertson and his Christian Broadcasting Network in 1966 and really caught fire in the late 1970s when dozens more religious radicals added their voices. "This nation was built upon a Christian foundation, upon a Bible foundation," declaimed Rev. James Robison, roaming from the pulpit and brandishing his Bible like a weapon as he decimated the Constitution in Jesus' name. . . . "I hope I live to see the day when, as in the early days of our country, we won't have any public schools," said Rev. Falwell. "The churches will have taken them over again and Christians will be running them. What a happy day that will be!"

Don't think these are ancient battles with no current relevance. The names in Lear's crosshairs are the same evangelicals who became central figures in the evangelical story of how Trump won in 2016 (Falwell now succeeded by his son). And since the election, Lear's public statements against President Trump have only intensified.

In August 1976, Tom Wolfe penned a lengthy essay for *New York* magazine: "The 'Me' Decade and the Third Great Awakening." Wolfe, who a decade later would accurately describe the *Bonfire of the Vanities* materialism of the 1980s, profiled the ballooning narcissism present in the seventies culture and the coming-into-adulthood boomers. Wolfe used religious terms to optimistically write about the coming wave of social trends, arguing that the "me" focus on the individual and self-fulfillment would bring on a "Third Great Awakening" that would permanently change the culture.

Three years later, historian Christopher Lasch wrote *The Culture of Narcissism*, a best-selling book that took a decidedly negative view of the "pathological narcissism" that he argued had become prominent in the postwar years. "The contemporary climate is therapeutic, not religious," wrote Lasch. "People today hunger not for personal salvation, let alone for the restoration of an earlier golden age, but for the feeling, the momentary illusion, of personal well-being, health, and psychic security."

TIME called Lasch a "biblical prophet" and Jimmy Carter called Lasch for help—bringing him to Camp David in July 1979 for counsel about the underlying problems of the nation's soul. A week later, Carter delivered what became known as the "malaise" speech: "The threat is nearly invisible in ordinary ways. It is a crisis of confidence. It is a crisis that strikes at the very heart and soul of our national will. We can see this crisis in the growing doubt about the meaning of our own lives and in the loss of a unity of purpose for our nation. The erosion of our confidence in the future is threatening to destroy the social and the political fabric of America." Though the speech diagnosed accurately the cultural ills of runaway individualism and materialism, the depressed economy and long lines for gas had the nation looking for a leader with competence and confidence to turn things around. Instead, the Iranian hostage crisis began in November.

One month later, Donald Trump began demolition of the Bonwit Teller department store in Manhattan to create the space for what would become his crowning achievement and home: Trump Tower. By the time the steel was going up for the new building, Reagan was being inaugurated as the nation's new president, and the hostages were on their way home.

After it opened on Valentine's Day in 1983, a *New York Times* architecture critic described the public space within Trump Tower as "warm, luxurious, and even exhilarating—in every way more welcoming than the public arcades and atriums that preceded it on 5th Avenue."

Since being elected, the security at Trump Tower has tightened greatly. But when it first opened, doormen with white gloves stood below the gold-and-black-lettered "Open to the Public" main entrance to Trump Tower. Once inside, Reagan's "Morning Again in America" theme incarnated itself with opulence and optimism. Nobody put on a sweater or turned down the thermostat in Trump Tower. Trump-style swank declared that the 1970s were over: gold plate, polished brass, mirrors and marble throughout, and high-end retail stores.

Even as Reagan's ad men were crafting "America Is Back" and "It's Morning Again in America" themes for his 1984 landslide re-election, Donald Trump moved his family into a three-story penthouse at the top of the Tower. In 2016, a writer for *The New Yorker* stated that "Half a lifetime after Trump built it, the tower still defines the man."

11

The Man Who Has Everything

With Lady Gaga performing the halftime show at Super Bowl 2017 just weeks after Donald Trump's inauguration as president, there was a palpable expectation that she would lace her singing with political protest. Instead, she opened with a medley of Irving Berlin's "God Bless America" and Woody Guthrie's "This Land Is Your Land." Of course, Guthrie originally titled his song "God Blessed America for Me" as a parody of sorts on Berlin's lyrics being frequently used as a call for divine blessing on whatever America happened to be doing at the moment. A decade later, in 1950, Guthrie signed a lease with Fred Trump—literally, Trump's signature is on the papers—to live in Trump's brand-new Beach Haven apartment complex near Coney Island. But Guthrie would grow to despise what he believed was the lack of racial integration in the complex and penned lyrics about "old man Trump."

Fred built and ran his apartments in accordance with the federal policies in place since the New Deal created the FHA in 1934. This was more than a decade before the Civil Rights Acts and at a time when the Federal Housing Administration (FHA) loans that financed Trump's projects still maintained "restrictive covenants" with code phrases like "inharmonious uses of housing," which meant homes in white neighborhoods were not to be sold to blacks. The Supreme Court ruled against restrictive covenants in 1948, and Lyndon Johnson signed the Fair Housing Act in 1968. In 1973, the Justice Department sued the Trumps for housing discrimination—just two years after Fred made Donald the president of the company. They countersued for $100 million, asserting their innocence and charging the Justice Department with making false statements. Two years later, a settlement was reached—but with no admission of guilt.

Hillary Clinton brought up the lawsuit during their first debate. Trump responded: "Now, as far as the lawsuit, yes, when I was very young, I went into my father's company, had a real estate company in Brooklyn and Queens, and we, along with many, many other companies throughout the country—it was a federal lawsuit—were sued. We settled the suit with zero—with no admission of guilt. It was very easy to do." Then Trump said, "I'll go one step further," and he told how he integrated his Mar-a-Lago Club, against the tradition of the existing country club scene in Palm Beach. "I opened a club, and really got great credit for it. No discrimination against African-Americans, against Muslims, against anybody. And it's a tremendously successful club. And I'm so glad I did it. And I have been given great credit for what I did. And I'm very, very proud of it. And that's the way I feel. That is the true way I feel."

It was in 1984 and 1985 that Trump bought his first casinos in Atlantic City and in 1985 that he bought the historic Mar-a-Lago—the twentieth-biggest mansion in the entire United States. These purchases serve as an opening bookend of sorts for the next decade—when Trump went from being famous in New York City to being famous everywhere. American culture during the 1980s became fascinated with peering into the *Lifestyles of the Rich and Famous*—the spectator sport of viewing the conspicuous consumption of the super-rich. And Trump began to position himself in the crosshairs of their gaze. Unfortunately, this was also the time when he overleveraged his business and began an affair that led to a nasty divorce from Ivana—all played out in the press.

•   •   •

In July 1986, the nation's eyes were on New York City as President Ronald Reagan and First Lady Nancy Reagan led a four-day "Liberty Weekend" party to celebrate the re-opening of the Statue of Liberty after two years of work to restore the landmark. Reagan had tasked Lee Iacocca, the auto industry guru, to lead a private sector fund-raising campaign: $500 million was raised, including $2 million in small change that schoolchildren sent in to support the effort. Their teachers worked through a year's worth of curriculum about American history, civics and the Constitution, and immigration.

Highlights of the celebration included numerous concerts, fireworks, and the largest flotilla of ships ever assembled. Supreme Court Chief Justice Warren Burger swore in new citizens in a ceremony on Ellis Island. Norman Lear produced the TV broadcast of the spectacle for ABC, and Americans watched in record numbers. On July 4, speaking from the deck of the USS *Iowa,* Reagan described the procession of ships in language echoing Emerson and Peale:

> Perhaps, indeed, these vessels embody our conception of liberty itself: to have before one no impediments, only open spaces; to chart one's own course and take the adventure of life as it comes; to be free as the wind—as free as the tall ships themselves. It's fitting, then, that this procession should take place in honor of Lady Liberty.

That night, just before the fireworks, Reagan spoke about the need for national unity—"the real obstacle to moving forward the boundaries of freedom, the only permanent danger to the hope that is America, comes from within." Reagan told the story of the decades-long partisan estrangement that came between Founders

John Adams and Thomas Jefferson, and how they reconciled their differences before they died as they reflected on their shared love of the country they had helped birth. Reagan noted how the two men died on the exact same day—and exactly fifty years after the original "Fourth of July" signing of the Declaration of Independence.

> It was their last gift to us, this lesson in brotherhood, in tolerance for each other, this insight into America's strength as a nation . . . that the things that unite us—America's past of which we're so proud, our hopes and aspirations for the future of the world and this much-loved country—these things far outweigh what little divides us. And so tonight we reaffirm that Jew and gentile, we are one nation under God; that black and white, we are one nation indivisible; that Republican and Democrat, we are all Americans.

Trump, having just turned forty a few weeks earlier, soaked up all these events with pride—as an American, a New Yorker, a fan of Ronald Reagan, a friend and future business partner of Lee Iacocca, and the son of immigrant parents who had sailed by the Statue of Liberty en route to citizenship and pursuit of the American dream. Trump even had a hand in making the weekend memorable for an eleven-year-old Vietnamese refugee, born right at the end of the conflict. She had won a trip to New York for the celebrations, but if the family claimed the prize, they would have lost their public assistance. Carl Icahn's TWA donated tickets to fly the family and Trump put them up at his St. Moritz hotel—so everything worked out, and memories were made.

The entire nonpartisan process of Lady Liberty's restoration and the capstone celebration involving people from every political, religious, and economic background created an immense surge of national pride, patriotism, and civic knowledge. One could make a strong argument that, apart from the days immediately following 9/11, this event was the last time our nation has been so united in purpose and spirit.

That October, on the true one hundredth anniversary of the Statue of Liberty, Donald Trump stood in the shadow of the statue as an inaugural recipient of the Ellis Island Medal of Honor. The award celebrates the conviction "that the diversity of the American people is what makes this nation great. Its mission is to honor and preserve this diversity and to foster tolerance, respect, and understanding among religious and ethnic groups." With a medal around his neck, Trump stood directly alongside Joe DiMaggio, Muhammad Ali, and Rosa Parks for photographers.

Reagan's secretary of the interior Donald Hodel, an evangelical Christian who would later serve as president of the Christian Coalition and then CEO of Focus on the Family, gave a speech that criticized the Soviet Union for "systematic and continuous abuse of the rights of its citizens." Hodel pointed at an empty chair on the stage and said it symbolized "the millions and millions of people throughout the world who yearn for freedom."

It was also on an October day, two decades earlier, that President Lyndon Johnson stood in the shadow of the Statue of Liberty to sign the Immigration and Nationality Act of 1965. This legislation ended the National Origins Formula of 1921, which had put restrictive quotas on immigrants from non–Northern European nations. Johnson said:

> This bill that we will sign today is not a revolutionary bill.
> It does not affect the lives of millions. It will not reshape
> the structure of our daily lives, or really add importantly to

either our wealth or our power. Yet it is still one of the most important acts of this Congress and of this administration.

For it does repair a very deep and painful flaw in the fabric of American justice. It corrects a cruel and enduring wrong in the conduct of the American Nation.

. . . The bill says simply that from this day forth those wishing to immigrate to America shall be admitted on the basis of their skills and their close relationship to those already here. This is a simple test, and it is a fair test. Those who can contribute most to this country—to its growth, to its strength, to its spirit—will be the first that are admitted to this land.

Though Johnson and the shapers of the bill sincerely did not believe it would have a revolutionary effect, they were wrong. As Tom Gjelten, a veteran NPR correspondent, wrote in *A Nation of Nations*: "In the decades since, America's founding myth of openness has been tested. Prior to 1965, three out of four immigrants came from Europe, and the country's cultural character reflected its Anglo-Saxon roots. Since then, nine of ten immigrants have come from other parts of the world."

During the 2016 election, it became fashionable to state that "White Christian America" was dying off and that White Christians were in lamentation and mourning over this fact, because they're opposed to immigration. But in reality, many American Christians know that Latin American immigration has been a vital source of energy for evangelicalism. Since 1970, Pentecostals in Latin America have increased from 4 percent of the population to 28 percent—an increase from 12 million people to 156 million. And during that same time, the Hispanic population of America increased from 4 percent to 18 percent.

So, based on these two facts alone, the evangelical electorate in America is less white as a direct result of the 1965 Act. Less white, but not necessarily less evangelical. Denominations which eschew Pentecostalism, like the Southern Baptist Convention, are 3 percent Hispanic. By contrast, two of the leading Pentecostal denominations are the Assemblies of God (25 percent Hispanic) and the Church of God (28 percent Hispanic). And contrary to the dire prognostications that showed Trump would receive historic low support from Hispanics, CNN exit polling reported that he won 28 percent of their vote—compared to 27 percent that voted for Mitt Romney in 2012.

In the summer of 1986, Donald Trump challenged New York mayor Ed Koch that he could fix the broken Wollman Ice Skating Rink in Central Park in six months for less than $3 million. The city had been working on the problem for five years and had spent $12 million, so this seemed to be arrogant bluster. Koch, prompted by a public outcry from citizens who wanted the rink functional again, agreed to let Trump take a crack at it. Four months later and 25 percent under the projected cost, the rink opened to the public in November 1986. And throughout the construction process, Trump made sure to have press releases and news of ribbon cuttings churned out to the newspapers. It was a win-win situation—the public got to ice skate again, the city stopped wasting taxpayer dollars, and Trump increased his name recognition and created goodwill among New Yorkers. Though fixing of the Wollman Rink involved only a fraction of what Iacocca did for the Statue of Liberty, this singular act probably marks a turning point for Trump regarding public activism and his eventual entrance into politics.

With the manuscript for his first book, *The Art of the Deal*, in the hands of publishers and set for a release in November 1987, Trump got busy creating publicity. And as everyone knows, nothing beats presidential political speculation for securing the attention of the press. In September, he paid for a full-page open letter about foreign defense to be placed in the *New York Times*, *Boston Globe*, and the *Washington Post*—just the kind of thing a billionaire with White House aspirations might do.

The next month, he flew up to New Hampshire and spoke at a Rotary Club: "I'm not here today because I'm running for the presidency. I'm here because I'm personally tired of seeing this great country of ours being ripped off." The press coverage of his speech noted that he drew a bigger crowd than men who had declared their candidacy for 1988: Bob Dole, Pat Robertson, and Jack Kemp.

In November, he released his book with a $160,000 party at Trump Tower. Two thousand people attended, including a young model and aspiring actress from Georgia named Marla Maples. The book held the number-one position on the *New York Times* bestseller list for three months and stayed on the list for nearly a year altogether. It has sold over a million copies since its release and probably did more than anything else, outside of *The Apprentice,* to make Trump a household name.

In December, Barbara Walters produced a segment on Trump for *20/20* called "The Man Who Has Everything." To say the least, she was enamored. "What do you feel like when you look at that wonderful skyline?" Walters asked Trump as they flew over Manhattan in his helicopter. "Do you say, 'I own that and that and that and that?' "

No, Trump didn't own most of Manhattan. But he *was* in the midst of making overleveraged purchases—both business and personal— that would be his temporary undoing, even as they increased the spread of his fame for being rich and successful. In addition to buying up three casinos in Atlantic City, Trump bought a million-dollar helicopter in 1987 (naming it *Ivana*), and an $8 million Boeing 727 a few months later. In 1988, he paid $29 million for a yacht once owned by a Saudi arms dealer, then spent $10 million more to have it refitted to his liking. He also bought the Plaza Hotel in the spring of 1988, overpaying by $100 million for it according to some estimates. With that purchase, Trump even admitted his hubris in a full-page ad he took out in the *New York Times* to explain himself: "I haven't purchased a building, I have purchased a masterpiece— the *Mona Lisa*. For the first time in my life, I have knowingly made a deal which was not economic—for I can never justify the price no matter how successful the Plaza becomes." And then in November of 1988, he responded to the pressure of all these commitments and debt by purchasing the Eastern Airlines Shuttle for $385 million.

And it was during this same time that his marriage to Ivana unraveled. On Christmas Eve 1987 they celebrated the signing of their fourth nuptial agreement—but by all accounts, the marriage was already in peril. Trump began an affair with Marla Maples around this time, and over the next two years the tabloids were full of stories about the sordid mess being made of the marriage. During Christmas in 1990, Ivana and Marla ended up on the same Aspen ski slope with Donald, and a highly publicized confrontation was photographed and shared with the world. They spent 1991 on their way to the divorce that was finalized in the spring of 1992.

Trump and Maples split up several times as a couple. Their daughter, Tiffany, was born in October 1993; two months later Donald and Marla wed. Dr. Arthur Caliandro, the successor to Norman Vincent Peale at Marble Collegiate, married them at the Plaza Hotel. The Reverend himself had been married twice, and would eventually marry a third time too—quite the contrast to Peale's sixty-three-year marriage. Over one thousand high-profile guests from business, sports, and entertainment attended the wedding— including O. J. Simpson, Howard Stern, Rosie O'Donnell, and Robin

Leach. While the couple honeymooned Peale died—on Christmas Eve 1993. Trump and Maples separated in 1997 and divorced in 1999—two weeks before Fred Trump died. Mary Anne Trump died one year later in August 2000.

Honestly, the preceding two paragraphs only skim the surface of all the debt, expenses, and expansion that Trump bought into during this eight-year period between 1985 and 1993. Entire books and hundreds of articles have been written to chronicle the wealth and women stories from these years. The premise and promise of this book did not involve trying to break new ground on the financial analysis of his business or tales of his love life. That said, we do have three brief points of analysis about these troublesome years in the life of Donald Trump.

First, the Bible does not lack clarity about our relationship to wealth or sexuality. Jesus said that a man who gains the entire world but loses his soul has made the foolish choice. Jesus was asked by a rich man, "How do I have eternal life?" Knowing the man's love and idolatry of his wealth, Jesus told the man to sell everything and follow him. The Bible says the man went away sad because he could not follow that teaching. The Apostle Paul wrote that the love of money (not money itself) is the root of all evil (1 Timothy 6:10). And the Apostle John wrote, "Do not love the world or the things in the world. If anyone loves the world, the love of the Father is not in him. For all that is in the world—the desires of the flesh and the desires of the eyes and pride of life—is not from the Father but is from the world. And the world is passing away along with its desires, but whoever does the will of God abides forever (1 John 2:15–17).

As for breaking one's marriage vows, adultery breaks one of the Ten Commandments God gave the Israelites at Mount Sinai (Exodus 20), and the basis for it is rooted in the Creation account itself when God instituted marriage as he brought one man and woman together (Genesis 2). And Jesus defined adultery in even stricter terms when he said that "looking at a woman with lust" was as the sin of adultery. To be clear, the Donald Trump of this period would have never been able to ascend to the White House. But America is the land of second chances—or even third chances if you live long enough.

Second, it seems too great a coincidence to not mention that the two most famous Christian televangelist sex-and-money scandals broke around the same time that Donald Trump began pursuing Marla Maples. Jim Bakker's scandal broke in March 1987, and Jimmy Swaggart's came in 1988, and again in 1991. And the profligate spending of ministry funds for personal use had been taking place for years. Such public scandals brought a lasting reproach upon the church and the Gospel. The outside world and the casual Christian would have no reason to respect God's morality when preachers played the part of a hypocrite.

Third, though we have avoided playing the part of an armchair psychologist with Donald Trump, several people we interviewed who consider themselves to be friends or on friendly terms with Trump stated their opinion that they don't believe Donald Trump's relationship with money flows from a heart of greed. Donald himself opened *The Art of the Deal* with a phrase that, in our opinion, is sincere: "I don't do it for the money." These off-the-record friendly interviewees sense that Trump's ambition stems from a deep-rooted need to command respect—a basic, simple drive to prove that he is the best. Prove to whom? The answers to that vary: the approval of the elites, the approval of the masses, the approval of his father Fred, or his own approval.

We won't attempt to answer that question about another man's soul. But Christian teaching has a word to say about these matters for all of us. St. Augustine, a man who pursued pleasures of all sorts before his conversion to Christ—a conversion that his devout mother had prayed for years to happen—wrote in his autobiography, *Confessions*: "You have made us for yourself, and our hearts are restless until they find their rest in Thee." Christian philosopher Pascal wrote, "There is a God-shaped vacuum in the heart of every man, and only God can fill it." And the Scottish Roman Catholic novelist Bruce Marshall had one of his priests say: "I still prefer to believe that sex is a substitute for religion and that the young man who rings the bell at the brothel is unconsciously looking for God."

12

Prospereality

When the bankers came after Donald in the early 1990s, they realized quickly that buildings and casinos with the name "Trump" at the top were worth more than if they killed off Trump financially and foreclosed on the properties. We'll spare you the details of how these Chapter 11 deals went down, and who got what, but suffice it to say, by the middle of the decade, Donald had retooled his business model to focus on the brand itself—the "Trump" name itself became his moneymaking juggernaut. One historian described it as a flash of genius because Trump was only an average CEO in terms of running a traditional, public company, but he was without peer in the arts of promotion, sales, and branding. From this point forward, Trump would shift from being mostly a developer to more of a promoter of a brand. "He's a wonderful promoter," a banker involved in work with Trump said. "He's the P. T. Barnum of the 21st century." It was also during the second half of the 1990s that Trump fully burnished his credentials as a Don Juan of sorts—a man with a beautiful woman on his arm, and preferably, a steady rotation of them at that. But by 2005, both of these Trump trends had played out in different directions.

Donald and Marla separated four years after they wed—ten years after they first met. And even before their divorce was finalized two years later, Trump began to be associated with a constant stream of supermodels. The Hugh Hefner playboy ethos—that a man should aspire to wealth, celebrity, and women—became a reality for Trump during these years.

In this, he was living out the ideals of puberty, learned at NYMA in camaraderie with his fellow cadets. "Our biggest advice in our lives came from *Playboy* magazine," Trump classmate Sandy McIntosh said. "That's how we learned about women." McIntosh recalled how Fred and Mary Anne visited Donald on the weekends and brought along a different, gorgeous young woman each time. This probably explains how he earned the label "Ladies' Man" in the school yearbook—despite there being no females at the school.

Trump biographer Timothy O'Brien wrote that if there are "three stereotypes" that are "tap dancing in Donald's mind and in his imagination of himself, it's Clint Eastwood, James Bond, and Hugh Hefner." In 1995, Eastwood's film adaptation of *The Bridges of Madison County,* about a four-day affair between an Iowa farmer's wife and a traveling photographer, became one of the top-earning movies of the decade. To say the least, *Bridges* leaves the viewer wishing there could have been some way the farmwife might have been able to keep both her good husband and kids while also having the steamy romance with Eastwood's character.

Trump, in a 1994 interview with ABC, talked about the years when he had both Ivana and Marla: "My life was so great in so many ways. The business was so great . . . a beautiful girlfriend, a beautiful wife, a beautiful everything. Life was just a bowl of cherries." Also in 1995, Pierce Brosnan made his first portrayal of James Bond—the first "007" movie to release since 1989—and the British MI6 agent promptly jumped into bed with beautiful women. The fictional James Bond character was not known for showing sexual restraint—you could even say that the dalliances were part of his job description. And Americans—including evangelicals—fund these culture-shaping products with their book purchases and ticket sales.

What is interesting is that the "playboy Trump" years began in earnest at the same time that Fred Trump was diagnosed and

fought a six-year battle with Alzheimer's. Two of the most forma-
tive real-world father figures in Donald's life—Fred and Peale—had
over one hundred twenty years of married life between them. Peale
died in 1993, the same year as Fred's diagnosis. It almost seems
as though when Trump lost the older generation, he responded by
returning to a "sow some wild oats" mindset of adolescence. But
this was not to be the final chapter written about Trump's marital
relationships.

In September 1998, Trump met Melania while on a date with
another woman, also a model. They began dating, with a couple of
break-ups mixed in and reported on in the papers. At some point
in 2001, Melania moved into Trump Tower. In 2002, Donald flew
to Slovenia to meet her parents. In January 2005, they married at
Bethesda by the Sea, an Episcopal congregation near their Florida estate, Mar-a-Lago. Fifteen months later, Melania gave birth to
Barron.

Two weeks after Trump and Maples married, his friend Rudolph
Giuliani was sworn in as mayor of New York, the city's first Republican mayor in twenty years. "The era of fear has had a long enough
reign," Giuliani, a former US attorney general, said in his inaugural
address. "American cities cannot survive as we know them if they
remain so violent . . . our problems may be big, but our people are
bigger."

Trump had served as a co-chair to a fund-raiser for Giuliani's
failed bid for mayor in 1989. Meanwhile, the crime in New York
continued to escalate. The murder rate in the early nineties hovered
around two thousand per year.

In 1989, a woman was raped, beaten, and left for dead in Central
Park. Five young minority men were arrested. Trump took out a
full-page ad in all the New York papers, to urge for the toughest

penalties on the accused: "Bring Back the Death Penalty! Bring Back Our Police!" He seemed to be incensed over both the crime itself and the response from City Hall:

> Mayor Koch has stated that hate and rancor should be removed from our hearts. I do not think so. I want to hate these muggers and murderers. They should be forced to suffer. . . . Yes, Mayor Koch, I want to hate these murderers and I always will. . . . How can our great society tolerate the continued brutalization of its citizens by crazed misfits? Criminals must be told that their CIVIL LIBERTIES END WHEN AN ATTACK ON OUR SAFETY BEGINS!

The accused were convicted and sent to prison, but the convictions were later overturned, and the men won a lawsuit against the city.

Then, in 1991, seventy-nine-year-old Mary Anne Trump was assaulted and robbed—thrown down to the pavement in Queens by a sixteen-year-old to steal what amounted to some pocket cash. The fall fractured her ribs, caused a brain hemorrhage, and led to permanent damage to her vision and hearing. The young man was chased down and caught by a witness to the crime, an African-American bread-truck driver. When Trump discovered the hero was in danger of losing his house to foreclosure, he cut him a check that kept the man in his home.

As mayor, Giuliani instituted many "broken windows" measures to curtail crime, along with more controversial policies like "stop and frisk." Crime decreased dramatically and continued to do so even after he finished his second term in December 2001. The murder rate is now as low as it was in the 1960s.

Endless studies have attempted to explain the reduction in crime as due to police tactics, demographic changes, or a nationwide decline in a time of economic prosperity. But as one who came of age in New York City in the 1970s and who saw firsthand the breakdown of "law and order" before moving away as an adult, I can attest to the shock of disbelief I felt when I returned to the city for visits during Giuliani's mayoral tenure. The city had rebounded.

One of the amazing stories of religion in New York City is the surge of evangelical churches during the past generation. This trend has affected the entire metro area, but Manhattan, in particular, has received much of the attention. Make no mistake, the city is incredibly diverse and pluralistic—every world religion can be found in the boroughs, to say nothing of secularism and irreligion. But seven out of ten evangelical congregations now in Manhattan were started since 1950. And four out of ten were started in the decade since 9/11. In hard numbers, since Trump landed the Commodore Hotel project in 1978—his first major action in Manhattan—about 120 of the roughly 200 evangelical churches in Manhattan have begun. Trump moved from Queens with dreams of changing the skyline of Manhattan; evangelicals came seeking to change the soul of the city. The verse of choice for urban church leaders became Jeremiah 29:7: "Also, seek the peace and prosperity of the city to which I have carried you into exile. Pray to the Lord for it, because if it prospers, you too will prosper."

Tony Carnes, the editor of the religion journalism website *A Journey Through NYC Religions*, explored this Manhattan Evangelical renaissance and gave this conclusion about the significance of religion in the city:

> In sum, no other city's ups and downs become part of the world's consciousness quite like New York's. Today, post-secular New York City is in a similar icon busting and

making stage. It is busting the image of the city as Sodom and Gomorrah and the Secular City. It is becoming the place where faith has an accepted public role in the fate of the city. . . . Truly, the city speaks a vernacular gospel that is also cosmopolitan in its impact. Whatever happens, a fundamental change in the role of faith in New York City will affect the mindspace of the world.

Three of the better-known examples are within only a mile or two of Trump Tower. For example, Times Square Church was begun by David Wilkerson in 1987, three decades after his ministry to gangs in the city inspired *The Cross and the Switchblade*. This church has a personal connection to me. I grew up in a "Jewish household" in Manhattan, but neither of my parents were very religious. I would go to temple and Hebrew school, and I had my bar mitzvah at age thirteen, so I was doing all the religious stuff, but I was just going through the motions. I never had any sort of understanding of God. All I knew was that I did these things because it was tradition.

In college, my girlfriend and future wife, Lisette (whom I had known since high school), started to talk to me about having a personal relationship with Jesus. I remember thinking, "What are you talking about? I don't need a personal relationship with God. I'm Jewish." The year after college, Lisette invited me to her charismatic church in New York City—Times Square Church. Something seemed to be tugging at my heart. I think the sermons about life and death and the idea of a personal relationship with Jesus Christ interested me on some level. But, more importantly, I was hearing this idea that you could have a personal relationship with the God of the universe. This was very foreign to me. We married the next year, in 1988, and shortly after I committed my life to Christ while living in Colorado.

A second well-known congregation, Redeemer Presbyterian, was begun by Tim Keller in 1989. Keller has become a best-selling author of books that people liken to the winsome apologetics of C. S. Lewis. Redeemer began a church-planting network that has helped bring one hundred congregations into existence throughout the city. Keller helped Christians realize the opportunity to "reach the nations" (Matthew 28:19–20) by coming to New York City—where all the nations live.

Finally, Hillsong is a congregation affiliated with the Australian Pentecostal mega-church by the same name. Carl Lentz, the current minister, has become known as "Justin Bieber's pastor" because of his ministry and spiritual counsel to the young singer—as well as numerous other celebrities. *GQ* profiled the church in 2015 "to find out if Christianity can really be this cool and still be Christian." When asked if the church tries to "cater to celebrities," Lentz answered: "I say, yes, we do. Celebrities deserve a relationship with God. Celebrities deserve a place to pray"—adding, "so do all of God's children." Ironically, Hillsong meets one block from the spot where Trump's great-aunts went to church in New York's first Pentecostal church—the church that celebrity preacher Aimee Semple McPherson preached at on her visits to the city.

In the early 1980s, Donald and Ivana Trump met Andy Warhol at his studio to discuss his creating some works of art that would hang in Trump Tower. Apparently, they didn't finalize a commission or price, but Warhol went to work and produced eight pieces that depicted Warhol's vision of the building. Donald, however, didn't like the pieces and chose not to buy them, causing Warhol to express his hatred of Trump—something he wrote about in his diary, which was published in 1989.

But in a rare case of Trump deciding not to counterpunch a fellow celebrity—at least not by name—he favorably quoted Warhol twice in his 2009 book *Think Like a Champion*: "Making money is art,

and working is art, and good business is the best art." That's Warhol, not Trump—though the sentiment is Trumpian, as his opening
lines from *The Art of the Deal* show: "Deals are my art form. Other
people paint beautifully on canvas or write wonderful poetry. I like
making deals, preferably big deals. That's how I get my kicks."

The greatest Warhol-Trump connection comes indirectly, through
the iconic artist's famous dictum: "In the future, everyone will be
world-famous for 15 minutes." Of course, both Warhol and Trump
grabbed a much larger share than fifteen minutes. But the TV-loving
Warhol's quote perfectly predicted the rise of reality TV as a tool
for turning nobodies into somebodies—even if briefly. Warhol may
have hated Trump in person, but he wouldn't have missed an episode of *The Apprentice*. For every Kelly Clarkson who grabbed her
"Breakaway" moment and found lasting fame and a singing career,
there are thousands of people who merely get fifteen minutes of TV
fame on their way to being cast off an island or hearing "You're
fired." Fame is the drug we're addicted to before we even get our
first score. As novelist Oscar Wilde had one of his characters proclaim: "There is only one thing in the world worse than being talked
about and that is not being talked about."

Trump understands that in America, no matter what your business,
your business is entertainment. Before launching into real estate
with Fred, Donald had even thought about heading out to California to try his hand in the movie business. And he even invested
some money in a short-lived Broadway play during that time. "I've
always thought that Louis B. Mayer led the ultimate life, that Flo
Ziegfeld led the ultimate life, that men like Darryl Zanuck and
Harry Cohn did some creative and beautiful things. The ultimate
job for me would have been running MGM in the '30s and '40s—
pre-television."

Trump has always understood the central role of entertainment in US culture. When he owned a USFL team in the eighties, Trump said, "It's crazy, but I could build a $300 million building, and nobody cares. I hire a coach and 400 reporters call. The priorities are ridiculous."

In 1995, John F. Kennedy Jr. launched a magazine called *George* that would merge politics, celebrity culture, and entertainment. The first issue had Cindy Crawford dressed as George Washington—if our first president ever wore a midriff-exposing half-shirt. But Kennedy died in a plane crash in 1999 and the magazine folded in 2001. Before it did, however, the editors put Trump on the cover of the March 2000 issue for an article discussing his "Exploratory Committee" as a Reform Party candidate. Trump was giving interviews all over the place during this time, and he filled them with highly quotable riffs on every subject. Larry King interviewed him and asked who he would have for a vice president. Trump said, "Oprah. I love Oprah. Oprah would always be my first choice. If she'd do it, she'd be fantastic. She's popular. She's brilliant. She's a wonderful woman." He told *The Advocate*, "I guarantee you this. If I do run, it won't be boring."

Trump did not run for president in 2000, but in January 2004 he started living out those earlier entertainment dreams by starring in *The Apprentice*. The show's ratings were incredible, as over 20 million people tuned in to watch at the height of its popularity. And the show secured his universal name-recognition status. From coast to coast, his face was everywhere—in everyone's living room—and people enjoyed watching his antics.

In fact, when he announced his candidacy in 2015, many people thought he was just building his brand some more. And since he wasn't seriously running anyway, why get bent out of shape about his statements? "Like an awful lot of people, I just flat out didn't take it seriously early on," conservative columnist David French said. "I just thought he was funny. My wife and I watched *The Ap-*

prentice from the beginning. We enjoyed the show, thought he had a funny persona. I also remember him from *WrestleMania*. That's kind of how I viewed him—a larger than life reality TV star and a quasi-business mogul, a walking-talking brand."

Robert Schuller, the late founder of the Crystal Cathedral and the *Hour of Power* Christian television program, inherited Norman Vincent Peale's legacy and spread the message of positive thinking—though he tweaked it slightly and called it "Possibility Thinking." In his autobiography, Schuller explained his turn from the Calvin-influenced theology of his denomination, the Reformed Church in America:

> I concluded that I'd have to present Bible truths in simple words and simple messages as Jesus had done. No heavy theology. No intimidation. No judgment. Just inspiring ideas that might bring people from doubt to faith. . . . I deduced that if I focused not on generating guilt, but . . . trust and positive hope, I would be preaching against sin via a creative, redemptive approach.

There doesn't seem to be any record of Donald Trump and Robert Schuller meeting, though they both made a splash at the 1988 Republican National Convention. Schuller gave an opening invocation where he speech-prayed about "Someday is today" and celebrated George H. W. Bush as "a humble man who was able for eight years to live under the towering shadow of one of the great presidents of our country, and never took advantage of opportunities to attract attention to himself. We celebrate a person with emotional health— such healthy self-esteem that he does not yield to boisterous and brash and flamboyant styles of behavior."

NBC's Chris Wallace interviewed Trump from the floor of the

convention, and CNN's Larry King brought Trump into his booth—but both asked the same question: They prodded Trump about the idea of jumping into presidential politics. "Well, I think I'd have a very good chance," Trump told Wallace. "I like to win—when I do something, I like to win. I like to do well, and I think I probably would have a very good chance."

Schuller, like his fellow Californian-from-the-Midwest friend Ronald Reagan, believed that possibility thinking helped people achieve the American dream of being successful. Like a character in a Horatio Alger novel, Schuller felt he had made something of himself as a result of his possibility thinking: "You can go anywhere from nowhere. My life is witness to that. I was born at the dead end of a dirt road that had no name and no number—in a flood."

If Trump ever heard Schuller's message, it must have come via television. Some people may think it is odd to suggest Trump would watch Christian TV, but these viewing habits of his are now an established fact. He and Fred would watch or listen to Billy Graham's sermons—either in the *Hour of Decision* radio format or the *Billy Graham TV Classics* that are broadcast on cable. Trump told an audience at Liberty University that he used to watch Jerry Falwell's program *The Old-Time Gospel Hour*.

And Trump loves the preaching of David Jeremiah, one of the best-known pastors in America and a writer of best-selling books with a conservative, evangelical message. When Jeremiah came to the Theater at Madison Square Garden in 2013 to celebrate the release of his study Bible, over five thousand people bought tickets—an event that included worship music and preaching and was more like a church service than a publicity show. Without any fanfare or special recognition, Donald and Melania showed up and sat in the front row. One person who sat close by said that if you didn't know this was Donald Trump, you would have assumed it was a Christian businessman at worship. Jeremiah and Trump spoke backstage at the event, and the two have maintained contact since; Jeremiah joined the faith advisory board for Trump in July 2016, and he attends the group's meetings at the White House.

Another preacher that Trump first discovered on television is Paula White, currently the pastor of New Destiny Christian Center in Apopka, Florida. At the time of their first contact, however, White was the co-pastor of Without Walls International Church in Tampa, which she founded with her husband, Randy White. Both of the churches White has pastored have been called a "mega-church" due to the size of their membership and budget, and from those resources, a television preaching ministry was birthed. And that's how Trump encountered White.

"I know that so many people have gotten to know Donald Trump through media," White said, "but I had the privilege of knowing Donald—Mr. Trump—as a person. The value of that has been invaluable."

Paula said she was in her office one day, about fourteen years ago, when she was told that "Donald Trump is on the phone for you." She had never met him, so she assumed the call was a prank. But no, it was Trump after all.

"I got on the phone, and he started to quote back to me three sermons that I'd preached—I mean, verbatim. I'd done this series about the 'Value of Vision,' and Trump said, 'You're fantastic.' He said the sermons really ministered to him. We began to have a conversation. He told me how he was confirmed Presbyterian but grew up in Norman Vincent Peale's church and how he was one of the greatest orators. We just began to communicate."

Trump asked White if she ever came up to New York. At the time, she was doing a Bible study for the Yankees (Tampa is home to the Yankees' Class A affiliate, playing at George M. Steinbrenner Field). She met with Trump in New York and gradually became friends with the entire family.

"I didn't know if he did or if he didn't have a relationship with the Lord," White said. "But God connects people strategically and sovereignly for purposes. I felt that the Holy Spirit whispered to my heart and said, 'Show him who I am.' And so that was my assignment—just to be his friend. Sometimes you just look at your phone and hope it is someone calling just to see how are you today. I wanted to be that person—simply a Christian, a living epistle."

White told Trump, "I don't want your money, I have enough of my own. I don't want your fame, I have enough of fame. I want your soul. I'm here for one purpose—to be your friend and show you who God is."

James Robison, a spiritual counselor to Trump since 2016 and a friend of White's, believes that her testimony of failures and flaws may have been what resonated most with Trump. "In Paula, he met a girl who had missed the mark and failed. She never turned loose of Jesus, and Jesus never turned loose of her. That impressed him. Paula never, never, never asked him for anything and never took anything from him. She just loved him and his family, and he watched her hold on to Jesus."

Robison was referring to the fact that White was converted to Christ as a young adult, and that her life has not always been a straight trajectory of sunshine and success. "I believe God raises up little people to do big things," White said. "I didn't grow up in church and never heard the gospel until I was eighteen. I truly had an encounter with God and got radically saved—and I dedicated my life to him. I stayed at an altar all night long one night, and said to God: 'If you can, then use me.' I gave God all the reasons that He couldn't use me: although I came from a well-to-do family, my father had committed suicide when I was five years old. Then, I had been sexually and physically abused in my childhood and had a child out of wedlock. I was just this young girl that believed that God could take anything and anyone and if they would believe that he could use their life as a transformed life. Fast forward thirty-two years, I still believe that one of the assignments in my life is to be like Naaman's maid, to go in and deliver the Word of the Lord" (2 Kings 5:1–19).

White also discovered that Trump loves Southern Gospel music and that one of his favorites is the Gaithers, having seen them on Christian TV. For a birthday or an anniversary, she would send him Bill Gaither tapes, along with books and sermons. "Have I had in-depth spiritual conversations with Mr. Trump? Absolutely," White said. "Let me say something very literally about our President: 100 percent, he has a relationship with God through the Lord Jesus Christ as his savior."

In 2012, Trump called White and told her he was thinking of running for president. There was a time of prayer as he pondered the decision. Of course, he didn't run then, but he called again in 2015 and told her, "'I really believe the Lord is speaking to me, that maybe I'm supposed to run for President.' I asked him, 'As my friend, what can I do for you?' He asked for me to bring some pastors in to him, and I did." Time and again, White and various pastors have surrounded Trump and placed their hands on his shoulders as prayers were spoken.

It was also during this season in Trump's life that he began to make new friends from within evangelicalism. Arthur Caliandro retired in 2009 from Marble Collegiate, and Trump admits they haven't been back there since then. But in 2010, he began a friendship with Ralph Reed, conversing about the worldview and values of the Christian faith. Through frequent interaction in the studios at Fox News, he and Mike Huckabee—an ordained minister—began to know one another. In 2012, Trump came to Liberty University for the first time, speaking to a record number in the audience for their regular convocation. In November 2013, he and Melania attended an invitation-only ninety-fifth birthday party celebration for Billy Graham. And, of course, as I mentioned in the introduction, my first encounter with Trump came in 2011 when I interviewed him at Trump Tower for CBN.

Of all the Christian leaders who showed support for Trump, few have known him longer than White. And among the group, nobody received as much scorn or personal attack as White did during the 2016 campaign. After yet another evangelical theologian called her a heretic a few weeks before the Inauguration, White responded with a written statement:

> In recent days, I have read a great deal of false information being reported about me, my theology, and my past. I have been called a heretic, an apostate, an adulterer, a charlatan, and an addict. It has been falsely reported that I once filed for bankruptcy and—my personal favorite—that I deny the Trinity!
>
> I have hesitated to even address such patently false accusations about my personal life and my beliefs so as to not dignify them with a response, but since these comments pose a potential distraction to an otherwise celebratory and historic time in our country, I would like to set the record straight in the hope of returning our collective attention to what's most important.
>
> First of all, I believe and have always believed in the exclusivity and divinity of Jesus Christ, his saving grace and substitutionary atonement made available to all by his death on the cross. I believe and have always believed that he was buried and on the third day rose again. I believe and

have always believed in the Holy Trinity. I believe and have always believed in the virgin birth, and the second coming. I also reject any theology that doesn't affirm or acknowledge the entirety of scriptural teaching about God's presence and blessing in suffering as much as in times of prosperity. In fact, I have preached and written as much on the lessons we must learn in times of trial in our lives as I have in times of abundance. Many of those sermons are themselves lessons I've learned in the difficult seasons of my own life.

My life and my decisions have been no-where-near perfect though nothing like what has been falsely conveyed in the media. Nevertheless, I am now a fifty-year-old grandmother who has learned from the good and the bad in my life. I thank God that he has plenty of grace for us all and that he knows that neither my faith, my life, nor my theology originates or is inspired by any other book than the Bible—which I believe is inerrant and God's truth. God also knows that I have poured my life in love and service to others.

I want to extend a hand of friendship and fellowship to all, even those who have made false accusations against me. Jesus taught us to "bless those who curse you and pray for those who insult you." This is what I have chosen to do, and I have done so genuinely from the bottom of my heart. I—for one—am willing to work with all those who find inspiration in the life and teachings of Jesus and a common cause in the well-being of our great America.

White hopes that people realize the long-term nature of the friendship and spiritual counsel she has given to Trump. "Way before his run for the Presidency, way before involvement in the Party, way before becoming a politician—he was a man seeking God. A man who was spiritually hungry, watching Christian television and listening to Southern Gospel music. We are this work in progress that is continually growing, as long as our heart is open to God and as long as we are seeking God."

PART
II

13

The Escalator

At the base of the sixty-foot-high waterfall, Ivanka Trump stood behind a podium adorned with flags. A crowd of journalists, spectators, shoppers, and Donald Trump fans sat in chairs or stood close at hand. She stepped up to the microphone and gave a spirited introduction to her father—who wasn't yet present.

Then, the recorded music of rocker Neil Young played loudly over speakers assembled on tripods. Trump, almost the same age as Young, consistently lists the rocker as one of his favorite musicians: "His voice is perfect and haunting. . . . He's got something special."

Young, a Canadian by birth, supported Bernie Sanders during the primary. The day after Trump's announcement, Young wrote on his Facebook page: "Yesterday my song 'Rockin in the Free World' was used in an announcement for a U.S. Presidential candidate without my permission. . . . Music is a universal language. So, I am glad that so many people with varying beliefs get enjoyment from my music, even if they don't share my beliefs. But had I been asked to allow my music to be used for a candidate—I would have said no." The campaign and Young went back and forth as to whether the Trump campaign had the right to use the music. Young let his final word on the subject be "F— you, Donald Trump"— said on stage and then posted on his Facebook page. For his part, Trump made his feelings known about the song on Twitter: "Didn't love it anyway."

Melania and Donald stood at the top of the escalator, waving to the gathered crowd below. At the precise moment that Melania

Trump's feet touched the top step of the escalator, Young's second stanza began, about seeing a woman holding a baby while standing next to a garbage can and looking for her next hit of drugs. The woman regrets that her kid won't get to go to school or fall in love.

With the juxtaposition of bleak dystopian lyrics echoing across the opulent atrium, Trump laid out the basic vision for his 2016 campaign. For large numbers of Americans, life sucks. Be realistic about that fact and elect a person who knows how to get things done—a successful person, the kind of person who could create Trump Tower. Do so, and things can turn around.

Though mocked without end on late-night talk shows, the escalator ride and music served as shrewd political stagecraft, worthy of comparison to anything Mike Deaver accomplished for Ronald Reagan.

In his opening remarks, Trump seemed to know that his launch had the right stuff, comparing it to what he saw as poorly planned launches by two of his fellow GOP candidates. Without mentioning their names, Trump mocked Rick Perry's heavy-perspiration launch in a hot Dallas airport hangar: "And, I can tell, some of the candidates, they went in. They didn't know the air-conditioner didn't work. They sweated like dogs." Then Trump lampooned Lincoln Chafee's launch (called "the worst campaign rollout of the year" by *The New Republic*) in an almost empty room. "And they didn't know the room was too big because they didn't have anybody there. How are they going to beat ISIS? I don't think it's gonna happen."

Though Trump's announcement speech seemed spontaneous, his most newsworthy lines came just two hundred words into his six-thousand-word speech. In journalistic lingo, Trump didn't "bury the lede":

The U.S. has become a dumping ground for everybody else's problems. [applause] . . . When Mexico sends its people, they're not sending their best. They're not sending you. They're not sending you. They're sending people that have lots of problems, and they're bringing those problems with us. They're bringing drugs. They're bringing crime. They're rapists. And some, I assume, are good people.

The outcry came immediately. Most pundits assumed a retraction would be forthcoming the next day. Such is the nature of modern political speeches that immediate retraction follows an uproar—whether the candidate meant what he or she said or not. In Trump's case, he meant it. Two weeks later, Kate Steinle died on the San Francisco Pier from a ricocheted bullet shot by Francisco Sanchez, an illegal immigrant from Mexico. Sanchez had seven previous felony convictions and had been deported to Mexico five times.

Trump wore his lack of verbal discretion as a sign of his straight-shooting honesty on the issues. At Trump Tower, he preemptively defended himself against the critiques of his poor speechmaking—by going on the offense against the other candidates' fine speechifying that lacked honesty about the issues:

But you don't hear that from anybody else. You don't hear it from anybody else. And I watch the speeches. I watch the speeches of these people, and they say the sun will rise, the moon will set, all sorts of wonderful things will happen. And people are saying, "What's going on? I just want a job. Just get me a job. I don't need the rhetoric. I want a job."

Trump even pulled in biblical imagery to explain the futility of following leaders who can't produce results:

. . . Well, you need somebody, because politicians are all talk, no action. Nothing's gonna get done. They will not bring us—believe me—to the promised land. They will not.

. If Trump recalled his Old Testament Bible stories, it was Moses who God used to lead the Israelites out of Egypt and to the promised land. And it was Moses who tried to get out of the job by pleading with God, "Oh, my Lord, I am not eloquent, either in the past or since you have spoken to your servant, but I am slow of speech and of tongue" (Exodus 4:10).

With a bit of superlative talk about how rich he is, Trump established an ethical premise of his potential governance—he couldn't be bought or bribed. "I'm using my own money. I'm not using the lobbyists. I'm not using donors. I don't care. I'm really rich."

When Moses established leaders who would judge disputes, he told the Israelites to "look for able men who fear God, who are trustworthy and hate a bribe" (Exodus 18:21). The Bible condemns bribery and influence peddling in public office because they destroy the office, damn the nation, and bring pain upon the innocent.

Trump found his fellow Republican candidates to be good men, but men of indecision—and he attributed that fault to their dependency on campaign funds flowing in from moneyed groups.

> But all of these politicians that I'm running against now, they're trying to disassociate. I mean, you looked at Bush, it took him five days to answer the question on Iraq. He couldn't answer the question. He didn't know. I said, "Is he intelligent?"
>
> Then I looked at Rubio. He was unable to answer the question, is Iraq a good thing or bad thing? He didn't know. He couldn't answer the question.
>
> How are these people gonna lead us? How are we gonna— how are we gonna go back and make it great again? We can't. They don't have a clue. They can't lead us. They can't. They can't even answer simple questions. It was terrible.

In the close of his speech, Trump put a dollar amount on his estimated wealth: "So the total is $8,737,540,000." Many found his statement to be crass—rightly so. And others found it to be a dishonest calculation of his own wealth—an overstatement by a little, or a lot.

Trump's point, however, went deeper than braggadocio about bank accounts. Trump uses his wealth to state two facts about himself: (1) I'm competent, and (2) I can't be bought.

> . . . I'm not doing that to brag because you know what? I don't have to brag. I don't have to, believe it or not.
>
> I'm doing that to say that that's the kind of thinking our country needs. We need that thinking. We have the opposite thinking.
>
> We have losers. We have losers. We have people that don't have it. We have people that are morally corrupt. We have people that are selling this country down the drain. . . .
>
> This is going to be an election that's based on competence because people are tired of these nice people. And they're tired of being ripped off by everybody in the world.

For those with ears to hear, Trump launched his campaign with moral argumentation. Not with the language of the ivory tower, mind you, but in the tongue and bluster heard at the counter of a local greasy spoon or Rotary Club. Trump argued that it's wrong to fail to protect your citizens when it's your duty as the head of the executive branch to do so. It's dishonest to say you're watching out for the country when you're really a puppet of special interest groups. These are moral arguments.

14

What Is Your Relationship
with God?

Iowa ranks first in the nation in corn production, edging out its neighbor Illinois. And Iowa also ranks first in pork production, producing three times more than second-place North Carolina. But since the 1970s, Iowa also holds the distinction of being the first state in the union to cast votes to decide who the Democrats and Republicans will nominate as their party's candidate for president.

Iowans caucus.

They do so in January or early February of an election year. That much is known. As for how caucuses work, it has yet to be proven that an average Iowan understands the process. The rest of us don't, yet we look on with curiosity once every four years.

Because they go first, Iowa voters receive massive amounts of exposure to the candidates. A mailbox in states with late primaries might not ever receive a political postcard. By contrast, Iowans often receive a half-dozen a day—for months on end. Politicians who never set foot in Iowa before feeling their Oval Office itch will suddenly camp out in the state, meet voters and eat pork chops on a stick at county fairs. The ambitious among them will even attempt the "Full Grassley"—the feat of visiting all ninety-nine counties—"Grassley" being the name of the state's US senator who makes a point of visiting all the counties each year.

All that is to say, you've got to learn the vocabulary of people who know hogs and corn if you hope to have a shot at the White

House. Likewise, with nearly 80 percent of Iowans claiming either Protestantism or Roman Catholicism as their religious preference, you also must learn the language of people who know Jesus. God-talk can't make you uncomfortable.

The Family Leader, Iowa's foremost conservative Christian political organization, hosts a "Leadership Summit" every July, bringing together politicians and preachers for two days of speeches and rallies. Several thousand Iowa conservatives travel to Ames to sit in Stephens Auditorium on the campus of Iowa State University. The event becomes a first opportunity for candidates to test their messaging out on live people. Dozens of national media cover the event, taking special note of who received the loudest and longest applause.

In mid-July 2015, one candidate heard both applause *and* booing: Donald Trump. Public opinion guru Frank Luntz sat on the stage with Trump for a one-on-one session of questions and answers, opening with a query about his education policy.

"Common Core has to be ended. It is a disaster," Trump said, earning applause by echoing every other GOP candidate's answer on the subject. But then he added Trumpian color: "It is a way of taking care of the people in Washington that frankly, I don't even think they give a damn about education, half of them. I am sure some maybe do."

"Do you want to use that word in this forum?" Luntz asked with a smile. The audience leaned in.

"I will, I will. Because people want to hear the truth, Frank," Trump said. "I watch you all the time; they want to hear the truth."

Applause erupted.

"I mean, exactly what Frank said is what is wrong with our country. We are so politically correct that we cannot move anymore."

More applause.

"We have to be able to express ourselves," Trump continued.

"But don't we go too far?" Luntz countered.

"Too far?"

Luntz asked Trump about the statement he made one month earlier: "Don't you feel that you went too far in what you call Mexicans coming across the border?"

"Not at all. No, not at all," Trump said—again to applause.

> Two things. I am so proud of the fact that I got dialogue started on illegal immigration. And people in the media, in all fairness, they were very rough on me in that first week, and now then many of them have apologized to me. And almost everybody—because it has turned out I was right. Beautiful Kate in San Francisco was shot by an illegal who was here five times, and they couldn't do anything about it, and believe me, Mexico kept pushing him back, because they didn't want him. Believe me, that's true. And now, everybody is saying that Trump was right. But I tell you, I took a lot of abuse.

Luntz challenged Trump about his calling Arizona senator John McCain a "dummy." One week earlier, Trump had held his second rally of the young campaign, and fifteen thousand Arizonans showed up in Phoenix. Up to that point, only Bernie Sanders had attracted such numbers. But when interviewed by Ryan Lizza of *The New Yorker*, McCain blasted the event: "It's very bad. . . . Because what he did was he fired up the crazies."

Now, to say that McCain is unpopular with Iowa Republicans would be an understatement. In his 2000 campaign, he skipped the Iowa caucuses altogether. And even in 2008 when he won the overall nomination, he lost the Iowa caucus—placing a distant third with 13 percent to Mike Huckabee's 32 percent. And Obama beat him by 10 points in Iowa during the general election that fall.

Trump responded with force when Luntz mentioned McCain: "Crazies, he called them all crazy. I said they were not crazy. They were great Americans. These people, if you were to see these people—I know what a crazy is. I know all about crazies. These weren't crazy. So he insulted me, and he insulted everybody in that room."

Trump could have left it at that. Instead, he reflected back to the 2008 election: "I supported him. I supported him for President. I raised $1 million for him. That's a lot of money. I supported him. He lost. He let us down. But, you know, he lost. So, I have never liked him as much after that, because I don't like losers."

The audience laughed.

"He is a war hero, he's a war hero," Luntz said, countering the "loser" label by bringing up McCain's military record.

Trump *could* have said, "Frank, when I called him a loser, you know I was *only* talking about the shellacking he took at the hands of Obama. As to his service to our country, of course, he is a hero—and I salute him for his service."

Instead, Trump infamously responded, "He hit me—he's not a war hero."

"Five and a half years . . ." Luntz said, referring to the number of years McCain spent as a POW, enduring torture.

But Trump barreled along: "He's a war hero because he was captured. I like people that weren't captured, OK? I hate to tell you. He was a war hero because he was captured, OK? And I believe—perhaps he is a war hero, but right now, he said some very bad things about a lot of people. So, what I said is John McCain, I disagree with him, that these people aren't crazy."

"Boos" spilled forth from the crowd. Journalist's keyboards started clicking.

Huckabee sat backstage at that moment. One of Trump's new Iowa campaign operatives walked into the room and said, "Well, I may have the shortest-lived contract in GOP primary history. He cannot survive this."

It was interesting because we were set up to interview Trump following his Q&A. It was all arranged ahead of time—a one-on-one, exclusive televised interview for CBN in a private room one floor above the stage. Then, between the "not a hero" and "forgiveness" comments, the other media folks were pretty much beside themselves: "You've got to be kidding me. This is going to sink his campaign before it even got started." There was such a flurry of activity, of journalists running around on cell phones, reporting back to whoever they were talking to—bureau chiefs back in New York—just to say, "I can't believe what he just said," and "This is a big story."

Trump held a press conference right after his time on stage—an impromptu press conference. He knew he had to address what he just said about McCain. And he didn't back down from it at all, which made the media go even more gaga for the story.

Here we are, waiting for the press conference to end, because he's supposed to come up to our room, a floor right above the press conference. Then, through our producer Tracy Winborn, I got a message from Hope Hicks: "David, I'm really sorry, but things are a bit hectic right now, and we're just going to have to reschedule."

As uncomfortable as the "not a hero" comments were, Trump produced even more quotables when Luntz probed him about his Christian faith and practice.

"Have you ever asked God for forgiveness?" asked Luntz.

"That is a tough question," Trump responded, seemingly unfazed by the fact that in such a setting, the only answer you're supposed to give is "yes." But what followed next was authentic Trump.

"I don't think in terms of—I have—I am a religious person. Shockingly—because people are so shocked when they find this out, I'm Protestant, I'm Presbyterian, and I go to church, and I love God, and I love my church."

Trump then went on to describe his deep fondness for his former pastor, Norman Vincent Peale. Luntz let him finish, then returned to the question at hand: "But have you ever asked God for forgiveness?"

The audience seemed amused, sensing that Trump had danced around the question. But Trump didn't seem to be evading—not at all. His answer certainly revealed his lack of a Billy Graham–basic take on the Gospel of Christ. But he answered without evasion or scripted pandering.

Trump's next words (printed in full) became one of the most often ridiculed statements he uttered during the campaign, especially by the mainstream media and his critics:

> I am not sure I have. I just go and try to do a better job from there. I don't think so. I think, if I do something wrong, I think I just try to make it right. I don't bring God into that picture. I don't.
>
> Now, when I take—you know, when we go in church and when I drink my little wine, which is about the only wine I drink, and have my little cracker, I guess that is a form of asking for forgiveness. And I do that as often as possible, because I feel cleansed, OK? But, you know, to me, that is important, I do that.
>
> In terms of officially—see, I could tell you, "Absolutely"— and everybody—I don't think in terms of that.

Ironically, if the truth of the matter is that Trump has never asked God for forgiveness, then if Trump had lied and said "yes"—

then he could have avoided criticism. That is, lying about his practice of confession would have kept him out of trouble with the piety-inspectors.

Two months later, I asked Trump about what he said about "forgiveness" here in Iowa. His response still led with sacramentalism ("I take communion"). But he also admitted something about his response to Luntz: "Maybe I was getting a little bit cute, and we were all having fun."

Trump, in a moment of candidness, was admitting that his "my little wine" and "my little cracker" comments flowed from a make-'em-laugh approach to the question.

"The audience, which was largely evangelical, gave me a standing ovation when I left," Trump concluded. "I got the biggest standing ovation of anybody. We were all having fun. I didn't know it was going to be such a big deal. And actually, it turned out not to be a big deal, because the polls came out right after that, and the evangelicals like me—so I was happy about that."

Of course, the truth of Christian doctrine doesn't depend on standing ovations and poll numbers. In fact, when it comes to orthodoxy, it's usually the exact opposite. TV shows and presidential elections depend on popularity for their survival. Christian theology does not. But Trump was right when he told me that it "turned out not to be a big deal," because the comments didn't sink him at all.

Luntz circled back around one final time: "So, again, you've gone into it. If I don't ask this question, this audience will be disappointed. Straight question, what is your relationship with God?"

"Well, I pray, I go to church," Trump answered. "I do things that are wrong? I guess so. You know, I'm a businessperson, I really do well at business, I've done great. I've made some of the great deals. I own some of the greatest properties in the world."

"Does God help you do these great deals?" Luntz asked.

"I think God helped me. . . . God helped me by giving me a certain brain, whether that's a good thing or a bad thing. . . . I went through phenomenal school, the Wharton School of Finance, which is said to be the greatest business school in the world. I did really well there. I was a great student. So, I mean, I was born with a certain intellect that is good for this."

Trump attributed his intellectual and financial success in life to God's gifting. Such attribution is a common religious practice—thanksgiving. A more nuanced tongue would be cautious here, making sure not to equate material success as proof of right standing with God—who Jesus said sends the blessing of sun and rain on the just and on the unjust alike.

The question about forgiveness would come back around at least two more times during campaign interviews—notably by Jake Tapper and Cal Thomas. In both instances, Trump never specifically expressed an evangelical understanding of salvation by grace alone—the "you must be born again" truth of Christian conversion (John 3:7). That would make sense in that it's not something he would have heard preached every day in his previous church experiences. But as we'll begin to see later on in his journey, that would change dramatically.

Jesus once told a parable to teach people "who trusted in themselves that they were righteous" (Luke 18:9–14). In the story, there are two men—a Pharisee (a religious leader) and a tax collector.

Both men were in the Temple praying. The tax collector begged God for mercy and confessed that he was a sinner. But the Pharisee looked up to heaven and gave a prayer of thanks to God "that I am not like other men, extortioners, unjust, adulterers, or even like this tax collector." He then went through a litany of his good deeds.

Jesus concluded the parable by commending the tax collector: "this man went down to his house justified" (made right with God).

"For everyone who exalts himself will be humbled, but the one who humbles himself will be exalted."

The spiritual disease of the Pharisee wasn't simply arrogance—though he had plenty of that. It was self-righteousness—thinking that his own religious works had earned God's smile. As if God's smile on us is a wage that we earn through good behavior. Like the Apostle Paul before his conversion to Christ, religious deeds can numb us to the reality of just how sinful we are—and how much we need the grace of confession.

Nothing that Trump said in Ames had an ill effect on his poll numbers.

"Trump violated every convention and norm that is known to politics," Huckabee said. "Every time he did something that would have killed anybody else, it only boosted him."

That's one reason why Huckabee believes that faith played a very minor role in the support for Trump. "The faith community—they were against Hillary and against Obama. They really didn't care whether Trump was a person of faith or not. That just didn't matter. I mean, it's pretty evident by the things that he said."

In late August, Trump traveled to Mobile, Alabama, for a rally deep in the heart of the Bible Belt. In the two months since his campaign launched, he had vaulted to the top of the national GOP polls. But lingering questions about his character remained. Going to Mobile would be the first test of Trump's viability among Southern evangelicals.

"Sweet Home Alabama" welcomed Trump to Ladd-Peebles Stadium. One week earlier, the campaign had been planning an event at the local civic center, with seating for two thousand. The free tickets got snapped up quickly, so they changed the venue to the forty-thousand-seat stadium.

Senator Jeff Sessions stirred up his hometown crowd and then turned the podium over to Trump for a speech lasting almost an hour. The crowd was energized in a way not seen since Obama's 2008 campaign rallies.

As soon as Trump finished his last word, Twisted Sister's "We're Not Gonna Take It" blasted over the speakers.

Trump then walked the line, shaking hands with the crowd. As he leaned in to give a baby a kiss, he told the mother, "He's a cutie!" A news photographer snapped a picture of the woman, a local school-teacher named Sydnie Shuford, capturing her in an expressive exclamation and smile.

A few feet behind Shuford in the photo, an outstretched arm held up a bright white poster board with red and blue handwritten letters that proclaimed: "Thank You Lord Jesus, For President Trump."

The resulting photograph went viral and became one of the best-known pictures of the campaign season. It also became a Rorschach test of your thoughts on Trump and people who came to his rallies. Some said Shuford looked "unhinged" or "amazingly creepy." Others said much worse about her and about Southerners in general. Clearly, the reaction to her joyous expression was an echo of McCain's "crazies" comment and a foreshadowing of Hillary's "basket of deplorables."

Peggy Noonan, penning one of the first warm-to-Trump pieces by a national Conservative commentator, wrote:

> A source of Mr. Trump's strength is that normal people understand how big donors have an impact on policy. Mr. Trump can stand where the people stand on such issues as immigration because the donor class doesn't have hooks in him. . . . Something in Mr. Trump himself—the fact that his candidacy has garnered such support in spite of his past and present heterodox stands—has revealed a Republican

base that is not as much in lockstep as it has been long portrayed, not as predictable. Things are shaking out in an interesting way.

Clearly, this was a key turning point in a couple of different ways. It showed Trump had real staying power. It was the first of the big campaign rallies, and it got him energized in a way that he probably had never been energized before. He kept talking about that for months and months afterward—about how there were thirty thousand people in Mobile, Alabama—in the Bible Belt.

You started to hear folks asking: "What's going on exactly?" The Spidey sense tingled. The antenna went up as people asked: "Wait a minute, why in the world were thirty thousand Alabamians showing up at a Donald Trump rally—this brash New Yorker?"

Something wasn't computing. But at the same time, because it wasn't computing, it made it all the more intriguing. And the media did a double take, not that they believed this was for real. This also seems to be when Trump started to realize all that was happening. And this rally was a beginning to the idea that Trump appealed to blue-collar evangelicals.

15

The B-I-B-L-E. Yes, That's the Book for Me

Within a week of the Bible Belt rally in Mobile, Trump talked about the Bible on national television. Mark Halperin and John Heilemann interviewed Trump for *With All Due Respect,* their Bloomberg Television talk show.

Trump Tower patrons strolled in the background of the interview as Halperin asked Trump to explain what he would say to a gay son, daughter, or grandchild if they asked him about his opposition to same-sex marriage.

"Well, it's the way it is," Trump began. "I mean, I wouldn't speak to them at all about it other than they are who they are. I want them to be happy, and I will love them, and I will cherish them."

"But how would you explain your personal opposition to same-sex marriage?" Halperin pressed the original question. "How would you explain it to them?"

"I've gone to gay weddings. I've been at gay weddings," Trump responded. "I have been against—from the standpoint of the Bible, from the standpoint of my teachings, as growing up and going to Sunday school and going to church—and I've been opposed to it. And we'll just see how it all comes up. If I was ever in that position, I'd just have to explain it."

Halperin jumped at the opportunity when Trump mentioned the word "Bible."

"You mentioned the Bible," Halperin said. "You've been talking about how it's your favorite book. And you said some people are surprised that you say that. I'm wondering what one or two of your most favorite Bible verses are and why?"

Trump's reply became the headline for the next news cycle.

"I wouldn't want to get into it because to me that's very personal. You know, when I talk about the Bible, it's very personal—so I don't want to get into it."

"There's no verse that means a lot to you that you think about or cite?" Halperin asked, swatting away the "it's personal" argument.

"The Bible means a lot to me, but I don't want to get into specifics," Trump doubled down.

"Even to cite a verse that you like?"

"No, I don't want to do that," Trump said with more emphasis.

Heilemann jumped in from a different angle. "Are you an Old Testament guy or New Testament guy?"

"Probably equal," Trump said without a pause. "I think it's just an incredible—the whole Bible is an incredible—they hold up *The Art of the Deal* [Trump's best seller], and I say 'That's my second favorite book of all time.' I just think the Bible is something very special."

While walking down the hallway of our CBN office in DC my phone rang. It was Donald Trump. I stepped into our green room and took the call.

He talked about the Halperin interview and the question about the Bible verse. Even with all the negative headlines about his response, I could tell that he thought it was a good answer.

It was, in fact, a purposeful non-answer. But using the logic of *The Art of the Deal* and how to handle the media, he thought it was the best way to handle the question because he didn't want to give them anything. As in, it's none of their business, and he wasn't going to play their game.

You might agree it's a good thing because he's not letting the media get to him, but most evangelicals would believe it to be their duty and joy to share some verses—if put in the same situation. Hence, the word "evangelical"—connected as it is to "evangelism"—the sharing of the Gospel using the Scriptures (Romans 10:14–17). Though Trump clearly wasn't going to attempt play-acting as an evangelical, a little more biblical meat would be nice.

And on that note, Trump asked me to send him some of my own favorite Bible verses. He also asked me why the Bible is so important to me.

The call ended. By the end of the day, I had emailed him my response to his questions.

As I reread the following email, I know that I would have written the same message to Hillary Clinton or Bernie Sanders. If any candidate or politician from any party—or *anyone* for that matter—asked me why the Bible is important, or if they asked me to give them some of my favorite Bible verses, then I would write what I emailed here. I'm a Christian first and foremost, and this episode during the campaign was evidence of that.

Mr. Trump,

As promised, below are some of my favorite Bible verses along with a short commentary to put them in perspective.

I pray these help you draw closer to God, as each one of us needs to do every day. I would encourage you to read a daily devotional that takes just a couple minutes to start you off in the morning. . . .

I commit to praying for you during this campaign. It won't be prayers for political victory (God has that covered) but rather that you stay healthy and full of endurance, integrity, and patience through what promises to be a presidential race for the ages.

Best wishes,
David

My email to Trump included verses about faith from the Book of Hebrews; grace from the Book of Romans; letting the Lord fight your battles from 1 Samuel, and God's plans for your life from Jeremiah.

One final note of clarity for the reader (Trump understood what I meant) about my line "God has that covered." I didn't mean that God was going to give Trump the victory. What I meant about God is that He is sovereign and free to shape the world and orchestrate human affairs in whatever way He sees fit.

As the Babylonian king Nebuchadnezzar testified, after being humbled by God most dramatically:

> *For His dominion is an everlasting dominion,*
> *and His kingdom endures from generation to generation;*
> *all the inhabitants of the earth are accounted as nothing,*
> *and He does according to His will among the host of heaven*
> *and among the inhabitants of the earth;*
> *and none can stay His hand*
> *or say to Him, "What have you done?"*
> (DANIEL 4:34–35)

Over fifteen thousand people showed up for a rally in Dallas in September, at the American Airlines Center—the home of the Mavericks and Stars. Robert Jeffress, the pastor of the historic and huge First Baptist Church in downtown Dallas, remembers this rally well because he met Trump for the first time that night.

"He had seen me on Fox News, and he reached out to me via Twitter," Jeffress recalled. "But that rally was the first time I actually met him in person."

Jeffress led the rally in prayer, earlier in the evening before Trump had even arrived at the arena. The pastor wasn't on the stage or part of the ongoing program after that point.

"But out of the blue, Mr. Trump called me to come up on the

stage with him," Jeffress said. "He thanked me publicly for my support of him. And that's where he first started using the line: 'You know the Pastor says I'm not a perfect Christian, but I'm a pretty good leader.' Everybody roared with laughter at that."

Like the Mobile rally, here was another event deep in the Bible Belt that drew the largest crowds of any GOP candidate.

"We filled up a whole basketball stadium," Trump told me. "It was a love fest. A lot of evangelicals, Tea Party people, Hispanics—everybody was there. I don't think I ever thought it would be this big this fast."

From a national media standpoint, the Jeffress "local pastor prays" angle wasn't much to write about. And once the event finished, everyone was focused on the second GOP debate to be held two days later at the Ronald Reagan Library in California. But there in Dallas, you witnessed Trump standing alongside the pastor who would preach a private sermon to him on Inauguration morning, five hundred days later.

With Trump, it's about having people vouch for him—especially people in groups that aren't his own natural tribe. Jeffress wasn't endorsing him at that point—and technically, he never did.

The next afternoon, my CBN colleagues and I spent several hours at Trump National Golf Course in Rancho Palos Verdes, California. Overlooking the Pacific Ocean just west of Long Beach, the fairways were a lush green and the clubhouse was regal.

We did part of the interview inside and then golf-carted out to the eighteenth hole. Along the way, he pointed out places where the camera angles would be best for getting a memorable TV shot. I took note, once again, of how Trump thinks regarding visual aesthetics and broadcasting. We talked throughout the entire time about a dozen subjects, but it was our conversation about the Bible that made the headlines.

Attempting to pick up where Mark Halperin left off, I asked Trump to explain why he says that the Bible is the best book.

"There's so many things that you can learn from it," Trump said. "Proverbs, the chapter 'never bend to envy.' I've had that thing all of my life where people are bending to envy."

Trump then compared the Bible to a great movie or a great work of art.

> I don't like to use this analogy, but like a great movie, a great, incredible movie. You'll see it once it will be good. You'll see it again. You can see it twenty times, and every time you'll appreciate it more. The Bible is the most special thing.

My colleagues and I left portions of the interview on the editing room floor. Such is the nature of broadcast news that you only use a small portion of the material you obtain. But we published the video and transcription of Trump's comments about the Bible. Then we got geared up for the debates that would take place the next day— just an hour north of the golf course.

I suppose that if I had been more deliberate during the interview, I might have asked a follow-up question about "Proverbs" and "never bend to envy." What verse is that?

But even though I don't remember all the proverbs myself, I felt as if I knew what he was talking about. In my mind, he was conflating together verses or themes like "do not incline your heart to evil" and "do not envy sinners."

After my interview with Trump, many mainstream media outlets and a few evangelical authors critiqued his Proverbs comments. The *Washington Post* wrote, "Donald Trump likes that Proverbs verse that might not exist."

What I found most interesting is that Trump still had no desire to take the easy road and simply memorize a couple of Bible verses for the next go-around with the "favorite verse" line of questioning. I had given him some of my favorite verses. A staffer could have come up with a few more, and even scripted some evangelicalish lines to sweeten the ears or stop the critics.

Honestly, I don't have any way of knowing what his "favorite verses" might be. He respects the Bible in a general way, but he admits that he has never consistently gone to a church that emphasizes expository Bible teaching and doctrine. However, the thirst for more knowledge seemed to be there during the campaign. He constantly had evangelical preachers around him and wanted to be in their company consistently. "If there's an evangelical on the plane, he wants them to sit beside him, and he just peppers him with questions," evangelical leader Richard Land said. "Peppers them with questions. Questions, questions, questions, questions, questions."

At any rate, since it was our reporting of the interview that was causing confusion, I reached out to the Trump campaign for clarity. In response, they emailed us the following statement from Trump, which we published:

> Proverbs 24 teaches that envy should be replaced with discernment. Wisdom builds and understanding establishes, whether it be a family, a house, or our community. For me, this is important, especially in this race for President of the United States as it shows it is important to rely on one's own wisdom and ability rather than follow others down the wrong path.

I concluded the matter with these words:

> Look, folks, Donald Trump is not Pastor Trump. He's not Mike Huckabee, and he doesn't pretend to be. It will

be up to evangelical voters in Iowa, South Carolina, and those crucial SEC Primaries to sort through all of this. I do think it's important for evangelicals to have a candidate rooted in their Christian faith. To what degree, I guess we will find out. Hey look; Mitt Romney was a Mormon, and plenty of evangelicals voted for him over some of the more evangelical-type candidates in 2012. It's not like the "most evangelical guy" wins.

A week later, Trump addressed the Values Voter Summit, an annual convention held in DC and sponsored by the Family Research Council. This event is a large-scale, national version of the Iowa event talked about in the previous chapter. Thousands of conservative and Christian citizens converge in a convention hall to hear dozens of politicians and pastors. All the candidates are invited to speak, but not all show up.

Trump came to the event with a Bible in his hand. Literally. This was the "Mary MacLeod Bible"—the Bible his mother gave him for his confirmation.

He's very proud of that Bible and mentions it in interviews, but that's the only time I've seen it up close was when I interviewed him backstage at the event. It's just an ordinary Bible, except that it connects Trump to his mother—and to formal religious experiences from his childhood six decades earlier.

Trump held the Bible up for everyone to see. The picture went viral.

"The word *Christmas*: I love Christmas," Trump said. "You go to stores now, you don't see the word *Christmas*. It says, 'Happy holidays' all over. I say, 'Where's *Christmas*?' I tell my wife, 'Don't go to those stores.' I want to see *Christmas*."

The crowd applauded in approval. Trump then promised them

that, if he were elected president, the phrase "Merry Christmas" would come back.

Some Constitutionalists in the crowd probably pulled out their pocket-size versions of the document, looking to see how Trump's promise fit with the Founders' intention for the powers of the Executive Branch.

Some Christians in the crowd probably looked at their wish for things they wanted Washington, DC, to do in support of Judeo-Christian values. Hearing more "Merry Christmas" probably wasn't on the list, but they were "picking up what Trump was throwing down." Trump's basic point: Christians are being marginalized in the public square.

The attendees participated in a straw poll to see which candidate the group wanted to send to the White House. The results:

Ted Cruz: 35 percent
Ben Carson: 18 percent
Mike Huckabee: 14 percent
Marco Rubio: 13 percent
Donald Trump: 5 percent

Similarly, a survey of evangelical leaders published the same month by *WORLD* magazine showed Trump with 1 percent support from that group. Clearly, he still had a lot of work to do to win over evangelicals—or at least, evangelical leaders and conservative activists (the type who travel to DC for conventions).

16

Pentecostals, Prayer, and
Dinner at the Polo

Imagine a group of men and women in dress clothes, standing huddled together around one central figure—a tall man with orange-blond hair.

Most of the group puts one hand in the air and one hand on the shoulder of the person in front of them. Those at the center of the ring put their hands directly on the tall man—on his shoulders, his head, his chest. Now imagine that everyone is in a mutual and simultaneous conversation with somebody else—someone not physically in the room. One person talks louder than the rest, but the rest are speaking too. And to top it off, everyone's eyes are closed. And there is an intensity to their voices.

Who are these people? What is going on?

If you thought "some folks are having a prayer meeting" then you might be a Christian—or even, an evangelical.

If you thought "some folks are laying hands on that man and praying for his special anointing," then you might be a charismatic or Pentecostal evangelical.

The meeting lasted roughly two and a half hours and ended with pastors gathering around Trump and laying their hands on him in prayer, asking the Lord to give the GOP presidential frontrunner wisdom, stability, and knowledge necessary to pursue this endeavor. They also prayed for America and for God's will to be done.

During the meeting, Trump talked about his Christian faith. At one point, he admitted that he may not have read the Bible as much as the pastors in the room.

As the conversation continued, a few of the ministers implored Trump to tone done some of his harsh rhetoric. Trump explained that he is a "counterpuncher"—that he doesn't hit first. He received the message by nodding his head, listening attentively and not being combative at all.

"He has a very high regard and a very deep respect for men and women of the cloth," Darrell Scott remarked.

Trump told the religious leaders and pastors that he will be a strong supporter of Israel and that defeating ISIS would be a strong part of his agenda. He also discussed trade, balancing the budget, eliminating the deficit, and tax reform. As for faith issues, he talked about how religious liberty and Christianity is under attack in America and that there is a lot of religious intolerance for Christianity in today's society.

Trump also had a challenge for the attendees. "I think you've gotten weak in speaking up and making your own voice heard," Lance Wallnau remembers him saying. "You, me included, as Christians have been spoiled by a long period when Christianity was acceptable."

The subject of race relations also came up when some of the African-American pastors in the room mentioned that there seems to be some detachment between him and the black community. While citing some polls to the contrary, Scott said Trump agreed with the overall assessment and would try to do a better job.

"People had a lot to say to him, a lot of advice. It was not a pep rally for Donald Trump," Christian book publisher Don Nori said.

During the prayers, Southern Baptist pastor David Jeremiah, known internationally for his radio preaching ministry, prayed that God would "bring into his life a strong African-American who can stand with him and represent that community so that his voice will be heard even in a stronger way there." Pentecostal preacher Kenneth Copeland prayed for God to "give this man Your wisdom" and to "make sure and certain that he hears. Manifest Yourself to him." He closed by thanking God "for a bold man, a strong man, and an obedient man."

When you have dinner with Donald Trump, you never know who's going to show up. Trust me, I know. One clear, starry late September night, it seemed appropriate that the "stars" were literally out for the evening at The Polo Bar in New York. That's where my wife and I met Melania and Donald Trump for dinner. It was a table for four . . . with plenty of celebrity guest appearances.

The establishment is owned by American fashion designer Ralph Lauren, who bills his eatery as "a casual yet refined setting for food and drink in the heart of NYC." But make no mistake: you don't just walk in and get a table. This is VIP seating only, and on this night, we were on the list.

A few weeks earlier, I had received word from one of his high-ranking associates that Mr. and Mrs. Trump would like to have dinner with us. It made sense: I was out on national television analyzing the presidential candidates and their chances with evangelicals, and Trump knew me to be an honest broker. He figured breaking bread with me simply made sense. Plus, we had known each other since 2011, and we're both from New York.

My wife and I traveled down the spiral staircase where we met the Trumps in a cozy, small dining room, complete with fine wood paneling and brass accents that seated maybe one hundred patrons.

It didn't take long for Trump to break the ice with the most unusual of first questions. Trump leaned in slowly and asked inquisitively, "How's your marriage?" It's not necessarily the first question you think a serious businessman like Donald Trump would ask. But what it revealed to me is a different side of him, a more caring and gentle side that is far more apparent in private than in public.

While we talked about immigration, evangelical politics, and the state of the race, by far the most interesting takeaway was the consistent way throughout our dinner in which Trump came across as normal. For example, Melania was speaking to my wife; he would interrupt but then quickly stop himself and say, "Oh, sorry honey. Please continue." Normal. Later in the conversation he showed care and concern when commending my wife for doing so much research on a pending court case regarding her former apartment in Manhattan.

And then there were the celebrities. Lots of them: George Lucas from *Star Wars* fame; owner Ralph Lauren; actor Michael Caine; legendary Broadway composer Andrew Lloyd Webber, and actor Michael J. Fox. They all came by the table one by one just to quickly say hello. There was no campaign talk at all. Instead, Trump showed his compassionate side once again by asking them about their lives rather than talking about his own.

We should add here that this empathetic side of Trump is more prevalent when the cameras aren't rolling. Evangelist James Robison has seen it too. "I've been back behind the curtain with him when he's with people nobody sees and he keeps noticing the crippled person . . . or the military person, or the person with the police force, or the person that looks like they're poor. Those are the people he goes to when nobody sees him. He notices them. He notices them when he walks out in the crowd. He'll notice the people that nobody else notices."

Oh, there was one more celebrity in the room. Trump leaned into me slowly. "David, don't look but you know who is sitting behind you over there?" I wondered who it could be. Maybe David Hasselhoff? Nah. Somebody much more popular. "Who?" I whispered. Trump paused for effect. "Oprah." Indeed, it was Oprah. She would later come over to our table to say hello to the four of us. At the end of the conversation, as we all got up to leave the table, Trump and Oprah had an exchange that I'll never forget. "Oprah, can you believe I'm having dinner with the Christian Broadcasting Network?" Trump bellowed with a smile. Oprah replied with a rolling laugh, "Never in a million years, Donald!"

17

Mr. Cyrus Meets Wrecking Ball

"Nothing evokes a stronger image of a lunatic-fringe Christian than calling someone a Dallas Evangelist," Lance Wallnau said with a laugh. "When journalists want to nail me, that's what they call me: Dallas Evangelist." Wallnau—definitely from Dallas, but definitely not an evangelist, though once a pastor over a decade ago—runs his own business, a successful consulting firm.

Wallnau keeps a tight watch on the news cycle, trends, and world events. But he did not plan nor foresee that he would be involved in national conversations during the 2016 election cycle. That's ironic, of course, as Wallnau prophesied publicly and correctly—during the pre-primary days in the fall of 2015—that Donald Trump would be the next president.

Wallnau had no personal reason to do so. He did not know Trump beforehand. He wasn't on the staff or a volunteer for the campaign. And being a conservative Pentecostal Christian, Wallnau had the same reasons as other evangelicals to lean toward one of the other candidates.

A fellow Pentecostal named Kim Clement was scheduled to attend a meeting at Trump Tower in September 2015. Clement believed he had a message about Trump—a "word from the Lord" as Pentecostals would call it. But Clement had a stroke and would not be able to go to New York. Somehow—and Wallnau doesn't know the details—he wound up getting asked to come to the meeting.

He traveled to Trump Tower and had a good time with a group of leaders and Trump—then flew home again. But he still wasn't sold on Trump. And that's when Wallnau said, "The Word of the Lord that was going to come to Kim about the Presidential candidate—it came to me. This was new territory for me, but I came home, and when I was standing in my study in my office, I heard these words: 'Donald Trump is a wrecking ball to the spirit of political correctness.' "

Wallnau said the words went from his left ear through to his right ear. "I heard that, and I laughed. I thought, 'Donald Trump is a wrecking ball to the spirit of political correctness.' So I started saying that. And that was the moment that I got behind Donald Trump. I was enthusiastic for him from that moment on."

There began to be many ugly altercations at Trump rallies as protesters—often from the Black Lives Matter movement—showed up at the events. And early on, a line in the sand seemed to be drawn by African-Americans for any of their own community who were thinking about giving support to Trump. The message was clear: Don't!

Enter Darrell Scott, an influential African-American Pentecostal pastor from Cleveland. Scott, who had been friends with Trump for several years, thought a false narrative about Trump had emerged, that he was a racist and a bigot. Scott worked to orchestrate a meeting between Trump and black religious leaders, to help heal the divide.

Scott also called Wallnau, whom he had met at the meeting in September, and invited him to come to the meeting with the pastors. Wallnau said he questioned why he should come, telling Scott, "I'm not involved with race issues. Not that I don't care—they're just not my forte. Secondly, I'm not a minority, and you're having a minority meeting with Donald Trump." But Wallnau said Scott just laughed it off and told him he needed him there because "you're a strategist . . . and besides that, you're a future minority. So you should show up just for that sake."

Wallnau decided he would come, but planned on just sitting off to the side as a spectator. This wasn't his event, and he didn't see that he would have anything to offer.

Before the trip, however, he had a second experience of hearing from the Lord. "I'm not one of those guys that's always hearing something," Wallnau said, admitting the sheepishness he had felt about the experience. "I'm mostly a teacher—I'm not telling people that I'm hearing from God. But I heard the Lord say, this second time, God spoke right to my ear, and said, 'The next President of the United States will be the forty-fifth president, and he will be an Isaiah 45 president.' I didn't even know who Isaiah 45 was talking about, so I opened it up—the Bible, and it says, 'Thus says the Lord to Cyrus whom I've anointed.' Right then I knew that Donald Trump corresponds to the Cyrus character in the Bible. And that he—the wrecking ball—would be the forty-fifth president."

Wallnau read further into the chapter: "And I will build for Israel my people's sake" and "Though you have not known me."

"That line freaked me," Wallnau said, because "I always teach that salvation's free but the anointing is given by God for certain tasks, and I always thought about it as a Christian currency, of being anointed or blessed. But in this case, it says God anointed a heathen ruler. And that was the moment I realized God was going to anoint someone who doesn't know him."

And then Wallnau said he "thought about 'common grace'—what the late Chuck Colson taught—that common grace is the grace that God puts upon unredeemed humanity such as judges and police and governors and rulers for the restraining of evil. If it was up to only the church to restrain evil, then the whole world would be chaos like 'Mad Max.' But God restrains evil through common grace. Saving grace is what gets a Christian saved. One aspect of common grace is that God establishes officials—even ones who are not believers—to restrain evil in society."

Ahead of the second meeting in New York, Wallnau told Darrell

Scott all these things that he had heard and thought about. "This is something two Pentecostal preachers might talk about in a phone call with enthusiasm," Wallnau explained, "but it's nothing you're going to say in front of other people."

The day of the meeting at Trump Tower arrived.

Wallnau recalled the sense of drama in the air just before the meeting. "We're all in that room, and you can tell there were a whole bunch of people waiting to posture themselves. I mean, 90 percent of the African-American community was politically aligned against Donald Trump. The African-American community is locked up for the Democratic Party, so you're struggling to find the objectivity. In my opinion, most of the folks who came out to Trump Tower for that meeting would be going back to deliver a report to their people on what they had done to set Trump straight. They weren't going there to find facts or to build bridges."

Trump came into the room holding his Bible, the one his mother gave to him. He held it out in front of him, like a shield. He paused, looked around the room, and said with a big smile, "Most of the time I bring this Bible as a prop when I'm sharing about my mother and my faith. In this case, I'm simply holding it for protection."

Trump took his seat at the head of the table, and the dialogue began at a fast pace. Wallnau recalled the gist of it: "We can't have this kind of insensitivity on the campaign trail. You can't have people beating up on African-American people. There has to be more compassion."

Wallnau remembers there being lots of back-and-forth between Trump and the pastors. Trump explained about people who were being planted at his rallies, paid to be disruptive. He said that the campaign was instructing security to be very careful about how they handle people. And that his campaign is not against anybody.

Then Trump got everyone's attention and asked, "Let me ask you guys a question: In your church, how do you deal with this. While you're speaking a good sermon if someone got up in the congregation and decided to storm the pulpit to get the microphone, or take over the meeting while you're preaching, how would you deal with it?"

Wallnau said that the reaction was instantaneous. "Nobody even stopped to say, 'Let's be careful how we answer this'—because, in an African-American church, the very thought of you getting up and interrupting the man—no, they've got more respect for the man of God, like the Catholic respects their priest. In the African-American church, you'd better respect clergy. They told Trump, 'We'd take the person out—and we may not even be pleasant on the way out the door. We wouldn't be worried about hurting your feelings if you're going to try to storm the pulpit when the preacher's preaching.' "

Wallnau said that Trump waited until they finished, then looked at them and said: "That's all I'm saying. The rallies are like my church service. I'm the preacher, and I'm trying to deliver my sermon."

"They all looked at each other," Wallnau recalled, "and there was this silence—this awkward silence as Trump had given resolution to what seemed to be an unsolvable problem. And all the racial tensions were just, like a balloon, out of the window."

In the midst of that awkward silence, Darrell Scott—while sitting next to Trump—turned and saw Wallnau "hiding in the corner of the room." He called out to him, "Dr. Lance, please tell Mr. Trump that word you told me."

Wallnau said he just froze. "You know, if I was sitting next to him, I could quietly say 'no'—but from twenty feet away, I couldn't. So, I asked, 'What part?' And he said, 'Tell him the whole thing.' I was like, dang."

Wallnau remembers that he pulled his Bible out of his briefcase—"one of those big King James Bibles"—and "plopped it open to Isaiah 45." He read the passage about Cyrus and explained how this prophecy had been spoken one hundred years before Cyrus came into office.

"I told Trump that the reason God's hand was on him was because of the grace of God—to restrain evil. And that he would be the forty-fifth president of the United States. And when it was over, Mr. Trump knew that I had prophesied over him."

Wallnau said that after that meeting, the staff couldn't remember his name, but people at the headquarters said just call him "the Cyrus guy."

"The 'Cyrus Guy'—what a stupid handle to have—but hey, listen, we take what we can get," Wallnau joked.

When Wallnau finished, Trump came up to him privately to say something in response. Once you've been in Christian circles long enough, you know what to say in such a moment, something like "that really touched me" or "that ministered to me."

"But Trump doesn't have any of that nomenclature down," Wallnau said. "Trump said, 'I don't know how to put it, but that meant a lot to me. And I'm going to think about that. It meant a lot to me.' "

18

3 Wings, 2 Corinthians, and February 1

Political campaigns use "guilt by association" as a regular staple of their advertising. If the opposition candidate ever stood for a photograph with someone whose mug is now infamous for misdeeds, then the picture also casts suspicion on the candidate.

For example, conservatives published an old photograph of Bill Clinton and Bill Cosby standing side by side with smiles on their faces. No politician would stand by Cosby now, given the sexual assault charges he faces. Yet there Clinton stands, with the implication being that "birds of a feather flock together."

Or when the Josh Duggar sex scandals broke during the primary season in 2015, a boatload of pictures hit the internet, showing Duggar standing alongside one GOP candidate after another. Again, the implication being that conservatives either lacked judgment about who they befriended, or even implying they might have similar skeletons in their closet.

And then there's the matter of unwanted endorsements. Campaigns don't want the endorsements of well-known people with checkered pasts and troubling views. Donald Trump received many such endorsements from people, and he would end up on the firing line of questions about whether or not he would accept their praise.

Likewise, campaigns do seek endorsements from well-known people with impeccable qualities—trusted persons who vouch for the candidate. And if they can't get an actual endorsement, sometimes just having an old picture of their candidate with the person will do the trick. After all, we're just talking about impressions that are made on voters, not actual substance or argument.

So, for example, in 1992 when Bill Clinton ran for president, his campaign made sure to play up a photograph of him as an eighteen-year-old shaking the hand of President John F. Kennedy at the White House. It is, of course, an incredible picture, especially since it was taken just months before Kennedy's death. But for the 1992 campaign, Clinton's use of the picture conveyed the idea that he was a true heir to Kennedy's Camelot.

Conservatives do the same thing with Ronald Reagan, pulling out any random snapshot ever taken with them and the Gipper, or Nancy Reagan, or even just a jar of jelly beans. Anything they can do to create the impression that Reagan, if he were but alive, would hit the campaign trail on their behalf.

One month out from the Iowa Caucus, the Rubio campaign launched an email and video intended to cement his evangelical bona fides with voters. The video showed Rubio talking about his Christian faith and how "our goal is eternity" and "to accept the free gift of salvation offered to us by Jesus Christ." The video went viral—and for good reason. Rubio articulated clearly a personal faith and claimed that his faith influenced his politics—just the kind of statement that evangelicals want to hear.

But the email didn't work out so smoothly. The January 8 email sent by Eric Teetsel, Rubio's director of faith outreach, used a Russell Moore quote published earlier in the day by *Roll Call*.

Moore stated: "I would say that Ted Cruz is leading in the 'Jerry Falwell' wing, Marco Rubio is leading the 'Billy Graham' wing and Trump is leading the 'Jimmy Swaggart' wing." Swaggart, of course, disgraced himself and Christianity through a series of sex and financial scandals during the late 1980s. And the late Falwell, though free from the taint of scandal, was a polarizing figure as a leader in thirty years of culture wars. By contrast, evangelist Billy Graham has sat near the top of "most admired American" lists for decades.

Moore, in his role at the Ethics & Religious Liberty Commission (ERLC), cannot give an explicit endorsement of candidates. But to communicate a tacit endorsement takes creativity—like the "Billy Graham wing" statement. And two days before the Iowa Caucus, Moore and Rubio teamed up to write an op-ed that appeared in the *Washington Post*—the first and only time Moore partnered with a candidate in such a manner.

The Moore-Teetsel-Rubio email seemed to backfire though, as it operated on the logic of mocking the constituents of Rubio's fellow GOP opponents. Columnist Doug Wead wrote, "Rubio's Blunder Helps Trump," explaining that Rubio had sought an endorsement from Graham—or even just a meeting—but had been turned down. Wead concluded that evangelical leaders "deeply resent the apparent manipulation" and "see Rubio as taking advantage of the aging Christian leader." At the very least, Bob Vander Plaats of Iowa argued against such rhetoric: "I don't think we want to divide Christianity along those lines. We all break off the same church." As David Lane, a Christian political operative, often says, "Politics is about addition and multiplication, not subtraction and division."

Twelve months after the "three wings" kerfuffle, representatives of all three so-called wings participated in the Inauguration events for President Trump: Franklin Graham and Paula White prayed at the Inauguration itself and Jerry Falwell Jr. read Scripture at a private worship ceremony held in the morning hours.

With Cruz leading in the Iowa polls and Rubio also gaining momentum, Trump traveled to Lynchburg, Virginia, to speak to fifteen thousand students at Liberty University's convocation.

The school makes a point to note that "our Convocation is not a chapel service"—meaning, it is not a Christian worship service. They do sing together and have a prayer, but the speakers vary from pastors to scientists, comedians, and yes, politicians. Bernie Sanders spoke the previous September, making sure the students knew (in case they didn't) that he had "very, very different" views than them "on a number of important issues."

Falwell took the stage and introduced Trump for fifteen minutes, foreshadowing the personal endorsement he'd make the following week. Falwell, a graduate of the University of Virginia Law School, doesn't speak with the manic cadence of politicians on the stump. But with the methodical and steady mannerisms of a middle-aged Southern gentleman lawyer, Falwell built a case for Trump's candidacy: "Matthew 7:16 tells us that by their fruits, you shall know them. Donald Trump's life has borne fruit, fruit that has provided jobs to multitudes of people in addition to the many he has helped with his generosity."

Falwell also compared Trump to his own father, explaining that these men were bold talkers when they needed to be and were often scorned by the established power. "Like Mr. Trump, Dad would speak his mind," Falwell said. "He would make statements that were politically incorrect. He even had a billboard at the entrance to this campus for years that read 'Liberty University: Politically Incorrect since 1971.' "

Trump spoke on his "Make America Great Again" campaign themes, but also added a new line: "We're going to protect Christianity. And I can say that. I don't have to be politically correct." He mentioned "what's going on throughout the world"—and referred to "Syria, where if you're Christian, they're chopping off heads. . . . Christianity, it's under siege."

Nestled in that discussion, Trump referred to a Bible verse that Liberty has inscribed throughout the campus—a theme verse of the university: "Now the Lord is that Spirit: and where the Spirit of the Lord is, there is liberty" (2 Corinthians 3:17).

Except, as everyone knows by now, Trump said "Two Corinthians" instead of "Second Corinthians."

Twitter went wild in mockery, sensing that Trump had finally proven with his own lips that he didn't know much about the Bible. In the Liberty auditorium, giggling could be heard.

Sarah Pulliam Bailey, the religion writer for the *Washington Post*, tweeted a plausible explanation for the misspoken reference:

> For what it's worth, 2 Corinthians (Not Second) is pretty common British speak. Granted, Donald Trump is not from England.

Bailey followed up with:

> One last note on Donald Trump and 2 Corinthians. His mom is an immigrant from Scotland, where I'm told 2 (not second) was likely common.

On Wednesday's *CNN Tonight with Don Lemon,* Trump explained the source of the wording. "Tony Perkins wrote that out for me. He actually wrote out the 2. He wrote out the number 2 Corinthians. I took exactly what Tony said, and I said, 'Well, Tony has to know better than anybody.' "

Perkins told us that he had gone to New York to meet with Trump in early January. Trump informed him he would be speaking at Liberty that month. Perkins mentioned to Trump that Liberty was his alma mater.

"Oh, well then why don't you send me a couple themes that might be good—since you know these folks," Perkins recalls Trump saying.

"So I emailed him a week later. I told him he should talk about religious liberty—because that's really an important issue," Perkins said. "And I wrote: 'You might want to work in 2 Corinthians 3:17, Liberty's theme verse.' Of course, this was in an email, written out as you would see it in the New Testament. That's the whole story behind it. It wasn't verbally communicated—just an email."

Perkins was not at Liberty that day but did listen to the speech live. "I heard that, and I cringed a little bit," Perkins said. He called Corey Lewandowski.

"I said, 'Corey, it was a good speech, but you know that's 'Second Corinthians'—that's how it's said.' He goes, 'It was a great speech. They loved it.' I said, 'Well you just need to have somebody who knows the nuances of those things—especially if you want to communicate with the evangelical world.' "

Perkins admits he didn't like how it played out in the press because "it made it look as if I was advising him" in a special way. "I had actually made myself available to all the candidates to help them."

Perkins said this also moved up his endorsement of Ted Cruz, as people were beginning to ask if he had joined in with Trump.

I was backstage at Liberty that day, preparing for a post-speech interview with Trump. When he said "Two Corinthians" I walked over to Corey Lewandowski and Hope Hicks in the green room and said, "You realize he just said 'Two Corinthians'?" They looked at me without much of a reaction, like "What's the big deal." I said, "He's going to get some flak for that. It's 'Second Corinthians.' You need to give him a heads-up because he's going to get asked about that—starting with me."

Moments later, I asked Trump about "Two Corinthians."

"Well, I've actually, over the years, heard it both ways. But I would say probably I prefer saying Second Corinthians. But I've seen it, as you have, both ways."

I then asked him why evangelical voters should vote for him. He went with the Gipper.

"Ronald Reagan wasn't totally— He didn't read the Bible every day, seven days a week. But he was a great president. And he was a great president for Christianity. And frankly, I would say that I would be a far better leader. . . . I'll be a much better person for evangelicals, but also for everybody else."

At a campaign stop that day, Jeffress prayed for Trump: "Today we come to thank you for Donald Trump, who is willing to selflessly offer himself for service to this nation for no other reason than his desire to make America great again . . . give them guidance as they seek your will for their lives."

Jeffress told crowd after crowd of Iowa voters that, as a pastor, he could not officially endorse a candidate, but "I would not be here this morning if I were not absolutely convinced that Donald Trump would make a great president of the United States."

"Wow, I want to thank the pastor—an incredible guy," Trump said. "I watched him on television a year ago, and he was talking about me . . . and he said, 'He may not be as pure as we think, but he's really good and a great Christian,' and that's what I wanted to hear."

The *Washington Post* published an op-ed by Falwell explaining the endorsement of Trump he made that day. Falwell saw a clear parallel to the financial crisis of the United States and the nearly bankrupt days Liberty University experienced in the late 1980s and 1990s. Falwell's basic argument became the talking points for evangelicals who supported Trump even ahead of his winning the GOP nomination. Falwell wrote, "Jimmy Carter is a great Sunday School teacher but the divorced and remarried Hollywood actor Ronald Reagan saved this nation when it was in nearly the same condition as it is today. Jesus said, 'Judge not, lest ye be judged.' Let's stop trying to choose the political leaders who we believe are the most godly because, in reality, only God knows people's hearts. You and I don't, and we are all sinners."

When we asked Falwell about the critics who told him, "Your father would be ashamed," he said that this was a misunderstanding of his father's politics. "Dad was a political pragmatist," Falwell Jr. said. "He understood that this is not a theocracy and we're not electing a pastor, we're electing a president. And when you elect a president, that person has to be president of all the people. In order for somebody to get the votes and to get elected, they can't be just like you, or like everybody in your particular interest group, because then they wouldn't get the support of others who are much different. Dad figured that out early on, and that's why he supported Reagan over Carter."

I interviewed both Falwell and Trump backstage at the Adler Theatre in Davenport, Iowa, a beautiful Art Deco building listed on the National Register of Historic Places.

I didn't even know I would be interviewing them until I got a call five hours before the Davenport event from campaign manager Corey Lewandowski. "Hey, I have an exclusive for you if you can get to Davenport in five hours," Lewandowski said. "Umm, sure. Let me work on that—since we're a three-hour drive away at this point!"

Trump surely deserved credit for lasting so long at the top of the pack. It was now six months since he'd jumped into the race, and he had maintained his lead for nearly the entire time—even with the various verbal miscues that probably would have sunk other candidates. Critics thought he'd be long gone by January.

I asked him about the final *Des Moines Register* poll showing him out in front with less than forty-eight hours to go before the Iowa Caucus: "It's a good result, and we're really happy about it, and with evangelicals, we're leading, and that's something that really made me happy, maybe even happier. I'm very happy about that."

"Those evangelicals could take you over the top?" I asked.

"Well, they're fantastic people. We love them."

When Cruz won the Iowa Caucus, Trump lost the credibility of his key self-label: winner. But he surprised everyone on two counts.

First, the exit polling data made people take notice. Trump won 22 percent of the evangelical vote in the state, beating Rubio (21 percent). Sure, Cruz won 34 percent of evangelicals, but he had made his "I'm one of you" the major theme of his outreach to those voters. If anything, the Iowa results caused people to realize that, for all his reputation that preceded him, evangelical voters were willing to vote for Trump.

Second, Trump lost graciously. For months, pundits predicted a Trump meltdown if he lost—that he would go off the rails after spending so much time and energy in the state. But Trump took it in stride, congratulating Cruz on his performance: "We finished second, and I want to tell you something—I'm just honored. . . . I want to congratulate Ted, and I want to congratulate all the incredible candidates—including Mike Huckabee, who has become a really good friend of mine."

Huckabee, the winner in 2008, got 1.8 percent of the vote, and Rick Santorum, the winner in 2012, got 1 percent. Both men suspended their campaigns after Iowa, but even before the voting took place both men had appeared with Trump at his fund-raiser for veterans that took place the night of the final Iowa debate (that Trump famously skipped). In doing this, they signaled to all their die-hard Iowa supporters that caucusing for Trump was a fine thing to do.

All this insider baseball serves to illustrate a basic point: Though they never seem to unite on a candidate early on—and although sociologists and theologians can't agree on a one-size-fits-all definition of the term—evangelicals still exerted great power over the GOP results in Iowa. "The truth is, the evangelical vote is always splintered," Huckabee said. "The big myth is that it unites. It didn't unite in 2008. If it had, I'd have been the nominee."

With the South Carolina primary three weeks away—and with Carson, Cruz, Kasich, and Rubio all still in the mix—evangelicals there would need to decide quickly who they were going to coalesce behind. The answer would shock everyone.

19

Pat, the Pope, and the Palmetto State Primary

Trump won the New Hampshire primary with 35 percent of the vote, or roughly the same amount as the next three candidates combined (Kasich, Rubio, Cruz). Now the focus shifted entirely to South Carolina.

I caught up with Trump in Charleston on the eight-month anniversary of the horrific mass murder of nine African-Americans at a prayer service at the Emanuel African Methodist Episcopal Church.

Charleston is, of course, the city where the Civil War began, with the bombardment of Fort Sumter. The killer—a young man—had soaked his life in white supremacy and draped himself, literally, with the Confederate flag. His actions reopened the debate over the public display of statues and symbols of the Confederacy. Nikki Haley, then South Carolina's governor, called for the flag to be taken down from the South Carolina State House.

When asked about the flag, Trump (who had announced his candidacy just one day before the shooting) said, "I think they should put it in the museum and let it go. Respect whatever it is you have to respect, because it was a point in time, and put it in a museum. But I would take it down. Yes."

Two weeks after the killings, TV Land removed *The Dukes of Hazzard* from its lineup of syndicated reruns. One week later, the flag came down at the State House.

• • •

In my interview that day, I asked Trump to "tell me about your core" and that "people want to make sure that you're going to be able to deliver." Knowing that a large portion of the audience at CBN is Christian (hence, the "C"), Trump first stated his reflexive triad, "I'm a Christian. I'm Protestant. I'm Presbyterian"—before launching into what would become a major theme of his campaign outreach to Christians, the Johnson Amendment: "I think Christians in our country are not treated properly. The bill that was passed during the Lyndon Johnson era is horrible because I see churches where they're afraid to be outspoken because they don't want to lose their tax-exempt status and I realize that is one of the problems. Essentially, they've taken a lot of the power away from the church. I want to give power back to the church because the church has to have more power. Christianity is really being chopped; little by little it's being taken away."

Trump would refer to the Johnson Amendment of 1954 repeatedly throughout the remainder of the campaign. When I interviewed him in the Oval Office, he explained that the genesis of it began when he was seeking the endorsement of some pastors at Trump Tower. "When I asked them for the endorsement they said, 'Well, we really can't do that.' And I said, 'Why is that?' They said, 'Because of the Johnson Amendment.' " That's how the whole amendment issue started. Trump researched it and then concluded soon afterward: "I thought about it for a month, and then I met with them again a month later, a large group, very large, probably fifty. And I met with them again, and I said, 'You know, I've been thinking a lot about the Johnson Amendment; I've done some research, and we've got to end the Johnson Amendment.' "

I also brought up the issue of defunding Planned Parenthood—an action which at the time many conservatives thought was a real possibility going forward. Six months earlier, some undercover videos had exposed a high-level executive with PP eating dinner and sipping wine while casually talking about the selling of fetal body parts obtained through abortion (though liberals believe the videos were selectively edited). As of today, that debate continues—though with the GOP in control of the House, the Senate, and the Oval Office, one could justifiably doubt the political resolve of the Republican Party when it comes to stripping taxpayer funds ($60,000 per hour—every hour of every day) from the organization.

I asked, "As president, if a bill came to your desk that would defund Planned Parenthood would you sign that?"

Trump's one-word answer was what the pro-life movement wanted to hear: "Yes."

But Trump also continued his explanation to say words that would never be on the talking-points page of a pro-life spokesperson. Never.

"Yes. As long as they do the abortion, I am not for funding Planned Parenthood, but they do cervical cancer work. They do a lot of good things for women—but as long as they're involved with the abortions—as you know, they say it's 3 percent of their work, some people say it's 10 percent, some people say it's 8 percent—I hear all different percentages, but it doesn't matter. As long as they're involved with abortion, as far as I'm concerned forget it, I wouldn't fund them regardless. But they do other good work. You look at cervical cancer. I've had women tell me they do some excellent work, so I think you also have to put that into account but I would defund Planned Parenthood because of their view and the fact of their work on abortion."

I let him finish, then countered: "All right, but there are other groups as well—not just Planned Parenthood—that do that fine work." My point being, other nonprofit groups do the "good work" for women, but without performing abortions. And while both sides of the abortion debate can argue about Planned Parenthood's role, the publicly available information shows that, among the pregnancy-related services of abortions, adoption referrals, and prenatal services, the majority of Planned Parenthood's work is, in fact, abortion-related. The abortion-rights organization will counter that when all services are factored in, it's not a majority. But in typical Trump fashion, he had a bottom line to the ongoing argument. "There are a lot of women taken care of by Planned Parenthood. So, we have to remember that, but I am for defunding Planned Parenthood as long as they are involved with abortion."

Abortion is, of course, a core issue of religious conservatives. No, it is not the only issue they are concerned about, but it is the one issue that weighs on the mind and determines whom to vote for— when the candidates differ on the issue. And at the national level of politics, the party platforms are miles apart. How many pro-lifers remain in leadership at the national level of the Democratic Party? How many Republicans in DC are pro-choice? As of 2017: two senators and three congressmen. The Republicans for Choice PAC, created in 1989 by the former wife of Roger Stone, spent less than $200,000 for the entire 2016 election cycle. By contrast, Planned Parenthood spent $38 million to support Democrats during the same period. Unless something fundamentally changes, each party is now set in stone on the issue.

I asked Trump, "Do you believe *Roe v. Wade* was wrongly decided, back in 1973?"

"Well, I do. It's been very strongly decided, but it can be changed," Trump said. But he noted, correctly, that such decisions depend on who sits on the US Supreme Court—and that is a slow process: "It's going to take time because you have a lot of judges to go."

That's true. You can't change SCOTUS overnight. On the other hand, when conservative justice Antonin Scalia died, the issue of picking judges for the highest court in the land became a central concern for the remainder of the primaries and the general election.

The horse race between Trump and Cruz had heated up coming out of Iowa. Without regurgitating that entire story, there were charges and countercharges that the Cruz campaign had done some campaign shenanigans in Iowa. Trump had taken to using a label for Cruz: "Lying Ted."

"Ted's been caught in a lot of lies," Trump told me. "He really lied with Dr. Ben Carson in Iowa. That's where I sort of got wise to him, and then he made the voter violation form which is a fraud as far as most people are concerned, and he lies a lot. . . ."

Just to be clear: We're not saying we agree with Trump's assessment of the Cruz-Carson imbroglio. You can go back and read about those events and make up your own mind.

But the point here is that Trump used that story to promote the idea of hypocrisy—something most people consider worse than outright infidelity.

"He does hold up the Bible," Trump said to me. "He holds up the Bible nice and high but he lies, and I think the evangelicals have figured it out because I'm leading with evangelicals by a lot."

"So are you questioning his Christian faith?" I asked.

"No, not at all. I'm just saying you don't hold up the Bible and lie."

Trump's unwillingness to question Cruz's Christianity contrasted sharply with what Pope Francis was saying about Trump on that very same afternoon: "A person who thinks only about building walls, wherever they may be, and not building bridges, is not a Christian."

The Pope made the remarks to journalists while on a flight across Mexico during a weeklong trip to the nation that had become such a focus of Trump's rhetoric during the campaign. Earlier in the day, the pontiff led a Mass in a border city on the Rio Grande—the very border, of course, that Trump famously said would have a wall built along to keep out illegal immigrants.

The Pope said he didn't plan on inserting himself into the US election, but concluded with this: "I say only that this man is not Christian if he has said things like that" and "We must see if he said things in that way and in this I give the benefit of the doubt."

After my interview with Trump, he drove about thirty minutes south, for a campaign rally on Kiawah Island. "I like the Pope," he said, as he read from a prepared text:

> If and when the Vatican is attacked by ISIS, which as every-one knows is ISIS's ultimate trophy, I can promise you that the Pope would have only wished and prayed that Donald Trump would have been President because this would not have happened. ISIS would have been eradicated unlike what is happening now with our all talk, no action politi-cians.

Then Trump addressed the personal nature of Pope Francis's comments:

> For a religious leader to question a person's faith is dis-graceful. I am proud to be a Christian and as President I will not allow Christianity to be consistently attacked and weakened, unlike what is happening now, with our current President. No leader, especially a religious leader, should have the right to question another man's religion or faith. They [the Mexican government] are using the Pope as a pawn and they should be ashamed of themselves for doing

so, especially when so many lives are involved and when illegal immigration is so rampant.

Trump went from 5 percent in the FRC straw poll in September to winning South Carolina five months later—on the strength of winning the highest percentage of the "born-again or evangelical Christian" vote. Evangelicals accounted for three-quarters of the GOP primary voters in South Carolina and gave their support to: Trump, 33 percent; Cruz, 27 percent; and Rubio, 22 percent (overall, Rubio came in second).

Many pundits speculated that had evangelicals coalesced behind either Cruz or Rubio (and remember, Carson was still in the mix too), their united vote would have blocked Trump in South Carolina. But polling—even among evangelicals—that asked "who is your second choice?" consistently showed inconsistent results: if not Cruz, a lot of people would jump to Trump; if not Rubio, many favored Kasich. So the idea that evangelicals allowed Trump to slide in the door by not joining forces in the primaries doesn't hold up. In the first Deep South state where evangelicals had an opportunity to block Trump, they supported him.

Now, at this point in the analysis, we're supposed to tell you that it was the "not a true Christian" evangelical who got on the Trump bandwagon. Evangelipundits, with deep concern that the brand identity of "evangelicalism" not be tainted, got busy trying to show that people from their tribe who are very active in their faith—regular church attendance, habitual Bible reading, tithing—were less likely to vote for Trump.

Did the ultra-devout go more to Cruz? Yes, but Trump still won a sizable chunk of them. The reality is that Cruz needed a much larger margin of the weekly churchgoer category to win—and he never got it. That's the takeaway. In other words, Cruz needed more of the devout to show up and back him. They didn't—they went for Trump instead. Cruz could have the "moral victory" of winning weekly churchgoers, but Trump still won upwards of 30 percent or more of this vote in some states. Looking at the empirical data from exit polling in state after state, it was the "white born-again weekly churchgoers" category that put Trump over the top and thwarted Cruz.

Trump won 46 percent of the vote in the Nevada caucuses, twice what either Rubio or Cruz collected. Though now being 0 for 4, Rubio did not drop out—despite a lack of historical precedent for being able to win a nomination after starting out with four goose eggs.

Trump took an overnight flight in his plane and arrived in Virginia Beach, Virginia, for a presidential candidate forum at Regent University. Founded by Pat Robertson—himself a onetime candidate for president and one of the pioneers of Christian conservative political involvement—Regent hosted as many candidates as would accept an invitation to these events. Bush, Carson, Kasich, Cruz, and Trump made it a priority to come.

I moderated the event by asking questions from the audience. Backstage, Trump and his people were all tired. But he didn't miss a beat once he got in front of the crowd. Pat told Trump: "You inspire us all."

This event, even though the primary season was yet young, showed a glimpse of the idea of continuity between the older generation's "Religious Right" and what was going on with evangelicals supporting Trump.

Pat asked him what criteria he would use to pick a Supreme Court justice.

"Pro-life. It starts with that," Trump replied. "Very conservative—a very, very smart—like Judge Scalia—would be perfect. He was a perfect representative."

20

#NeverTrump

Very early in the primary season—even before the Iowa caucuses—Christians on both the left and right began to float the idea that they would never get behind Trump's candidacy.

Or to phrase it in Twitter hashtag lingo: #NeverTrump.

Peter Wehner, a senior fellow at the Ethics and Public Policy Center, a conservative think tank, wrote what may have been the first column along these lines when he penned "Why I Will Never Vote for Donald Trump" in mid-January 2016, just weeks before the Iowa Caucuses. Because Trump would redefine conservatism, Wehner argued, "his nomination would pose a profound threat to the Republican Party and conservatism in ways that Hillary Clinton never could."

Then in July, after Trump had secured the GOP nomination, Wehner said Trump "embodies a Nietzschean morality rather than a Christian one." Finally, even as Trump was being inaugurated in January 2017, Wehner added another #NeverTrump article: "Why I Cannot Fall in Line Behind Trump." His subtitle stated, "Conservatism is a philosophy, not just a policy checklist."

Others, like *National Review* columnist David French, evolved into their #NeverTrump position during the primary. "Early on, I said something like, 'Well, I'm not going to take my ball and go home. I mean I'd vote for him in the general election. Absolutely I would.'" But when Trump went after Jeb Bush—and then called G.W. a liar on Iraq—"That's when Trump really lost me. That's when I thought, 'No. Not him. No.'" Eventually, French would give serious consideration to running as a third-party candidate, supported by William Kristol. When he chose not to run, Evan McMullin stepped into that role.

Republican keyboards across America began clicking out a case for why true conservatives should join #NeverTrump. William F. Buckley would have been proud of the effort. But even beyond the pages of *National Review* and *The Weekly Standard*, some in the faith community began to define and align with the position of absolute resistance to Trump.

Many evangelical theologians and ethicists spent both the primary and general election seasons constructing arguments that attempted to show the #NeverTrump position to be the best stance to take in light of Trump. Some of them, like Danny Akin, the president of Southeastern Baptist Seminary, did so with a proverbial tear in their eye: "the saddest political situation in my life."

One week before the election, Bruce Ashford, a sharp young theologian at the seminary Akin leads, wrote "Mr. Trump and Secretary Clinton: An Evangelical Assessment." He assessed for sixteen pages, then concluded: "For the reasons stated, we will not vote for either nominee."

Let's be honest here. In 2016, you would have looked in vain for one single Southern Baptist Convention seminary professor who supported pro-choice Hillary. Not going to happen. Of course, we Christian Conservatives go through the motions of assessing national Democratic candidates as a formality because of the constant accusation of "being captive to the GOP." But then Trump came along. #NeverTrump voices found his candidacy to be a perfect opportunity for disproving the old theory: Christians will come around for any Republican candidate. Plus, within their own conscience, they simply couldn't vote for him because of what they saw as flaws in his personal character.

• • •

On April 29, fifty faith leaders of the Christian Left signed a document titled "Christians Called to Resist Trump's Bigotry."

> Donald Trump directly promotes racial and religious bigotry, disrespects the dignity of women, harms civil public discourse, offends moral decency, and seeks to manipulate religion. This is no longer politics as usual, but rather a moral and theological crisis, and thus we are compelled to speak out as faith leaders.

Although the statement claimed to be "absolutely no tacit endorsement of other candidates," many of the signatories would eventually give a personal, if tacit, endorsement of Clinton during the general election. Therein lies the difference between the #NeverTrump of the Christian Left as compared to the Christian Right: The Left can usually find a way to vote for a pro-choice candidate, thus taking away the horns of the dilemma about whom to vote for.

On the other hand, we asked Brian Kaylor, a leader among moderate Baptists in Missouri, if he regretted staying on the sidelines—speaking out against Trump but not voting for Clinton. "We're responsible for what values we push and who we align ourselves with," Kaylor said. "And to me, Clinton was still a bridge too far. It's not that I wanted evangelicals to vote for Hillary, but if we evangelicals had just had a larger block that just refused to vote for either one, we wouldn't be in the same boat as him, and not be held responsible for what's happening."

On the third of May, Indiana handed Trump another victory—a conservative state that Cruz had spent a lot of time and resources on, and where he had the endorsement of then-governor Mike

Pence. CNN exit polling showed that "born-again or evangelical" Christians favored Trump (51 percent) over Cruz (43 percent). As a result, Cruz suspended his campaign. In just over ten months of campaigning, Trump had vanquished sixteen other candidates—including at least a half-dozen who were explicitly "evangelical" in their approach—and secured the GOP nomination.

After ignoring him for a year, Trump finally responded to a year's worth of opposition tweets and opinion pieces by Russell Moore, the head of the Ethics and Religious Liberty Commission (ERLC) of the Southern Baptist Convention, by tweeting out a personal attack:

> @drmoore Russell Moore is truly a terrible representative of Evangelicals and all of the good they stand for. A nasty guy with no heart! (May 9, 2016)

Any fair assessment of Moore's tweets about Trump (or his tweets about Trump's evangelical supporters, like Falwell and Jeffress) would show that the Southern Baptist had already taken the fight to a personal level—and often laced it with intelligent condescension and biting sarcasm. Such is the nature of political mudslinging.

Robert Jeffress entered the fray by saying that Moore had led the way when he "launched numerous vitriolic attacks not only against Trump's policies but about his own character and integrity." Jeffress noted that Moore "absolutely does not speak for all Southern Baptists even as I don't speak for all Southern Baptists" and that "no one should be surprised that Trump would respond to such attacks."

Richard Land, the previous head of the ERLC, was never enthusiastic about Trump during the primaries. "My first choice was Marco Rubio," Land told us. "My second choice was Jeb Bush. My third choice was Ted Cruz. My last choice was Donald Trump. He was my eighteenth choice out of seventeen. I mean, I'd have even voted for Rand Paul over him."

But once the primaries ended, Land did not even consider joining the #NeverTrump movement. "When a decision gets really tough, albeit to the point of challenging your core beliefs about how to participate in democracy, it is extremely tempting to use a convenient doctrinal nuance to take the easy way out. Theology, politics, and the nature of fallen man are a lot more complex than that." Land admits that 2016 was "an excruciating choice" and that he "went into the polling booth with less joy and lower expectations than I had in any election—including my votes for Nixon. I would say that we had lower expectations and we've been pleasantly surprised."

When we asked Family Research Council president Tony Perkins if he ever felt institutional pressure from within FRC to take a #NeverTrump position, he replied immediately: "No, that was foolish. I give an account to God for what I do. I take it very serious. This is what I've been called to do. This is where I spend my life—looking at and interacting with the political landscape—so I'm not going to apologize for providing the leadership that's necessary. If I can stand before God knowing that what I'm doing I have pursued through prayer and seeking his guidance, then I'm not going to apologize to you. I'm not going to try to make any excuses."

Perkins said that some have come back to him and told him he was right and they apologized. Others who had been against his position on Trump haven't said anything to him about the election—but "the evidence speaks that I did the right thing," Perkins said.

In mid-May, Trump released a list of twenty-one names—judges he would choose from in nominating the next Supreme Court justice. Ralph Reed told us this was the first of three key hinge points that brought evangelicals on board with Trump. "Not someone in a certain model," Reed said. "Not someone like this or that—but that he would choose someone from that exact list. No one had ever made that kind of commitment before."

One week later, Trump passed 1,237 pledged delegates—more than enough to secure the nomination. Nonetheless, *National Review* editor Jonah Goldberg wrote, "Sorry, I Still Won't Ever Vote for Trump":

> I honestly believe that a President Trump would do enormous, perhaps fatal, damage to the conservative movement as we know it. I also believe that without the conservative movement, this country is toast. But I further believe that Hillary Clinton would do obvious and enormous damage to the country. That's why I'm not voting for either of them.

"Fatal damage to the conservative movement" versus "enormous damage to the country"? To be sure, Christians had legitimate concerns about the character of Donald J. Trump—and some even staked out a position of #NeverTrump on that basis. But when you describe an election in such binary terms as Goldberg wrote, most Christians opted out of the Clintonian "enormous damage to the country" plan.

21

Coalesce or Two Evils?

As spring moved into summer, a lingering question remained: Would evangelical leaders make the turn and support Trump—or would they merge with the #NeverTrump group?

In June, I traveled to the annual conference put on by Ralph Reed's Faith & Freedom Coalition. With several thousand in attendance, Trump promised to "restore faith to its proper mantle in our society" and to "respect and defend Christian Americans. . . . We'll uphold the values our founders gave us."

Afterward, I asked Trump if he believed America is a Judeo-Christian nation. "That's the way it is—and it's been," he affirmed, before going on to say that freedom and good things are for all citizens in the United States—but that without leadership committed to keeping citizens safe, the threats of "radical Islamic terrorism" would keep people in fear—not freedom. "We have to be smart. We have to be vigilant. And we have no choice."

I changed gears and told him that the word on the street was that would-be supporters wanted Trump to "tone down the rhetoric." What did he think about that?

"Well you have to be who you are," he responded, and then laid out the facts: "I've gotten the largest number of votes in the history of Republican politics—by far. I want to keep doing what we're doing." Then he added cheekily: "But if you ask me to tone down, I'll tone it down."

Jennifer Rubin, who holds the "Conservative columnist" slot at the *Washington Post*, called the conference "the Christian conservative confab's shameless Trump cheerleading." Trump had not lost the esteem of Rubin—he never had it. Of course, just about all candidates not named Bush, Rubio, or Kasich could expect Rubin's columns to excoriate them for not being the type of conservative she could support. She wrote that Trump's speech "broke the hypocrisy meter" and was "simply out to flatter the evangelicals."

We talked to Reed about his relationship with Trump, seeking to discern what made these Christian leaders embrace him so suddenly. Reed explained that "suddenly" did not do justice to the relationship he had with Trump. "I had an advantage over other Christian leaders in that I had known Trump since around 2010," Reed said, "when he started to get more politically involved during the Tea Party period."

When, in early 2011, Trump explored a potential run for president, Reed invited him to come to the annual Road to Majority conference. Trump came, meeting privately with Reed at the event and then again at Trump Tower. He also came and spoke to some key pastors and state leaders affiliated with Reed. And then he came back again—three more times.

Reed had, of course, seen Trump on TV throughout the years, and he went into the relationship not expecting to like him based on Trump's public image and caricature. But in person, Reed found him "disarmingly charming, smart, and impossible not to like." And Trump surprised Reed by being "incredibly accessible"—almost to a fault. "It wasn't like he was my phone pal," Reed said. "I didn't call him up at eleven at night just to talk. But if I ever needed to reach him, I called his office and could get him on the phone in fifteen seconds. I don't even remember him having to call me back."

But what about the issues that Faith & Freedom cared about? Reed said that the two of them privately talked about abortion, marriage, and religious freedom. They talked a lot about politics, the

Obama administration, and his own potential future (including how people urged him to run for governor of New York).

"I knew him and knew where he was on the issues," Ralph explained. "He told me why he became pro-life and why he took the positions he did. I found every one of our conversations to be candid and compelling and convincing."

Before the primaries began, Reed's board members met and agreed that they would all remain neutral in the primary, as individuals and as an organization. When they held Faith & Freedom events or candidate forums, all candidates would be invited and everybody would be treated the same. They agreed to wait until the field had narrowed down to two people, and only then would they have a conversation to decide whether or not one of the remaining two was unacceptable. And when it came down to Trump and Cruz, Reed said they felt they could work with either one of them. Their consensus: "This is a win-win."

"We would not try and put our finger on the scale—we'd let the market decide," Reed said. "Even though I was a lot closer to Jeb than I was to Trump . . . and after that I was closer to Kasich than I was to Walker . . . and I was closer probably to Marco than I was to somebody else. But we stayed strictly and studiously neutral."

When Trump won the nomination, Reed's group once again evaluated him on the issues: "He was pro-life. He had just released his list of twenty-one judges for the Supreme Court; he was pro–traditional marriage; he was pro-Israel; he was against the Iran nuclear deal; he was for defunding Planned Parenthood. He was solid on every key issue that we cared about," Reed said. "And Trump was the only candidate who made one of the central promises of his campaign—at least to social conservatives—the repealing of the Johnson Amendment and the restoring of First Amendment rights to churches and ministries."

But what about "pandering"? Was Trump playing a part in

2016—reading a script for evangelicals? Reed refuted that idea, saying that there was never a time—from 2010 to the present—where he doubted Trump's sincerity and his conviction when they talked.

"We had very heartfelt and transparent conversations that were not in the context of a candidacy," Reed said. "I was very direct in sharing my views with him and he was very direct in sharing his views with me. I didn't flatter him. I gave him the best unvarnished understanding of my views."

Reed reminds people that he is a political operative—not a prophet. And he founded a public policy organization—not a ministry or a church. So it's all about where a candidate stands on issues. "We believed that he was not only solid on every issue that we cared about—every public policy priority that we had—I believed he took positions that were as good or better than we had ever received from any Republican nominee in my career."

Trump was no Johnny-come-lately to evangelicals or to their concerns.

Johnnie Moore first came to Liberty University as a student. His speaking and leadership abilities caught the attention of Jerry Falwell Sr. and Moore began to work for the famous pastor, political activist, and university president. After Falwell's death, Falwell Jr. took over as head of the school and Moore eventually moved into the position of vice president of communications—serving in a variety of ways, including as a campus pastor.

Though now in his thirties, Moore still looks barely out of college, with a contagious smile. He left his job at Liberty to found a media firm, picking up dozens of high-profile evangelical faces. He even worked on projects with Mark Burnett, the creator and producer of *The Apprentice*.

Like Reed, Moore's relationship with Trump predated the election by several years. It began with a conversation Moore had with his boss, Falwell Jr., to plan for future convocations at Liberty. "I was really concerned about the decline of the free market and how the free market was being perceived as a negative thing," Moore said. "I told Jerry that we ought to invite the most famous business-man in the country to come: Donald Trump."

Jerry gave his blessing on the idea, so Johnnie picked up the phone and made a cold call to Trump Tower—literally, calling the main number listed for the building.

"I said, 'This is Johnnie Moore, senior vice president of Liberty University, calling for Jerry Falwell.' Forty-five seconds later, I was on the phone with Rhona—Trump's lead gatekeeper. We had an invitation sent to them by the end of the day. Ten days later, Trump had waived his normal speaking fee. He hopped on his plane, flew to Lynchburg, and spoke to a record number of students in the Vines Center—and more than that in overflow space." This all took place in September 2012.

Moore said that before the big day, Trump called personally, to make sure that Liberty had received a picture of his confirmation—and that they would be ready to show it. "It was clear he valued his faith and he wanted our community to know that he was not an outsider," Moore said. "That he was actually an insider—he was part of us. That was important to him and of value to him."

Given that many Liberty students come from Baptist backgrounds—where confirmation is not part of the spiritual pilgrimage—Trump's picture might not have packed the desired punch with the student body. But for Trump, the picture is a reminder of where he came from: "Christian. Protestant. Presbyterian."—and it established some common ground with the students, at least on the first two counts.

Moore recalls not knowing what he would think of Trump in person. How would the big, famous TV superstar Trump—firing people all the time and being brash—respond to students and staff at Liberty? But Moore said he was "struck by his kindness and his humility" from the moment he stepped off the plane. "There was not a person he didn't talk to. He greeted every single person—and even canceled his schedule for the rest of the afternoon, and spent it hanging out and taking pictures with students all over campus. That's when I knew that this is not just a celebrity—this is a person who had character and compassion. To me, in my sort of Christian way of viewing things, it was like fruit of the Spirit. That's what it was."

Near the end of convocation, Trump answered questions texted in from the students. One student asked a generic question: "Do you have any advice for us as future leaders?" Trump leaned into the microphone and answered directly: "I always say don't let people take advantage—this goes for a country too, by the way—don't let people take advantage. Get even."

The crowd loved that. But, of course, it caused controversy, so Johnnie and Jerry ended up doing several different radio and TV interviews in Trump's defense. Moore wrote an op-ed for Fox News, arguing that Trump's essential point wasn't necessarily counter to the example of Christ:

> Of course, as a Bible-believing evangelical, I do not believe that Christians should treat people maliciously, take revenge or fight with others arbitrarily. I believe we should show extraordinary restraint. But, when someone asked me if I thought God would "get even" with people, I decided to make a nuanced, theological point: "God would, and he did, get even." In the end, God won.

During the 2016 election cycle, Moore launched "My Faith Votes," which catalyzed efforts to move Christians to the voting booth.

He also helped put together a June 2016 meeting at the New York Marriott Marquis hotel, where a thousand evangelicals met with Trump and began to unite. As the primaries had shown, the grassroots Christian voter gave Trump the nomination. But institutional Christianity—the think tanks, national ministries, media giants, pastors, and activists—had been fighting for "anyone but Trump" as recently as one month earlier.

Two groups—United in Purpose (led by Bill Dallas) and My Faith Votes (led by Johnnie Moore)—spearheaded the event called "A Conversation About America's Future, with Donald Trump & Ben Carson," along with others like Tony Perkins and James Dobson. Perkins had previously endorsed Cruz, though he is quick to note that his organization never attacked Trump. But even before Cruz dropped out, Perkins's team began making private contact with the Trump campaign, and once the nomination was secure they moved "full speed ahead" with plans for the meeting in New York. "All of a sudden it turned out that the event was the hottest ticket in town," Perkins recalled. "We were having to turn people away."

"Up until that point, there were several of us who were with him," Huckabee said, "but most of the people were either very hostile, or they were skeptical—and certainly noncommittal. I think that particular day turned the corner, because you had a number of people who began to openly say good things about Donald Trump. I thought that meeting was a pivotal moment."

Huckabee recalled how it was Ben Carson and Paula White who had told Trump he needed to work more on the evangelicals—to talk to them directly and all at once. "He had a number of different meetings that he'd had with smaller groups of pastors. But he had never brought in the 'heads of the families'—to use a mafia term—for a united meeting with all the 'mega-stars' and all the leaders that might not be marquee names. We ended up packing the ballroom—way more than anyone thought would happen."

Mike Huckabee had met Trump back in 2008 when the former governor and two-time candidate for president started his own Fox TV show. Trump was one of the early people interviewed on the show, and appeared several times. The two men also visited occasionally with each other in Trump's office.

"He and I had developed a good rapport," Huckabee said. "Every Monday he was doing *Fox and Friends.* I would do my interviews with him from Trump Tower. He seemed to like me—and I liked him. I found him intriguing and I liked his brash honesty."

In April 2011 when political prognosticators began to forecast who might run for the GOP nomination, the Gallup poll put Huckabee and Trump in a tie for first place with 16 percent (Romney came in third with 13 percent). Friends and family urged Huckabee to run again. But one month later, he went on his Fox show and told the nation: "All the factors say go, but my heart says no. Under the best of circumstances, being president is a job that takes one to the limit of his or her human capacity. For me to do it apart from an inner confidence that I was undertaking it with God's full blessing is simply unthinkable."

What is fascinating about Huckabee's announcement—and remember, this was in May 2011—is that immediately after he finished his monologue, the show broke to a prerecorded "Huckabee Alert" video of Donald Trump sitting behind a desk at Trump Tower.

I'm Donald Trump and this is a special announcement. Mike Huckabee is not going to be running for president. This might be considered by some people—not necessarily me—bad news because he is a terrific guy. And frankly, I think he'd be a terrific president. But a lot of people are very happy that he will not be running—especially other candidates. So Mike, enjoy the show—your ratings are terrific.

You're making a lot of money. You're building a beautiful house in Florida. Good luck.

The following Monday, Trump released his own "I'm not going to run" statement—adding in some characteristic New York swagger for good measure: "I maintain the strong conviction that if I were to run, I would be able to win the primary and, ultimately, the general election."

Five years later to the month, Trump did secure the nomination, leading evangelicals to this time of decision. Trump sat on stage for a Q&A session, with Huckabee as the emcee. Huckabee remembers telling the crowd that "Everyone here knows the Bible better than Donald Trump." Huckabee likes to say, "If you handed Donald Trump a tabbed Bible, he'd have a hard time finding John 3:16." People chuckle at the way Huckabee puts it, but he lets them know he is serious: "I just don't think it's a book about which he's deeply familiar."

Huckabee, a former Southern Baptist pastor and two-time president of the Arkansas Baptist Convention, believes Trump "has a God consciousness about him that's real." He says that for all of Trump's vulgarity and secularist attitudes and life, Trump has a "deep, abiding respect, not just for God, but for all people who truly follow God. I think he's intrigued by it. I think it almost is something that he just finds amazing and fascinating. He has real respect for people of faith. I've been around enough politicians who would curry favor with the faith community, and they even learn to say the right things. But it was so obvious that it was phony. But with Trump, even in the private moments when no religious people were around, he never said derogatory things. Or frankly, he never said the kind of things that faith people say about each other." Michael Cohen, Trump's longtime friend and lawyer, echoes Huckabee's views on Christian duplicity. "Trump is not the guy you're going to see kneeling in the pew, but he prays in his head and his heart on a regular basis. I'd rather be around someone who has religion in their head and heart than someone who just goes through the motions for optics."

The meeting in the ballroom took eight hours, with speeches and prayers by evangelical luminaries like George Barna, Franklin Graham, and Eric Metaxas surrounding the two hours of "conversation" with Trump himself. But Trump also met with smaller groups of leaders, including a meeting of about forty that took place in the early-morning hours.

Jerry Falwell introduced Trump as "God's man to lead our great nation at this crucial crossroads in our history." Franklin Graham prayed and then James Dobson began a time of frank questioning of the candidate: "Sir, if you are elected president, how will you protect our religious liberties? Will we have to fight another revolutionary war to secure those rights to worship, think, and speak?" Moore noted that the theme of religious liberty surfaced throughout the entire day.

Another participant in the early-morning meeting was Samuel Rodriguez, the president of the National Hispanic Christian Leadership Conference—"the world's largest Hispanic Christian organization." Rodriguez had been no fan of Trump's during the primaries and he had voiced his concerns repeatedly. But he had also been vocal about the charge of "racism" directed at Trump—and, as a result, the campaign had taken notice of him.

Rodriguez appeared on Univision's *Al Punto*—the *60 Minutes* of the Hispanic-American community. The program's host, Jorge Ramos, had famously gotten into verbal brawls with Trump at news conferences—even to the point of Trump having Ramos removed from the room. So when Ramos interviewed Rodriguez on the show, he asked: "Is Donald Trump a racist?" Rodriguez answered, "No."

Later, Heather Sells of CBN repeated the same question to Rodriguez: "Do you believe Donald Trump is a racist?

"No, in my understanding—Donald Trump is not a racist," Rodriguez remembers telling Sells. "Trump engages in rhetoric that is inflammatory and it's not the sort of rhetoric I would use—but I don't think it's racist."

Rodriguez explained to us that he grew up in a part of rural Pennsylvania that was not ethnically diverse, to put it mildly. He said he experienced racism firsthand—eggs thrown and his car scratched with a key—so he doesn't toss the word around without reason. "Before I plant that label on any human being, I want to know that there is way more than just rhetoric," Rodriguez said.

During the primaries there had been attempts to meet with Rodriguez, but it didn't work out. "It wasn't an issue of my not wanting to meet with him," Rodriguez said. "Quite the contrary, I did because I sought clarity on the immigration issues. I resonated with Mr. Trump on ICE, on religious liberty, and on limited government. I also resonated with him on 'peace through strength'—having a robust military."

Rodriguez appeared on *Fox & Friends* before heading over to meet Trump. He explained his agreement with Trump on immigration—though disagreeing with his rhetoric. "I told them I want him to build a wall but he must simultaneously build a bridge toward the Hispanic-American community."

Then, in the smaller meeting with Trump, the group was introducing themselves one at a time, working around the big conference table—Trump seated at the end, just like in *The Apprentice*.

"I began, 'My name is Reverend Samuel Rodriguez. I'm the president of the National Hispanic Christian . . . '—but Trump interrupted me.

" 'Sammy,' he said, 'you were amazing this morning on TV. I saw the entire interview. You were amazing, and I mean truly amazing. You're well-spoken. I need to hear from you. What do you have to say?'

"It became an awkward moment," Rodriguez recalled, "really, awkward. But I just began to share how I agreed with him on immigration, but that he needed to be careful with the rhetoric—and I laid out some preferable terms for him to use."

Rodriguez continued: "Mr. Trump, you can speak to the issue of limited government and multigenerational dependency on Uncle Sam. We're creating a class of citizens dependent on entitlements in perpetuity. But you have an opportunity here to shake things up— not just for the white community with the populist message—but for African-Americans and Latinos too."

Trump heard Rodriguez's entire pitch and affirmed it there in front of the other leaders. "That began the relationship," Rodriguez said. "I met with him again and was continuously emailing the campaign with ideas and concepts and terms and descriptors and so forth."

By the end of the day, Trump had put a lot of evangelical leaders at ease. "He listened," Perkins said. "He did some talking—but he did a lot of listening. And though there was still some skepticism— the feedback from the evangelical world that we got coming out of that meeting was very positive."

One tangible result of the event was the formation of a twenty-five-member Evangelical Executive Advisory Board. Members made clear that their presence on the board did not mean a public endorsement of Trump—and several said they would have accepted a similar invitation from Hillary Clinton. The meeting and the advisory board may not have been an evangelical coronation of Trump, but it was at least a coalescing around Trump. They showed they were willing to stand beside him.

For evangelicals yet skittish about Trump, his next action—choosing a running mate—would need to be stellar.

22

Cleveland Rocks . . . and Prays

It was perfectly appropriate for Cleveland, Ohio, to be the scene of the 2016 Republican National Convention. The city's unofficial anthem is "Cleveland Rocks," written by Ian Hunter, who felt his adopted home was always made fun of and never given the respect it deserved. Sound familiar? Donald Trump, welcome to Cleveland! But three days before the GOP presidential nominee made his way to town, he had some unfinished business to take care of: picking a vice president, a guy by the name of Michael Richard Pence. You may have heard of him.

When I sat down with President Trump in the Oval Office, he relayed an interesting spiritual aspect to the story of when he met Pence in mid-July at the governor's mansion in Indiana to discuss the vice presidency. "When I left, he [Pence] said, 'Let us pray.' And I said, 'That's great.' And he prayed." So what did Trump think when the evangelical Pence laid that line on him? "Well, first of all, I said, 'This is very different,' because you don't see that too much coming out of a New York real estate office," President Trump said. "But I thought it was great and we get along very well." The praying hasn't stopped since. "We do that often," Trump said. "Mike Pence has been my friend; he's been great. He's a spiritual person; so am I. It was a wonderful choice as vice president. Really a wonderful choice. And he's somebody that you can count on."

The importance of Trump's Pence pick can not be emphasized enough. Forget the political ramifications for a moment. Forget even the explosive impact this would have on how evangelicals viewed this president. According to those intimately involved in the vice-presidency deliberations, Trump genuinely wanted a deeply religious man as his number two, thus revealing something about Trump's deeper, inner-core beliefs: faith matters to him.

Meanwhile, evangelicals were doing spiritual cartwheels over the choice. For those who had their doubts about Trump, Mike Pence eased fears among the majority of evangelicals who remained skeptical.

"I think it was a huge development and it was critical to him winning the support of evangelicals," Ralph Reed, chairman of the Faith & Freedom Coalition, said. "It revealed so much about Donald Trump's judgment, his decision-making process, and his own priorities. He was choosing his partner in governance, and he picked the one person that would have been near the top or at the top of every single vice presidential list in the pro-family community."

Sammy Rodriguez, one of the most influential evangelical leaders in the country, puts it succinctly. "Mike Pence is like the quintessential antacid sort of pill that you take that calms everything down . . . he's a blessing indeed!" With Pence now in the fold, it was off to Cleveland, where evangelicals were setting the spiritual mood with a new form of expression for the city: "Cleveland Prays."

Two days before the week's political festivities got under way, thousands of Christians gathered at Cleveland State University to pray and worship at an event called The Response. Donald Trump wasn't the focus: Jesus was. Specifically, the mega-gathering was a call for spiritual revival in our country, asking God for mercy on an America that they believe has lost its way spiritually and biblically. Worship bands blared "Sound the alarm!" while those on stage asked God for "healing in this nation and in this state [of Ohio] by the powerful name of Jesus Christ." Truth be told, evangelicals fully understand that Donald Trump will not heal America. Trump is just a vessel. God does the real healing.

The country was in desperate need of healing in the summer of 2016. In the weeks leading up to the convention, racial tensions were extremely high. Shootings of African-American men in Louisiana and Minnesota by police, coupled with the murders of five cops in Dallas by a gunman on the hunt for white people, had everyone a bit on edge. Convention organizers feared for the worst, especially with a nominee who had come under great criticism by his detractors for stoking racial flames throughout the presidential campaign.

What's ironic, however, is that despite the brewing of racial anxiety in the country that week, Darrell Scott, an African-American pastor from Cleveland and early Trump supporter, was busy preparing for his prime-time address to convention delegates. As the mainstream media continued their lazy story line about how Trump harbored racist feelings, it turns out that it was the white Donald Trump who requested that the black pastor speak in prime time. They had been close friends since 2011, when Michael Cohen, Trump's Jewish lawyer, introduced them. Cohen and Scott went on to be the closest of friends. "That's one of my very, very best friends. I love that guy," Scott said. So there you have it: A charismatic black preacher, a white Presbyterian businessman, and a Jewish lawyer (sounds like the beginning of a joke) all coming together to "Make America Great Again." The mainstream media conveniently ignored that scenario. Didn't fit their narrative. Too much racial harmony.

On the Sunday before convention week, Scott was working up the congregants from the pulpit at the sprawling New Spirit Revival Center, a twenty-minute drive from Quicken Loans Arena, where Donald Trump would soon deliver his personal "sermon on the mount" to delegates. But for now, Scott was in full "fire and brimstone" mode as he preached from the Book of Romans and Second Corinthians about the need to pay more attention to your inner spiritual life than what people see on the outside. With an organ rhythmically accentuating each of his passionate biblical pleas, he called for the binding of "the devil in every way, form, and fashion." He was working up a sweat in his snazzy dark gray suit and finely pressed white shirt. He sure had come a long way.

Growing up on the streets of Cleveland in the late seventies and early eighties, Darrell Scott wasn't selling Christ. He was selling drugs, lots of them. But in 1982, his life turned around after he and his wife, Belinda, became born-again Christians. A redeemed life led both of them into full-time ministry and with hearts to help those lost to drugs and abuse. Their lives were humming along, and then in 2011, they received an invitation from Pastor Paula White to meet with Donald Trump in New York. He was considering running for president and "The Donald" wanted to get a bunch of clergy together to seek their advice. Isn't it interesting how God works: a former drug dealer from the streets of Cleveland called on to give godly counsel to a future president of the United States. "Nobody but God could have done something like that," Scott said.

One thing about Darrell Scott, he's a straight shooter, just like Trump, and so the pastor from Cleveland didn't mince words when he first met Trump at that meeting in 2011. "Why do you think black people will vote for you, because word on the street is you're a racist," Scott remembers telling Trump. "He [Trump] looked at me in my eyes and said, 'You know, I'm about the least racist person you ever want to meet. I work with all kinds of people in my walk of life. I can't be racist doing what I do.' " Scott liked Trump's forthrightness.

When I talked to Scott's wife, Belinda, in Cleveland the day before the convention began, she told me that she liked something else Trump said at that first meeting with the clergy. "He said, 'You all have been pursuing your higher calling, your relationship with God, while I was building buildings.' He said, 'Now it's time for me to catch up.' That was real deep. Being pastors and being Christians, we're very discerning of spirits, and we discerned that he was being very authentic and very genuine." Darrell Scott saw a humbler side. "In the company of the preachers, he adopted the position of the lesser, and he actually acknowledged the preachers in the room as the greater. . . . He has an old-fashioned respect for clergy. You don't see that anymore. He's got that 1950s respect for clergy."

But what about his walk with the Lord? Trump talked plenty in that meeting about how the religious liberty of Christians is severely threatened. But what about that relationship with Jesus? How was that going? "He really is pursuing a deeper spiritual life. I can sense it," Belinda Scott said. "My prayer for Mr. Trump is that he will be more sensitive to God than he ever has before . . . something is going on." As you get older, many times that happens. You become a whole lot more introspective. "He's the first one to admit, 'I'm flawed. I'm not perfect. I need to do better. I need to be better,' " Darrell Scott admits. "But he [Trump] believes in the afterlife. He believes in Heaven and Hell. He wants to go to Heaven."

Trump also wanted to get to 1600 Pennsylvania Avenue, and it was pastors like Darrell Scott who helped get him there. Trump values loyalty and Scott never wavered. He was given eight minutes for his prime-time convention speech, and he didn't disappoint. He whipped the crowd into a frenzy, channeling his inner "New Spirit Revival Center preaching style" and declaring in a rising voice, "I can think of no stronger leader who will place their left hand on a Bible that they believe in, raise their right hand and solemnly swear to faithfully execute the office of president of the United States, and to the best of his ability, preserve, protect, and defend the Constitution of the United States of America than Donald J. Trump." Exit stage left. Scott rocked Cleveland.

While Pastor Darrell Scott helped give Trump political cover among African-Americans, mega-pastor Paula White came to Cleveland with one goal in mind: to prayerfully cover Donald

Trump. She's known him since the early 2000s and has essentially morphed into one of his closest spiritual mentors. She doesn't want a single thing from Trump. She's there to offer spiritual guidance and to bring others alongside of him to shower him with prayer and advice from godly men and women. That includes not just Trump but members of his family as well. She remembers one night in Cleveland during the convention when she was in a car with Trump's son Eric and his wife, Lara. Eric asked her for prayer. "We were praying over a few personal things," White told me that week in Cleveland.

Her prayers in Cleveland weren't just for Trump and his family; they were for a nation. Trump asked her to give the benediction prayer at the end of the convention's first night. It's the first time a woman has ever done that prayer at the Republican National Convention. She was truly humbled and a bit nervous. "My heart was racing," White said. "I yielded myself to the spirit of God." And with that, her prayer, shown in part below, went forth in full biblical preaching style:

> *Help us to pray like we mean it and help us to pray like it*
> *matters.*
> *Protect us from all of those who aim to destroy us and make*
> *America safe again.*
> *Give us eyes to see a brighter future for America.*
> *We believe in faith that*
> *It's time for darkness to be dispelled.*
> *It's time for this nation to live out its holy calling in the*
> *[world].*
> *It is time for us to bridge the divide and become one again.*
> *We believe in faith that*
> *It's time for us to become the light that this world so*
> *desperately needs.*

It is time for this nation to uphold truth, proudly and boldly.

We choose by faith

To stand for the way of our God.

To walk in love

To seek peace for the generations to come.

We choose by faith

To raise up a standard against the forces of evil.

To have a heart for your presence

To have a thirst for your righteousness.

Dear God

We confess that we need you as never before.

*We need your guidance. We need your blessing. We need
    your help. We need your anointing.*

*We remember the many troubled waters that you have
    brought us through by Your grace and mercy.*

*We remember Red Seas that have been parted, and the
    mouths of lions that have been pacified.*

We remember the miracles of those times . . . and in our time

We remember the miracle of America.

*In it all we find our hope that we can be great and we can be
    good as we stand in Your righteousness.*

Lord—as we leave—lead us

*so that future generations in this land know of your
    goodness.*

May you bless us, and keep us.

Make your face to shine upon us.

May you show us your favor and give us your peace.

*In the name of Jesus Christ who gives us hope through his
    empty tomb,*

*and whose life has brought us new life and all the hope in the
    world.*

Amen, Amen and Amen and Amen.

Watching Paula White deliver her prayer that evening was a reminder of how God loves to use flawed people for His glory. Before God got ahold of her, White had her share of huge abusive obstacles to overcome. Yet God is using her in ways that she could never imagine. But that's how God operates. Abraham was old, Joseph was abused, Moses had a speech impediment, Samson was a womanizer, and don't even get me started on King David! As for Donald Trump, clearly, God is using this man in ways millions of people could never imagine. But God knows and that's good enough.

While prayer was in full force during the convention in Cleveland, another "P" word was also taking place: preparation. The Republican Party's policy platform takes shape every four years, and the presidential nominee and his staff lead the way in signing off on the final version. What would Donald Trump do? Evangelicals were watching to make sure he didn't stray away from socially conservative principles. It turns out, the platform was widely viewed as the most conservative of all time. It contained strong pro-life language, opposed same-sex marriage and transgender bathroom choice. It also reaffirmed the role of traditional parenting.

Tony Perkins, president of the Family Research Council and someone actively involved in making sure the Republican Party platform stayed true to the pro-family agenda, was pleasantly surprised. "We faced no opposition from the Trump team. In fact, they worked very closely with us on a number of issues." Perkins rejoiced, considering that in years past, the Bush, McCain, and Romney teams opposed them on certain items. "Trump didn't distance himself from it, . . . I think that communicated volumes to evangelicals because this was the most pro-life platform the party has ever produced. It was solidly pro-family, pro–traditional marriage, pro–religious liberty. I think that was critical for him."

• • •

With the party platform nicely sewn up, Perkins was ready to endorse Trump right there in Cleveland. It was an important endorsement considering Perkins went for Cruz in the primaries. It indicated evangelical solidarity heading into the general election. "Going into the convention and based upon what happened with the platform, I was determined to move forward and again they worked with us, so that's why at the convention at the request of [Trump campaign manager] Paul Manafort, I spoke at the convention and endorsed Trump. We didn't look back after that point."

All that was left now was the cherry on top: Donald Trump's speech to convention delegates. It would come amid controversy, with some delegates protesting Trump as the nominee. Ted Cruz took to the convention floor and refused to endorse Trump, leading to a cascade of boos. It all made for great television, but in the end, it didn't matter.

In Trump, evangelicals had a candidate that channeled many of their same desires. Tired of political correctness, they wanted to see a stronger, more patriotic America again; they wanted to see the return of "Originalist" Supreme Court justices and to see a president who will not be ashamed of defending their religious liberties in the public square. The good news for evangelicals is that in Trump they had someone who is loyal. He understood that without them, he wouldn't be in Cleveland. And so Trump made sure to give them a full-throttle acknowledgment in his speech:

> I would like to thank the evangelical community who have been so good to me and so supportive. You have so much to contribute to our politics, yet our laws prevent you from speaking your minds from your own pulpits. An amendment, pushed by Lyndon Johnson, many years ago, threat-

ens religious institutions with a loss of their tax-exempt status if they openly advocate their political views. I am going to work very hard to repeal that language and protect free speech for all Americans.

While Donald Trump's convention speech would go down as a passionate (his critics would say "mean") law-and-order manifesto, for evangelicals it was a speech that just made sense: enforce the laws of the land, work hard, do what you say, etc. But beyond that, it was a speech that told the world that both America and this future president would need to be taken seriously.

With Cleveland in their rearview mirror, Trump and his newly minted evangelical running mate Pence hit the road for a week of campaigning together. The night before they were to go their separate ways, the vice presidential candidate received, at least at the time, an unusual request from the man at the top of the ticket. "He said to me, 'Before you and Karen take off tomorrow, before we split up, would you mind us having a little prayer time together?' I said, 'Sure, that'd be great.' He knew the importance of faith in our family's life." After a short night's rest, morning came and Donald Trump was eager to start his day right. "He came out of the back of the plane and just said, 'Can we pray?' " Pence said. "I said, 'Yeah, that'd be great. You know the best prayer in our household is my wife.' He said, 'Great, let's go.' We just bowed our heads and my wife held forth a prayer on the plane, and it was a very special moment. I could tell he was touched by it, and said thanks and appreciated it very much."

23

Pastors and Pews

Omar Mateen called Orlando's 911 to state his allegiance to ISIS before walking into a local gay nightclub with murderous intent. Before dawn broke, fifty-three people were injured and forty-nine were dead—the highest number of fatalities in a single mass shooting in US history (until the Las Vegas shooting in October 2017).

Immediately after such an event, the blame game begins: radical Islam, Christian homophobia, and, of course, guns.

CNN's Anderson Cooper and the *New York Times* argued that people who are against same-sex marriage and transgendered bathrooms have little moral ground to express outrage at the Orlando massacre. Meanwhile, Trump tweeted: "Appreciate the congrats for being right on radical Islamic terrorism. I don't want congrats, I want toughness & vigilance. We must be smart!"

Two months later, Trump came to Orlando to speak at a "Pastors and Pews" event organized by the American Renewal Project and its founder, David Lane. Though Trump's campaign had only confirmed his attendance one week earlier, Marco Rubio—fresh from the realization that he did want to get reelected to the Senate—had been publicized as a keynote speaker for the event. LGBT activists labeled the American Renewal Project speakers "some of the most hateful anti-LGBT persons" and said they were "dedicated to oppressing LGBT people." They called for Rubio to cancel his appearance: "This is not the America we want. God will not be found anywhere near that event."

Rubio stood his ground, offering a counter-description of the

ARP—the group that had helped him surge in the Iowa polls when he spoke to pastors at one of these events. "Leave it to the media and liberal activists to label a gathering of faith leaders as an anti-LGBT event. It is nothing of the sort. It is a celebration of faith."

Huckabee introduced Trump to the seven hundred, mostly clergy (and their spouses), in the audience. Teleprompters had been set up for the speech, but Trump had them taken away, and he spoke instead from some notes on sheets of paper that he pulled from his vest pocket. He said that though some professional had written a speech for him, he didn't want to put them to sleep and instead would just talk about an issue he knew would hit their buttons: religious liberty and the Johnson Amendment.

On the way to the event, Huckabee had a chance to read the original speech. "I told him, 'There's no way you can give that speech,' " Huckabee explained later. Whoever wrote it had no clue how to speak to evangelicals—no direct understanding of their concerns. Trump spoke almost entirely about the Johnson Amendment, noting at the end that "I've explained it in more detail than I ever have."

Trump doesn't just bring this subject up in public. Privately, he ruminates about it with his evangelical advisory council. One time it led to an interesting spiritual-based discussion, according to Johnnie Moore, who sits on the council. "We all knew he was saying it in jest, but what he said was, 'I figure that repealing the Johnson Amendment is my best bet to get to heaven.' We all laughed, and we knew he was joking, but I remember at that moment James Robison chiming in right there."

Robison continues the story from there. "I just spoke up quite boldly. I said, 'Sir, this is James. I just need to correct something. There's nobody going to get to heaven because they did something. You can get rid of the Johnson Amendment, but it's not going to get you to heaven. Only one thing gets anybody to heaven, and that's what Jesus did on the cross. There's simply no other way to heaven. That's the only way.' And he kind of indicated, 'Well I was just kind of joking.' "

Richard Land closes out the story: "Mr. Trump said, 'Thank you for reminding me, James.' Now I got to tell you, I don't know too many people who have been nominated for president of the United States that would have that reaction to that statement. George W. Bush would have, and Reagan would have but I'm not sure any of the others might not have gotten their back up a little bit, but he didn't."

Back at Pastors and Pews, David Lane told Bloomberg News that rescinding the Johnson Amendment is a "good first step," but religious liberty involves so much more. He referred to the photographers, bakers, and florists who had, in recent years, lost either their religious liberties or their business—or both—over same-sex marriage issues. "Doesn't the First Amendment give us all a right to our beliefs?"

Lane said the response to Trump had been good, especially since he "didn't make himself out to be something that he wasn't." There was no "He has the voice of Jacob but the hands of Esau" feeling among the pastors.

Events like this one would be crucial to Trump if he wanted to beat Hillary Clinton. The reality is that evangelical pastors are a truly key ingredient to mobilizing the masses. They hold great power over a captive audience every week in the pews. Trump needed them to be engaged. When they are, the flocks will typically flow—a bottom-up approach that affects turnout exponentially. The top-down approach of receiving key endorsements doesn't do squat unless the evangelicals sitting in the pews are motivated.

Lane received an email from Paul Manafort, Trump's campaign manager, to say he was looking forward to being in Orlando the next day.

"Let's you and I talk," Manafort wrote. "I want to get your take on the campaign."

Lane had never met Manafort, but responded by suggesting they meet up in New York the next week.

"So, on Tuesday morning—the sixteenth—I was in my hotel room getting ready for the meeting, but I was running late," Lane said. "My phone rang, and it was a friend, a farmer—a chicken farmer."

"How are you doing on the $18 million?" he asked.

About eight months earlier, Lane had put together a proposal that called for a massive mobilization campaign in a dozen key battleground states—hence, the need for the $18 million.

"I haven't raised a dime," Lane said.

"You haven't raised a dime?" the chicken farmer asked.

"Nope."

"Where are you now?"

"In New York."

"What are you doing there?"

"I'm going to see Paul Manafort," Lane said.

"What's going to happen?"

"Probably, he will narrow down my plan to five or six states."

Lane was trying to get his tie on and lace up his shoes, to get out the door for his meeting—which, by now, he was going to be late for. As the two were about to hang up, the chicken farmer said: "Well, I'm in for $5 million."

Lane just smiled and thought, "You've got to be kidding." He hadn't raised a dime since coming up with the plan, and now he had a commitment of $5 million.

Lane went to his meeting and, as expected, Manafort picked apart the Pastors and Pews plan for the first half of the hour-long meeting—then asked, "How much do you need per state?"

"One point five million," Lane answered.

Manafort chose six states he wanted to hit: Florida, Ohio, Pennsylvania, North Carolina, Missouri, and Virginia.

"You know, money is hard to come by—there's no money," Manafort said.

Lane had not yet told him about the $5 million. He went through the money shuffle with Manafort for the next fifteen minutes—right up to the end of the meeting—and then said: "I'll tell you what I'm going to do. I've got five million if you can bring four."

"You've got five million?" Manafort asked.

"I do."

Manafort said, "Give me two days."

Lane went back to his room and loosened his tie. His phone rang. It was the chicken farmer: "What happened?"

Lane related the meeting to the man, including how Manafort said he'd be back in two days with a response.

"So do you think he's going to do that?" he asked Lane.

"In fundraising, you never know," Lane said, "but with your five, we'll go into Florida, Missouri, and North Carolina. If Manafort brings the money, we'll add Ohio, Pennsylvania, and Virginia."

"No, let's not do that," the farmer replied. "This is already the third week of August. You've just got September and October to go."

"What are you saying?" Lane asked.

"I'm good for $9 million. Make it happen."

Later that afternoon, Kellyanne Conway texted Lane: "We're so excited." He thought it was strange, because he didn't know Conway that well. The next morning, however, the Trump campaign announced that Paul Manafort had resigned and that Conway would become the campaign manager—so the text suddenly made more sense.

Lane ran his plan entirely with the $9 million from a chicken farmer, the unsung hero of everyone whose worst nightmare was a Hillary Clinton presidency.

• • •

Lane describes the sudden investment of $9 million as "a miracle of God"—and a timely one too. Wayne Hamilton, Lane's friend and a partner at a huge political consultancy firm in Texas, had used $100,000 to train "field generals" over the past sixty days in preparation for a ground assault of voter mobilization. But then their money fell through—something that happens in politics and campaigns. They were sickened because they were letting all that $100,000 worth of training go back home unused.

But, as Lane puts it, "the Lord took the engine—the $9 million—and hooked it to that train sitting on the tracks."

The very next Monday the operation began in those six states, and within sixty days, they had knocked on a million doors and had made a million phone calls. "We targeted low-propensity evangel-ical voters who had only voted once in the last four cycles," Lane said. "And one of the genius ideas, coming from Dave Carney, was to hire seventy bi-vocational pastors to help organize and orches-trate those calls and door knocks."

On November 8, Pennsylvania voted Republican for the first time since Bush—George H. W. Bush that is. Florida and Virginia voted Republican for the first time since 2004. Missouri overwhelmingly voted for Trump, and in so doing also helped to usher in a GOP governor and senator by small margins.

In five out of six of the states where Lane poured resources into mobilizing the faith community to vote—making no mention of any particular candidate—Trump won. And in several of the states, the margin of Trump's win was less than the total number of contacts that Lane's group had made in that state.

This effort sprung from Lane's message to Christians: "Unless politicians see scalps on the wall, they will never respect our poli-cies, marches, sermons or prayer rallies. Registering people to vote prepares the constituency to move to the voting booth, and remove politicians who have a tin ear to Christian values and no appreciation for God-given rights."

For Lane, it's all about the ground game of getting out the vote—a point he made following the Orlando event. "Trump cannot make the same mistake that Romney did in 2012: talking to evangelical national heads through conference calls and national meetings, thinking that will trickle down to evangelical and pro-life Catholic Christians. Those types of calls are necessary, but they don't produce a ground game."

In his article "How White Evangelicals Won the 2016 Election," author and presidential historian Doug Wead concluded that one man, though a mysterious figure due to lack of self-promotion, had been an outsized influence on the 2016 election: David Lane.

> He did not start out supporting Donald Trump. In fact, he didn't start out supporting anybody. He focused on organizing Evangelicals to be participants in the process, regardless of who won the nomination. He arranged for any candidate to meet and interact with Evangelical Christians. In the process, over a seventeen-year period, he built an effective ground game of pastors and activists. And Lane achieved something more. He united the Evangelical leaders in a way that their competing trade organizations and rival denominations could not. Lane just kept coming at them, letting petty jealousies and competition roll off him like water off a duck's back. He became the Movement's common denomination.

Wead is right about Lane's significance in mobilizing pastors and those in the pews. But there's a second unsung character in this story—a friend of Lane's who went to work for the RNC in a position created, literally, for this man and his vision: Chad Connelly.

In 2012, Connelly was the state chairman of the South Carolina Republican Party. After the fall election, he sat down with Reince Priebus—at that time the CEO of the RNC and the future chief of staff for the White House—and told him "we've been blowing this."

"We had maximized the faith vote in '04 with Bush," Connelly told Priebus. "Then in 2008, McCain's people ignored the faith vote—so we grew the numbers backward from four or five million. When Romney's people ignored the faith vote too, the numbers grew backward again. So, I told Reince that we're ignoring the base—ignoring the faith community."

Now it might seem counterintuitive to argue that the GOP doesn't reach out enough to faith communities. But remember, in national elections the margin between winning and losing is so small that even a little more effort spent in outreach to a specific group can change the result of an entire election.

Connelly says he wasn't looking for a job. He just wanted Priebus and the RNC to do better by sending out people who knew how to talk to faith voters. By the time he finished explaining the mindset of pastors (as he had once been), Priebus created a position—national director of faith engagement—and told Connelly to get to work.

And that's exactly what he did, starting with pro-life groups and pastors he knew. He had been a public speaker already, so he had the beginnings of relationships with pastors and churches. He reached out to them, got them on board, and then asked them for names of friends they could reach out to together.

"The biggest group I spoke to was twenty-five hundred folks," Connelly said, "but really it was mostly one-on-one coffees and talking to two or three people in a pastor's study or a conference room in a hotel. I'd just speak about the importance of doing voter registration and educating their flock about the issues. I did hundreds of coffees and luncheons and small meetings with less than five people."

We asked him to estimate how many pastors he had talked to since taking the position.

"Pastors specifically? Over eighty thousand in the last four years."

Then Connelly added, without a hint of swagger: "I believe what the Lord's letting me do is to have some of the best relationships across denominational and ethnic lines—better than anybody has ever done in reaching out to the faith voters of the conservative base. We built these relationships across all the most theological conservative denominations—not just the groups from my own faith tribe."

Connelly said his mandate didn't involve telling people to vote for the GOP. Instead, his message to pastors was simple: Get your people registered and challenge them to vote biblical values.

"See I knew that historically speaking, 78 percent of the evangelical vote goes for a conservative," Connelly said. "So you don't have to beat their head about it. Just make sure they vote."

And what was Connelly's goal right from the start in July 2013?

"We had never hit 80 percent. Evangelicals in a presidential election had never given a presidential candidate 80 percent of their vote," Connelly explained. "I wrote a memo to Reince when I came on board. I wrote that if we ever hit 80 percent, then the liberals wouldn't be able to win."

If you earned 80 percent of the evangelical vote in a national election, Connelly was convinced that you would win the office.

Eighty percent. That's what Connelly recommended to Priebus—in 2013. And then, they went to work and hit that number.

24

What the Hell Do
You Have to Lose?

Tony Perkins stood next to Donald Trump many times during the campaign, but the one time that probably had the greatest impact was an event that Perkins would have avoided if he could have. He lost his home to the Louisiana floods of August 2016.

On Saturday, the thirteenth, flood waters engulfed Perkins's house—along with about sixty thousand other homes in his parish. He and his family were making their escape from the waters when his phone rang. It was Paul Manafort.

Perkins talked for a minute but then said: "Paul, I'm going to have to get back with you. Our house is flooding, and we are escaping in a canoe."

Over the next four days, the whole world turned upside down for Perkins, his family, the members of the large church he served as interim pastor, and his extended community. Everyone in the area was affected. Unfortunately, outside of Louisiana, it seemed that nobody had taken notice of their plight.

"Four days into it, there was still no media attention," Perkins said. "I had called Franklin Graham, and he and Samaritans Purse came on site at our church to do some relief work. No real government assistance. No President Obama. No Hillary Clinton."

On the following Wednesday, Perkins called Trump and the campaign—first speaking to Manafort, then suddenly to Conway and Bannon instead—to say, "We could use your help—just by bringing attention to this situation. And, quite frankly, this would be a great opportunity to show that you can be more presidential than our President."

Perkins got word Thursday afternoon that they were coming, and Friday morning they arrived—Trump and Pence too.

Given the nature of a presidential campaign, news media were there for parts of the interaction. But then, Franklin, Perkins, Pence, and Trump got into a vehicle and went out to survey the neighborhoods—without the cameras.

"Trump was visibly taken aback by how significant the devastation and destruction was," Perkins said. "I could see it was genuine. He told the Secret Service to stop the cars, and he got out and went up and met residents in the neighborhoods. He was so warm and genuine in his concern." Jimmy and Olive Morgan experienced that side of Trump firsthand. When he met them, the couple, in their seventies, were at their lowest point: The home they had lived in for decades was destroyed and they were just sitting in their front yard looking numb. Trump approached Jimmy. Mike Pence recalls it vividly. "The [now] President is talking to him and says, 'What are you going to do? You're going to rebuild?' The guy says, 'Well, we're both getting up there and I don't know if we got it in us.' The President reaches over, grabs him on the shoulder and says, 'You're going to rebuild. I know you're that kind of guy. You're going to rebuild.'" Jimmy got emotional. "Here in this critical moment, a moment of crisis, what proceeds out of him is compassion and encouragement," Pence said. An important footnote to the story: Pence would return to see Jimmy and Olive nine months later. They had rebuilt. Perkins notes that Trump is the opposite of most politicians or celebrity types in that his compassionate and caring side comes out the most when he is out of the public's eye.

Perkins himself was actually the recipient of some of Trump's behind-the-scenes compassion. After spending time with Trump,

Pence, and Franklin Graham throughout the day, something happened during that car ride with the foursome. Trump, feeling moved by what he saw in Louisiana and seeing how Graham's ministry was coming to the rescue, looked over at Franklin and told him he wanted to give his organization a hefty six-figure check. When he asked where he should send it, Graham didn't miss a beat, telling him to send it to Perkins's church, which had been through so much and helped residents in such a significant way. This is vintage Trump. He may love the cameras when it comes to branding and publicity for his projects, but when the cameras aren't rolling what you see are acts of kindness like this that he has no desire to let anyone know about.

Trump has a history of unseen kindness. Back in 2010, Trump saw a *60 Minutes* report about how the Maytag plant in Newton, Iowa, was shutting down, affecting the small business community. Owner David McNeer, who was featured, received a call out of the blue from the billionaire mogul offering to help. McNeer eventually began working with Trump's hotels and later manufacturing Trump campaign merchandise. Michael Cohen, his longtime lawyer, was there when this happened. "The first thing he thought of was the Judeo-Christian principle of help and charity," Cohen said. "Many people don't know about stories like this because when one gives to charity, the right thing to do is to keep it private. Unfortunately, because he's Donald Trump, nothing in his life remains private."

As for the flooding in Louisiana, conservative author and Louisiana native Rod Dreher—who by that time in the campaign had already committed himself to a #NeverTrump position—wrote an article blasting the lack of national response to the flooding.

> But: Trump got to Louisiana before Obama or Clinton. And in so doing, he struck a chord resonating profoundly with the emotional and political climate of the moment. The

president is coming down on Tuesday, but he's missed his moment. Trump got here first. When Obama arrives, the thing a lot of people will be thinking is, "You're the President of the United States. What took you so long? How come you let Trump beat you here?" As for Hillary, forget about it.

One of Perkins's staff wrote an FRC blog post that week that, in hindsight, seems very prophetic: "If Donald Trump wins this election, I think historians will point to a critical visit to flood-ravaged Louisiana as its turning point."

Jeff Nolan, a well-sunned Louisianan in his fifties with a white beard—a self-described "Trump supporter"—stood in front of a Samaritans Purse emergency food trailer parked in front of Perkins's church. Nolan wore a red polo shirt that Trump had signed the back of when he stopped by earlier. A reporter covering the flood for the local ABC affiliate asked Nolan, "What did you lose?"

"Um . . . let's see . . ." he said, as he began to get choked up. "I didn't lose anything . . ."—now, the tears were welling up in his eyes—"compared to . . . what a lot of people lost . . . I'm ok . . . it's materialistic things—and they can be replaced" he said, voice cracking.

The reporter asked, "Having Trump here, did that mean a lot to you?"

Nolan regained the strength of his southern voice quickly: "Oh yes, yes! . . . Hell, America's gotta wake up. Donald Trump is the way to wake us up—He's waking America up—He's gotta get busy. And America has gotta get behind him. Without America getting behind Donald Trump, we're going to lose—and we're going to lose bigger than this flood ever did."

The next night Trump stood before a crowd in Dimondale, Michigan—a suburb of Detroit, but close enough to the financially distraught Motor City to warrant his bringing out what would become his ongoing theme to the African-American community: the Democratic Party has screwed you.

> Tonight, I'm asking for the vote of every single African-American citizen in this country who wants to see a better future. . . . Look how much African-American communities have suffered under Democratic control. To those, I say the following: What do you have to lose by trying something new—like Trump?

The crowd cheered, blew air horns, and started chanting: "Trump! Trump! Trump!" Buoyed by their enthusiasm for those lines, Trump continued, moving off the teleprompter's script for the next minute or so:

> I say it again. What do you have to lose? Look, what do you have to lose? What do you have to lose? You're living in poverty. Your schools are no good. You have no jobs. Fifty-eight percent of your youth is unemployed—What the hell do you have to lose?

Trump came back to Detroit for a closed-door meeting with a large group of African-American pastors, led by Bishop Wayne Jackson of Great Faith Ministries International and the president of the Impact Network on television. Bishop Jackson, a lifelong Democrat, had invited both Trump and Hillary Clinton to speak to his congregation. Clinton declined. Trump jumped at the opportunity. He arrived amidst plenty of protestors outside and media inside. Then, something remarkable happened. "When he got out of the SUV, the Spirit of the Lord told me that that's the next president of the United States," Jackson said. "The Lord said, 'That's the next president.' "

After the Saturday-morning interview with Jackson, a mini-problem ensued. Trump was ready to give a speech to members of the church, but Jackson was told before the visit that he wouldn't be delivering a speech and so he told the assembled media there would be no speech. He didn't think it would be right to change it now. Trump's handlers pleaded strongly with Bishop Jackson to let him speak, but to no avail. Then Trump spoke up. "He took his speech, his famous one-page piece of paper he had when he wanted to talk," Jackson said. "He folded it up and put it in his pocket and he said, 'Whatever the Bishop says, that's what we're going to do.' No resistance. He went on his way right into the fellowship hall to meet the people. As he was going out the door, the Holy Spirit said, 'Let him speak.' I said, 'Uh, Mr. Trump, what is the speech about?' He said, 'It's a very good speech that I wrote and I would like to say it to the African-American community.' I said, 'Okay, you can do it, but it can't be political.' He said, 'No, it's not.' "

First, however, Trump took part in the worship service. In the video of the event, Trump can be seen swaying along with the congregation—and there was a genuine look of gladness on his face. Later, he described the worship as an "amazing experience."

When Trump came to the podium, he delivered prepared remarks—not at all his normal stump speech. In a slow, methodical cadence, he made a statement of spiritual solidarity with African-Americans—and more specifically, the black churches of America:

For centuries, the African-American church has been the conscience of our country. So true. It's from the pews and pulpits and Christian teachings of black churches all across this land that the Civil Rights movement lifted up its soul and lifted up the soul of our nation. It's from these pews that our nation has been inspired toward a better moral character, a deeper concern for mankind, and spirit of charity and unity that binds us all together.

The African-American faith community has been one of God's greatest gifts to America and to its people. There is perhaps no action our leaders can take that would do more to heal our country and support our people than to provide a greater platform to the black churches and churchgoers. You do right every day by your community and your families. You raise children in the light of God; I will always support your church, always. And defend your right to worship . . . so important.

I am here today to listen to your message, and I hope that my presence here will also help your voice to reach new audiences in our country and many of these audiences desperately need your spirit and your thought. I can tell you that.

Christian faith is not the past but the present and the future. Make it stronger. . . .

We're one nation, and when anyone hurts, we all hurt together. That is so true. So true.

We're all brothers and sisters and we're all created by the same God. We must love each other and support each other and we are in this all together. All together.

I fully understand that the African-American community has suffered from discrimination and that there are many wrongs that must still be made right and they will be right. I want America prosperous for everyone. . . .

Now, in these hard times for our country, let us turn again to our Christian heritage to lift up the soul of our nation. I am so deeply grateful to be here today and it is my prayer that the America of tomorrow—and I mean that—that the America of tomorrow will be one of unity, togetherness, and peace. And perhaps we can add the word prosperity. OK? Prosperity.

I'd like to conclude with a passage from 1 John, Chapter 4. You know it? See, most groups I speak to don't know that. But we know it. If you want, we can say it together: "No one has ever seen God, but if we love one another, God lives in us and His love is made complete in us." And that is so true.

After Trump finished, Bishop Jackson came to him on the platform. "The Lord said, 'I want you to give this Elijah prayer shawl to him and I want you to prophesy over him and give him this Jewish Study Bible. The Lord says that the next president will be a very strong supporter of the nation, Israel. . . .' I was telling him about what the tassels mean, about the meaning of the tassels was that they would not stray away from God and serve other Gods and remember God and so forth and so on. I said, 'When you put it on, remember that we have prayed over this Tallit and there are going to be some hard days, some days that are going to feel like you're alone.' I went on to say all of that and then he said, 'Well, would you please put it on me now?' "

Bishop Jackson received an immense amount of criticism from within the black community for having Trump at the church. He was accused of being paid off by the Trump campaign—likening the bishop to Judas selling Jesus for thirty pieces of silver. Jackson denied all the accusations of impropriety. "I love my people," he said. "I feel that we should be better off than what we are. This is not an endorsement. This is engagement, for him to tell us what he wants to do." Jackson said he took the Christian approach. "We're Christians and if candidate Trump or anybody else would come into our church, we are told by Scripture to love them. The Bible says to love your enemy and do good to those who despitefully use you. That's our Christian faith."

"I love his movies. I hope he makes another one real soon," Trump said, pointing to actor Jon Voight, who had just introduced him at the Family Research Council's Values Voter Summit in September. Perhaps he was referring to Voight's portrayal of FDR—a Manhattanite who became the president—in the 2001 movie *Pearl Harbor.* Or maybe it was when Voight played the bad guy versus Tom Cruise in the first installment of the Mission Impossible franchise?

Trump stood to give his speech to this mostly evangelical convention of conservative voters—the same convention that had straw-polled him at fifth place just twelve months earlier. His winning over the evangelicals during the primary had been a "mission impossible" that he made look easy. But now, with just sixty days to the election and with the national polls showing him behind Hillary—anywhere from 5 to 15 points—Trump knew he would need the strongest support and turnout from the evangelicals since they sent Reagan into the White House in 1980 and returned George W. Bush to the Oval Office in 2004.

Trump spoke about the "power of faith" to heal and unite. "It's the power to make all of us live better lives—all of us. Our nation is divided. . . . It will be our faith in God and his teachings, in each other, that will lead us back to unity."

He also spoke about ISIS and the dangers of radical Islam and terrorism, giving a religious-war explanation for what motivated the terrorists:

"ISIS is hunting down and exterminating what it calls the nation of the cross. ISIS is carrying out a genocide against Christians in the Middle East. We cannot let this evil continue. . . . We must also establish a bipartisan goal in the United States and an international goal with our allies of defeating radical Islamic terrorism—words that our President won't use and words that Hillary Clinton won't use. Just like we won the Cold War by identifying our enemy and building a consensus to guide a long-term strategy, so too must we do the same with Islamic terrorism."

A week later, an Islamic man planted explosive devices throughout New York City, and Mayor Bill de Blasio responded by calling them "intentional acts"—but didn't use the word "terrorism" or mention that the man had immersed his mind in radical Islamic teaching on the internet. Conservative columnist Hugh Hewitt said de Blasio "certainly gave Trump a little extra lift with that winner of a phrase late Saturday night. Call a bomb a bomb, please, and terrorists with knives terrorists."

As Trump said to the FRC crowd: "It's a very imperfect world, and you can't always choose your friends. That's life. But you can never fail to recognize your enemies."

Every campaign has unexpected moments—things that happen that you might not have expected or could predict.

Phyllis Schlafly, an intellectual matriarch of Goldwater-Reagan conservatism and an early supporter of the Religious Right (and opponent of the Equal Rights Amendment), impacted the 2016 election in three ways. First, she endorsed Donald Trump early in the primaries. She had officially endorsed Trump in March, though she admired Cruz and hoped that President Trump would make the Texas senator his first appointment to the Supreme Court.

Second, she died two months before the general election. In the middle of September—crunch season for a campaign—Trump traveled to the beautiful Cathedral Basilica of St. Louis to attend the funeral Mass for Schlafly. Trump spoke at the funeral, calling Schlafly a "truly great American patriot" and that "a movement has lost its hero."

Third, the day after her death, Schlafly's final book was released: *The Conservative Case for Trump*, which argued that conservatives and Christians should support Trump. The book became a best seller, just like her first had—*A Choice Not an Echo*. That book, released five decades earlier, went on to sell three million copies and became a manifesto for conservatives who sought to buck the GOP establishment by electing Goldwater in 1965. Sixteen years later, Schlafly's work in defeating the ERA ran parallel to the Religious Right's backing of Ronald Reagan in 1980. So, in a very real sense, when Schlafly attended the 2016 RNC in Cleveland and gave a speech in support of Trump, it connected the nominee to fifty years' worth of anti-establishment, grassroots, Christian, Republican Party politics.

During the 2016 campaign, Trump supporters were often described as crazed, nationalistic, gullible, and bigoted—to name just a few of the pejoratives. Many people kept their support of Trump hidden so as not to receive such scorn from neighbors, co-workers, and family.

Clinton, speaking at a Democratic fund-raiser in New York, let these lines rip: "You know, to just be grossly generalistic, you could put half of Trump's supporters into what I call the basket of deplorables. Right?" Clinton said. "The racist, sexist, homophobic, xenophobic, Islamaphobic—you name it. And unfortunately, there are people like that. And he has lifted them up."

Ironically, many pundits believe Clinton's statement sent a large number of undecided people over to Trump's side. President Obama had derisively labeled them as people who "bitterly cling to their guns and God." On the other hand, Mike Huckabee described them (and himself) as people who like "God, Guns, Grits, and Gravy." Had Clinton taken a cue from her fellow former Arkansan instead of her fellow former Chicagoan, she might have kept from needlessly offending a basketful of American citizens. After all, nothing gets people knocking on doors in support of a candidate like when the opposition insults them.

Situated in Adams County, Pennsylvania, the area is roughly 95 percent white and plenty blue-collar too. What a delectable place for a Trump-Pence message to resonate. It's a conservative area where the theme of "God, Guns and USA" echoes loudly. As Mike Pence delivered a rousing "Make America Great Again" speech, many in the crowd who had been undecided spoke of the Pence pick as being critical in the ability to sway their vote for Trump. In a place with plenty of Catholic and evangelical votes for the taking, bringing Pence here became a logical choice. He grew up Catholic and later converted to evangelical Christianity. In my sit-down interview with him after the rally, Pence echoed a theme that many evangelical leaders had prayed about and seen as well: God directs all things—yes, including Donald Trump becoming president of the United States. "I believe in providence for the course of this nation," Pence told me that fall day in Gettysburg.

The principle of God's providence was something Trump himself was keenly aware of. In January, Pastor Robert Jeffress was along for the ride aboard Trump's luxurious campaign plane. The senior pastor at First Baptist Church in Dallas had been an early and staunch advocate for Trump, and over the course of time they became good friends. With that backdrop, after the two of them finished munching on Wendy's cheeseburgers, the topic turned to things of God. "I said, 'Mr. Trump, I believe you're going to be the next president of the United States,'" Jeffress recalls. "'And if that happens it's because God has a special purpose for you.' " Instead of shrugging off the provocative comment, Trump looked at Jeffress and asked, "Well, tell me something, Pastor, do you believe God put President Obama into office?" Jeffress replied simply and succinctly. "Yes sir, I do. I think every leader who holds a place of authority is there by God's predetermined plan."

25

What Happens in Vegas

During the 2016 election cycle, Samuel Rodriguez, president of the National Hispanic Christian Leadership Conference, often appeared on the major Spanish-language television networks Univision and Telemundo to talk about the candidates and how their policies would impact Hispanics in general—and Christian Latinos in particular. "They all were saying about Trump that he would walk out with single-digits of Latino votes—5 to 7 percent, that's it," Rodriguez recalled. "But I made the prediction that Trump would actually come out with a greater percentage of the Latino electorate than Mitt Romney did. They all laughed, but I told them that they were denying the faith component. I said it came down to this: Do we ignore his rhetoric and vote for religious liberty in the Supreme Court, or do we bow down to his rhetoric and let the Supreme Court go to waste and lose our religious liberty?"

Rodriguez felt that the Latino community is so Christian that the Supreme Court trumps Trump. "My prediction is that you will see a surprise come November."

As part of his outreach to Hispanics, Trump visited a key Latino congregation, the International Church of Las Vegas (ICLV), not once but twice in the month of October. The visits by Trump had their origin in an August meeting with Hispanic business leaders, hosted by the Republican National Committee at the sixty-four-story, golden-window Trump Hotel—the tallest structure in Las Vegas.

Pasqual Urrabazo, the associate pastor of ICLV, attended the meeting. "It was just the RNC people and not Trump," Urrabazo recalled. "There were seventy-five to eighty of us in a room. A young man who works for the Republican Party came up to me, asked to speak with me. He said, 'Donald Trump is here, upstairs. Would you like to meet him or can he meet you?' "

Urrabazo had not been part of the Trump campaign or a supporter, so he wondered what this was all about—and what would come of it. He said to the staffer, "Listen, before I go up there, I need to be honest with you. I'm a Hispanic pastor in the community here, and I don't need him to talk bad about Hispanics and stuff because I won't put up with all that."

The staffer led Urrabazo upstairs discreetly and into a room with a long conference table. There were fifteen or twenty people in the room—all businesspeople. He was the only pastor in the room. They sat Urrabazo right next to the chair that Trump would be sitting in. "Are you sure you want me to sit there—next to Trump?" he asked. The staffer said, "That's where you're called to sit. You need to sit there—we can't move you. That's the way it's been set up."

Trump came in the room and walked around greeting everybody. Then he sat down at the table, turned to Urrabazo, and said, "Glad you're here, Pastor. It's good to have you here with me." The conversation with the group got under way and Trump peppered everyone with questions—and he was answering the questions they were tossing at him. It was lively and productive.

"Then, in the middle of the conversation," Urrabazo said, "Trump stops everybody, turns around, and looks at me and said, 'Pastor, you know I'm a Protestant.' He was grabbing my shoulder and arm as he said it. I replied, 'Yes, sir. That's great.' "

The meeting continued; more conversation and questions. Then, abruptly Trump stopped the meeting again. "Pastor, I'm going to help the church. I'm going to remove the Johnson Amendment, so the church has a voice."

"Oh, that's great, sir," Urrabazo replied. Then the meeting carried on until a lady raised her hand and shouted, "Mr. Trump, the pastor sitting next to you has something to say to you."

Trump said, "What do you want to say to me?"

Urrabazo felt the conversation they were having in the room wasn't getting anywhere. Trump was looking to hear solutions from the Hispanic community leaders and business community, but nobody was offering any.

"So I just gave him solutions," Urrabazo recalled. "I said, 'Mr. Trump, the last time Obama came through and he won Nevada, he beat Romney. He won because he did something that got the Hispanic vote—because he did something that the Republican Party would not do. He came in and rented the Mandalay Bay, did a party there for the young Hispanics and the party lasted like for two or three days. They ate. They had music. The reason why Obama won was because he stopped by. He got to the people's heart. Now biblically, what you call this is 'breaking bread' or 'having fellowship.' Obama came, met the people, broke bread with them, fellowshipped with them—and he won Nevada. Mr. Trump, this is not just a platform. You got to come off the platform and go among the people."

Urrabazo said that Trump called over his executive and said, "I want to do what the pastor is saying." The remainder of the meeting was taken up in talking about dates and schedules and plans for the "breaking of bread" with people in Las Vegas—and Hispanics in particular. And before they departed, Trump told Urrabazo: "I'm going to come to your church."

Senior Pastor Paul Goulet, a naturalized US citizen who hails from Canada, founded ICLV twenty-five years ago. He was a "Ben

Carson guy" originally, even serving as state campaign chairman for the candidate. After Urrabazo met with Trump, Goulet received a call from the campaign to set up a time for Trump to come to the church. Goulet had hosted Carson and knew firsthand how distracting it is for attendees to have to submit to the Secret Service. Goulet countered with a different idea—"Listen, we'd love for him to come see our school. It would highlight the battle we are having in our state for school choice."

So, on October 5, Trump walked in the door and was greeted with "God Bless America" sung by over two hundred students in the foyer. As for Urrabazo, he recalled that when Trump walked in the door of the school, he walked up to the pastor and said, "I told you I was coming. I'm a man of my word. I came to you. I came to visit." And then he added, "But I still want to go to church." Goulet led him into a first-grade classroom, where the students presented Trump with a "Vision Bible." Trump then met the soccer academy students, before sitting down with a group of Latino and African-American leaders from Las Vegas.

"We love to build those bridges," Goulet said, "so we put together a VIP meeting where we asked him questions and let him share his heart. It was really a personal moment. We asked him about his dad's impact on him as a counselor—that kind of thing. My desire was really to kind of see his heart, to see where he was going. And he really started winning me over."

Goulet said that ICLV is very multicultural and has Democrats, Republicans, and Libertarians. As a pastor, he doesn't tell people whom to vote for. He said that Trump treated everyone with great respect and honor. And they prayed over him too. In fact, that's when something funny happened.

"A pastor friend of ours, Troy Martinez, was there. He has a massive role in helping kids in our city. He's very well recognized and respected. But he came from a really rough background to become a major leader in our city. And Troy is probably 260 pounds, with a full Fu Manchu—he looks like a biker. So while we're praying for him, he says, 'Mr. Trump, can I anoint you in oil?' And Mr. Trump says, 'Yeah. You can.' But you could tell that the Secret Service—I mean, they just turned and looked at him. It was hilarious. Pasqual and Tony said, 'Pastor, pray for him'—and that's what I did. That day was a really amazing first event with him. And in my observation, I thought that the man that was represented in the media was not the man that I was meeting."

Speaking of the media, Goulet got a firsthand lesson in false reporting. They got calls asking about the "massive protest" at the school, when in fact nobody even knew Trump was coming—it was a confidential, non-publicized event. Then, a story went out that the church and school were getting paid off by the campaign to make Trump look better with Hispanics. Finally, one story even reported that Trump had terrified several students in the first-grade class— though the entire visit was filmed and reveals nothing but delighted kids. "I just couldn't believe how distorted some of it was," Goulet said. "It wasn't even an effort to be fair and balanced—it was just outright slander and malice."

@DonaldJTrump tweeted later: "Beautiful morning—thank you @ICLV!"

Then, right into Trump's steady climb in the polls, the *Access Hollywood* tape dropped like a bomb.

The reaction among evangelicals was unequivocal in its condemnation of the lewd comments, though there was much disagreement about what should happen next in terms of the continuation of the campaign. Major political and religious leaders called for Trump to step down from the campaign and let Pence be the candidate. Across America, the individual secretaries of state were looking into their state's campaign laws and reporting what would happen if Trump were to step down with less than a month to go. The details varied, but one thing seemed eminently clear: Hillary Clinton would win the White House.

Richard Land, a seminary president and the former head of the Ethics and Religious Liberty Commission of the Southern Baptist Convention, related that "About twenty seconds after the *Access Hollywood* tape came out, I got a phone call from a reporter for a major newspaper who said, 'Professor Land, are you still voting for Donald Trump?' I said, 'Well, is he still running against Hillary Clinton?' "

Lance Wallnau created a Facebook video that went viral with millions of views, to explain how to think about the tape. As he had written in his newly released book, Wallnau argued that when Trump married Melania, he "decided that he was going to judge the one area of his life that was out of control. The guy doesn't drink, he doesn't smoke—but he was a womanizer billionaire. And he ended that. He got committed to Melania, and he's been dedicated to her and to having a rebranded family image ever since then." Wallnau told us that the reason why the *Access* video came out when it did was that "the Lord wanted to circumcise him. He wanted to cut away from him any basis for boasting that it was his own strength. He got into the White House by the grace of God, not because of a perfect campaign—because that *Access Hollywood* thing would have torpedoed anyone other than someone God's grace was on."

Johnnie Moore said that the day after the video came out he initiated a phone call with the evangelical advisory board. "We did not invite any campaign people—nobody affiliated with Trump was on the call. It was just us alone so we could talk about the video and our response. All of us agreed to stand behind the candidate at that point. We all agreed to it. We had all the grace in the world for this man who had sacrificed his entire life, in my viewpoint, and supported us. How could we not support him? We all believed he was a different person, but even if he wasn't, it demanded all the more that we were people of grace with him."

Politically speaking, the leaked tape couldn't have come at a worse time for those who had been working to get #NeverTrump leaders to lose the "Never." Robert Jeffress recalled his going to a private meeting at Trump Tower on September 29, to "mediate a meeting between then candidate Trump and a group of religious leaders—evangelicals and Catholics. Many in that group were Never Trumpers, and you could tell they came ready to give him a piece of their mind that they probably couldn't afford to lose. When he walked into the room, and I introduced them, he listened to them, he delayed his departure, and by the end of the meeting he had them eating out of the palm of his hand."

But with the release of the tape, fence-sitting ceased being an option, and those who were already committed to the #NeverTrump position solidified their argument even more: "Never Trump is our best chance to actually make America great again." Longtime evangelical allies appeared on cable talk shows to argue against each other, admitting on-air that it would have seemed impossible to imagine such a scenario where they'd be at such opposing poles regarding a national election. Albert Mohler, who had already pledged he would abstain from voting for either Trump or Clinton, wrote that "Donald Trump has created an excruciating moment for evangelicals"—asking a poignant question: "Why now? The Donald Trump revealed on the 11-year-old tape did not reveal anything that evangelicals should not have already known about the Republican nominee. Plenty of venality was in abundant evidence, even in the candidate's own books."

"It was a pretty unforgettable weekend. It's something I'm never going to forget for the rest of my life," Ralph Reed told us in his account of the *Access Hollywood* events. "That Friday afternoon I had just finished securing some final commitments I needed to complete Faith & Freedom's get-out-the-vote effort. So to de-stress a little bit, I decided to walk across the street to the mall and catch a movie, which I'll never forget what movie I was watching—*Sully* with Tom Hanks. About halfway through the movie, my cell phone started vibrating, and it just wouldn't stop—every thirty seconds— *Zzz. Zzz. Zzz.* I'm thinking, 'What's going on? Did somebody die? Did war break out?' I looked down at my phone to see what was going on and I saw—*Washington Post, New York Times*, AP, *Wall Street Journal*—everybody was texting me to get a statement. So I sat there in the theater and banged out my statement, that I found Trump's remarks to be offensive and inappropriate, but I didn't think it was going to weigh nearly as heavily in the hierarchy of concerns of evangelical and other faith-based voters as the issues facing the country."

Further, Reed said at the time and repeated to us that "the Donald Trump I had gotten to know was not reflective of what I saw on that tape. I was with him in many private settings in his office, backstage at political events, in private meetings, including times when women were present, and I never saw him treat any woman with anything but dignity and respect, including my own daughters."

Reed believed that evangelical voters would be repulsed by Trump's decade-old comments, but that still wouldn't overturn their sense that handing Hillary the White House could do irreversible damage to the country. "It turned out that I was correct in that judgment," Reed said. "I didn't know whether I was right or not, but it turned out that that was definitely the case."

In the third presidential debate in October, there was an exchange between Trump and Clinton that many evangelicals consider to be a campaign-defining moment, and it wasn't about a topic that had been the focus of attention by the media. Ralph Reed identified these few minutes of debate as "the third hinge point" of the campaign. Trump explained in detail the vicious details of partial birth abortion and his opposition to it.

The talking heads went ballistic at the violent rhetoric Trump used. The pro-life community, less concerned about the rhetoric and more concerned about the violence committed on the babies, asked themselves if *Access Hollywood* was worth losing the election to Clinton with a candidate like Trump being willing to say things that respectable Republicans were unwilling to say.

Eight months later, the pro-life Center for Medical Progress released an undercover video showing a Planned Parenthood official talking about how they would use forceps to hold a fetus inside a mother to accomplish the abortion of a late-term baby. Mallory Quigley, communications director for the pro-life Susan B. Anthony List, said, "That's exactly what Donald Trump said in the third and final presidential debate. He was ridiculed by the media at the time, but in their own words, these abortionists are proving the president was spot on in his analysis about what's happening."

The fact that Trump did better in the debates than anyone expected could be chalked up to low expectations. But spiritually speaking, the tone was set early, before the first debate, at Hofstra University, in Hempstead, New York. His campaign manager Kellyanne Conway remembers being in the holding room with advisers Steve Bannon and David Bossie when she approached the candidate. "I said, 'Would you mind if I led us in prayer?' He said, 'Okay.' We grasped hands and bowed our heads and I said a prayer for him and with him and asked God to bless him and give him wisdom and for the protection of him and his family and for God to let His will be done with respect to the direction and leadership of our nation. He appreciated that."

• • •

With just a little more than two weeks to go until Election Day, the Trump team had some important decisions to make: which states would their candidate visit? With polls showing Trump behind, any wrong move could prove disastrous. It surely wouldn't be Virginia, right? In early October, the Trump campaign pulled some resources out of the critical swing state as polls showed Hillary Clinton with a solid five-point lead. So where did Trump go? Virginia. Of course he did. The reason? He made a promise to an old friend by the name of Pat Robertson.

After Trump won the nomination, Robertson called him and asked if he would come to Regent University, the school he founded that centers on Judeo-Christian principles. Some in the Trump camp argued that going to Virginia at this point in the campaign didn't make sense, but Trump was determined to go. "I promised Pat, and I'm gonna do it," Robertson recalled Trump telling him. "That's the kind of person he is. He's loyal to his friends, and he gives you a promise that he's going do something."

After the rally, Robertson recollected a memorable exchange with Trump about Alicia Machado, the winner of the 1996 Miss Universe Competition from Venezuela. She had been critical of the GOP nominee, claiming he treated her like "trash" after she started gaining a lot of weight. Trump fought back against the charge, making it an even bigger media story. Robertson wanted Trump to move on. "I said, Donald, no more women. He said, 'I've got to answer.' [Rudy] Giuliani was there, and he says, 'I hope he listens to you.'" Eventually, the Machado controversy faded away but not before Trump would have his say. As for the state of Virginia, Clinton ended up winning the state, but for the purposes of this book, the political loss in Virginia isn't the takeaway. When it comes to the "faith of Donald Trump," one steady characteristic has always been that he is loyal to his friends. Proverbs 20:6 says, "Many will say they are loyal friends, but who can find one who is truly reliable?" Indeed, Pat Robertson found out that weekend in Virginia Beach that Trump was "truly reliable."

With just ten days left in the campaign, he would take a few hours off the campaign trail and head to a ribbon-cutting ceremony in Washington, DC, to celebrate the grand opening of Trump International Hotel. The media was aghast that he would spend valuable minutes away from key swing states, but did they not understand by now that, when it comes to the spotlight and attention, Trump knows exactly what he's doing? For the business mogul, this was a chance to tout a project with his name on it that came in under budget and ahead of schedule. Branding.

Trump's new playground, just blocks from the White House, used to be the old historic post office. Instead, he turned it into a palatial hotel, complete with a four-thousand-square-foot presidential suite and a sixty-three-hundred-square-foot "Trump Townhouse." While I didn't experience any of those amenities, I received something even better: a sit-down interview with Trump (and his wife Melania) for what would be our ninth and final interview during the presidential campaign.

Why in the world would Trump, a man who's not exactly the poster boy for evangelical Christianity, sit down with the Christian Broadcasting Network so many times? The easy, lazy answer is that he did it for political purposes, knowing that without the evangelical base of the Republican Party he had no shot. Well, of course, that's true, but if you stop there, you miss the deeper meaning. It should also not be lost on anyone that Trump's true DNA is that of an outsider: fearless, authentic, and free from the shackles of consultants and GOP operatives.

Past Republican nominees like Mitt Romney and John McCain would come in front of a Christian audience but only minimally, knowing it was a political rite of passage to do so. The conventional thinking is to be wary of "Christian TV" for fear of saying something that might get you into trouble. Trump, on the other hand, not only did substantially more interviews with us, his staff didn't even bother to ask us what we planned to talk about. Why? Because Trump is Trump. He just speaks from the heart and lets it rip the way he sees it. Can it cause more headaches for him at times? Sure. But it's far more refreshing to see, and it's one of the main reasons evangelicals flocked to him in the first place. Conservative Christians were tired of being thrown some lines of rehearsed GOP talking points. With Trump, they understand he wasn't perfect, far from it. But at least they felt he was shooting straight with them.

Before we began the interview, Trump, looking more relaxed than I had ever seen before, went for some small talk. "Have you lost a little weight?" he asked me. "You look good." Imagine if I was a woman and he said that? CNN would have milked that line for a week, but for Trump, it's just who he is. He calls it like he sees it. He went on to warn of the dangers of a Clinton presidency. "If Hillary Clinton gets in, you're not going to have religious liberty," Trump said. He also played pseudo–fortune teller, exclaiming to me that if evangelicals show up and vote, "we're going to win the election." They did. He was right.

Donald Trump wasn't leaving anything to chance. Interviews with CBN would help him immensely, but heading into a place of worship would work even better. So it was back to the International Church of Las Vegas. Pastor Goulet was in Texas at a school reunion when he got a call from his wife: "Donald Trump wants to come to church tomorrow."

"What?"

"I'm not kidding. He wants to come to church tomorrow," she replied.

"No, that won't work."

"Why not?"

"Because it's crazy with the Secret Service and I don't want that for our people—and I'm not there, and so I can't help manage that."

Denise said, "Trump promised to come incognito. No one's going to know he's coming to ICLV. He just wants to come to church."

Pastor Goulet thought, "Do I really want to say no to somebody who wants to come to church?" Even though he had taken a beating in the media for the first visit Trump had made four weeks earlier, Goulet decided to green-light his coming—especially since he intended on just slipping into the service. But Goulet said he told his wife, the co-pastor of the church: "Baby, I'm not flying back tonight. I'm preaching tomorrow here in Texas. Besides, I really believe that he needs to see a woman preacher—someone like you, strong and anointed, and fearless."

So, the next morning, Trump was in the front row of ICLV with his team, "worshipping God, just like a normal person," Urrabazo recalled. "Hands clapping, moving, shaking, glad. At one moment, he said, 'There's a lot of electricity in this room.' Then I got up on the platform and announced 'Donald Trump is here with us,' and the whole church went crazy—excited that he was here. We show honor to people because the church is about honor."

Urrabazo told the congregants, "Why don't you surround him right now and pray for him. We're going to pray for him." The Secret Service looked up and all of a sudden the people just swarmed all around Trump—"they were touching, praying, and we were prophesying from the platform. Then we called him to the platform, and I said, 'Mr. Trump, can you open your hands like this [palms up]. Open this up like this. This is a prophetic sign of you receiving.' He said, 'Oh, okay,' and he opened his hands up."

Urrabazo then prophesied over Trump, speaking over him a word about the need for our nation to be both generous and good stewards.

"Then Pastor Denise prophesied over him," Urrabazo recounted. "It was an excellent word. And then he stayed for the preaching. Denise preached, and the word was 'Pray for the servant that he would open his eyes.' I was sitting next to Donald Trump, and when Pastor Denise said, 'You can see that there's more for him than against him,' I leaned over to Trump and said, 'Did you hear what she just said? She said that there's more for you than there is against you.' " Trump smiled and said, "That's great. There's more for me than there is against me."

Nine days later, Trump was elected president.

26

The Art of the Unreal

The second Tuesday in November had finally come: November 8, 2016. Election Night. Or as Democrats like to call it, "Hillary and the Terrible, Horrible, No Good, Very Bad Day." All the "professional pollsters" had Trump losing "big league" to her. Trump, a man of extreme confidence, wasn't sure what to expect that night. "I don't know, Jerry, these exit polls look bad," Trump told Falwell during an Election Night phone call. "No, no, no, you got it," Falwell Jr. responded. "I just have a feeling. You're going to win it. I know it. Too much has happened that's been miraculous this year for it not to be of God. You're going to win." Later that evening another phone call took place between them. "Jerry, we're about to win. They're about to announce that we're going to win Pennsylvania," Falwell Jr. recalls Trump telling him. "That's the game," Falwell Jr. replied. Trump responded, "Yup, that'll be the game." Game. Set. Match.

Evangelicals delivered Trump over the finish line. "I think it was a very important victory for people of faith," President Trump told me from his desk in the Oval Office. "I think that our country was becoming unbelievably one-sided and going in the wrong direction . . . you saw the rules and regulations that they were instituting against faith. And it was getting really bad. . . . It was almost like they wanted to stomp it out."

Evangelicals agreed in spades. Eighty-one percent to be exact, a record turnout for a Republican nominee for president. Yes, running against Hillary Clinton helped, but that's the easy tale to tell. The evangelical connection to Trump goes much deeper than that, beyond nominating strict constructionist Supreme Court justices or choosing Mike Pence as his running mate. At the heart of it, Trump, of all people, became the ultimate fighting champion for evangelicals, confirming that God indeed has a sense of humor. "President Trump represented to the evangelical community a warrior to fight the encroachment of the federal government in their lives and in their institutions," said Robert Costa of the *Washington Post*, who has covered him extensively. "In spite of his many differences with the faith community and in spite of his personal foibles over the decades, he was seen as someone who would fight for religious voters. In a sense, they forgave him for all of his personal misdeeds because they believed he could be a strong man in taking away regulations or different federal guidelines that they saw as a burden for their church, or for their religious institution."

Trump also had something else evangelicals liked: authenticity. He never pretended to be someone he wasn't. The occasional "hell" or "damn" flew from his lips just as easily in front of evangelicals as any other group. In a counterintuitive way, something was refreshing about that. The human nature inside all of us leans toward a desire to know where you stand with someone. Put another way, it's called the "give it to me straight" principle. Evangelist James Robison, who became close to Trump during the campaign, remembers giving Trump some advice. " 'Don't use religious talk. It'll backfire.' . . . He did it. He never tried to prove to you or anybody else he's a great spiritual giant. I made it clear that he was growing in his faith. But here's what he knew. 'I can't win without evangelicals and professing Christians.' "

With the new title of president-elect, Trump quickly turned his attention to the transition process, and during it, evangelicals saw clear signs of Trump's genuine dedication to evangelicals. He chose

Ken Blackwell, a board member of the pro-family Family Research Council, to run his domestic policy transition team. His cabinet nominees read like a Believers in Politics all-star team: Attorney General Jeff Sessions; Housing and Urban Development Secretary Ben Carson; CIA director Mike Pompeo; EPA chief Scott Pruitt (a deacon at First Baptist Church in Broken Arrow, Oklahoma); Energy Secretary Rick Perry; Education Secretary Betsy DeVos; Agriculture Secretary Sunny Perdue; US Ambassador to the United Nations Nikki Haley.

In many cases along the way, Trump was consulting key evangelical leaders he trusted for counsel. "He asked me to help him check out some of the people he was looking at and asked my opinion," James Robison said. "I was the first person, as far as I know, to bring [Rick] Perry up as energy secretary."

This faith-filled cabinet ended up producing some spiritual fruit when Trump's administration began holding weekly Bible studies inside a conference room in the Health and Human Services building. Ralph Drollinger, head of Capitol Ministries, leads them and says a Bible study like this hasn't existed among cabinet members in at least a hundred years. "It's the best Bible study that I've ever taught in my life," Drollinger told Jennifer Wishon of the Christian Broadcasting Network. Rick Perry was so excited about it he called James Robison. "He said, 'James, the Cabinet is praying!' He said, 'This is phenomenal.' "

The forty-eight-degree temperature on Inauguration Day 2017 would go down in the record books as the fourth-warmest January inaugural temperature ever. But there was another record set that day: more prayers were read during Donald Trump's inaugural ceremony than at any other presidential inaugural in American history. There were a total of twelve: six religious prayers, three benedictions, three invocations, and a partridge in a pear tree! And we haven't even included the truly remarkable private prayer ceremony that began the day.

Since 1933, St. John's Episcopal Church, sitting across the street from the White House, has been where presidents go for the time-honored Inauguration morning prayer service. In Trump's case, what was waiting for him was some good ol'-fashion preachin'! With his family next to him in the pews, the president-elect heard from his good evangelical buddy James Robison, host of *Life Today TV* (remember, Trump loves to watch Christian television!). Robison said Trump asked if he would deliver personal remarks and a prayer for him. There was a reason the president-elect wanted Robison to share this special day with him and his family. Over the course of the presidential campaign, they developed a very special bond. As we all know, Trump is a force of personality and when it comes to talking about Jesus, so is Robison. Trump got a heavy dose of it from him throughout 2016.

One of the most memorable encounters came on the airport tarmac in Panama City, Florida. They arrived there after Robison flew with Trump on his campaign plane from Dallas to attend a campaign event that evening. Afterward, when they made their way back into an SUV, Robison turned to Trump and felt led to pray for him. One of Trump's assistants joined in. Robison remembers it clearly. "I put my hands on those shoulders and I said, 'Sir, we're going to give this big, rugged piece of clay straight into the hands of the master potter, every bit of it. And we're going to ask God to shape you into a vessel of honor.'" So what did Trump do? What came next was one of the most tender, private moments of the campaign. "He listened and was unbelievably sensitive and yielded even as I prayed for him," Robison said. "When I walked around the Suburban I didn't know what he would say. He gave me a hug, pulled me up against his chest firmly and said, 'Man, I sure love you.' " Trump asked Robison to come with him to his Mar-a-Lago home in Florida, but Robison couldn't make it. Still, Trump wasn't done with him yet. "Before he actually stepped into the door of the plane he turned around one more time and said, 'Man, I sure wish you were going with me. I sure love you.' It was an expression that you wouldn't expect from someone who had been counseled to really take some hard serious looks to some approaches which I continue to do today."

So on Inauguration Day, here they were again: Trump and Robison: face-to-face as the evangelist was about to dispense more biblical wisdom, not on a tarmac but at an Inauguration church service. Boy, did he deliver! He asked the president-elect to rise in front of everyone and then told him the following:

The first time you and I talked, I shared with you something I thought was very helpful—and knowing you and watching you, sometimes you would wonder if there is any way possible. I said, "Let me talk with you about humility and meekness, with the emphasis on meekness. It's not weakness." I said, "It's taking great power and submitting it with the kind of biblical direction that enables it to fulfill what its strength enables it to do. . . ." I said, "It's like taking the power of a thoroughbred like Secretariat and yielding it to the wisdom and guidance of a 100-pound jockey." I said, "Sir, the meekness that God has given you is as great as any I have ever witnessed—and ability to move and motivate people that is nothing short of a divine, supernatural enabling." I said, "Sir, if you yield the gifts of God and the strength that He put in you, not for your purposes but for His kingdom's purpose, you'll win a triple crown. You'll win an election and you'll save the day, even the future of freedom, and restore the foundation and the walls essential to protect it. . . . I think you have been designed and gifted by God for this moment. If you, too, together will submit to the wisdom God freely offers, it is going to be an amazing journey."

And then came his prayer for the president:

We believe, dear God, that the stage is set for the next great spiritual awakening, and I believe with all my heart it is absolutely essential. I want to thank you from the depth of my heart for giving us a leader who is fearless, who is tireless, who is committed and who has so obviously, by his very manner and the way he treats people and expresses appreciation for them, and the way he has forgiven those who have been unkind, and even given them an opportunity to serve. God, I want to thank you that we have seen the transformation of his own heart and mind in his actions. I pray, dear God, that those actions would continue to always speak louder than words.

Afterward, it didn't take long for the reviews to come pouring in from the Trump family. "I immediately began getting texts from Eric saying, 'Dad is talking about what you said. Everybody in the car is so grateful,' " Robison said. It kept coming throughout the momentous day. "They're texting over dinner to tell me how much my message meant to them and the family and they're sitting there in the White House talking about it on their first evening together in the White House. Thanking God for what I shared."

The spiritual meat offered up at St. John's Episcopal Church that morning seemed to never stop. Up next in the "evangelical hit parade" was a man Trump came to love and respect deeply: Pastor Robert Jeffress of First Baptist Church in Dallas. The night before, Jeffress was coming under attack from media outlets like the *Washington Post*. The newspaper claimed Trump was going to hear from "a Southern Baptist pastor who has a history of inflammatory remarks about Muslims, Mormons, Catholics, and gays." Despite the uproar and potential for distraction, Trump never pulled the plug on Jeffress, thus revealing one of Trump's key character traits: steadfastness. "You know, many administrations would have pulled back on that, and would have canceled that, but not Donald Trump," Jeffress said. "He went right ahead, he knew that was an unfair attack, and I'm appreciative of his willingness to not throw me overboard."

Jeffress delivered an impactful sermon, entitled "When God Chooses a Leader," in front of Trump and his family on Inauguration Day. He likened the president-elect to Nehemiah in the Bible, who helped rebuild the city of Jerusalem and knew a thing or two about building a wall! "I thought there was just some natural parallels between Nehemiah, the biblical character I cited in my message, and Donald Trump," Jeffress said. "Neither Nehemiah nor Donald Trump are politicians by profession, they were builders. Yet God used both of them to rebuild a nation that was in disrepair. . . . God uses special people with special gifts for critical times in a nation's history. More than the building of the wall I saw some characteristics in Nehemiah's life that I believe were going to be important for the president if he moved our nation forward. He refused to allow his critics to distract him. He refused to allow setbacks to stop him, and he sought God's supernatural power. I see Donald Trump doing all three of those things, and I think that's critical to the success of his administration and also the success of our nation."

With the private preaching and prayers complete, it was time for the main course. Trump loves numbers, whether it's crowd size, ratings, you name it. As we noted earlier, the number of prayers recited at his Inauguration ceremony now holds the all-time record. To grasp the philosophy of the faith of Donald Trump, it's imperative to understand some of the prayer participants on that stage.

Franklin Graham is a household name and has an excellent relationship with the President. "He's a great guy and is very much a friend of ours," President Trump told me. "Franklin has been terrific." Trump recalls watching Billy Graham sermons with his father on television in the 1950s, so this was a bit personal for him. "My father was a fan of Billy Graham," the President told me. "He liked him a lot. He would go to the 'Crusades,' at Yankee Stadium." "He told me that he remembers his dad listening to Billy Graham's sermons many, many times, and that made an impression on President Trump," said close personal friend Robert Jeffress. "I think one reason he is such a fan of Billy Graham is his dad was a fan of Billy Graham's." As for the younger Graham, he knew the election was a potential turning point in American history, and while not officially endorsing Donald Trump, he went around the country to all fifty state capitals praying and preaching about Judeo-Christian values, imploring Christians to get out and vote. In an interview with the Religion News Service, Graham concluded, "I think maybe God has allowed Donald Trump to win this election to protect this nation for the next few years by giving maybe an opportunity to have some good judges."

Bishop Wayne Jackson of Great Faith Ministries, a lifelong Democrat, became good friends with Donald Trump on the campaign trail. Earlier in the book, we described the fascinating scene when Trump attended his predominately African-American church, complete with him swaying to the music in the pews, being prayed over, and having a Jewish prayer shawl draped over him. Jackson seemed the perfect man for the job, considering he calls his church a "praying and fasting and Bible-believing church." "I believe when he was in the church, he felt the energy of the Holy Spirit through praise and worship and also the love that was displayed to him because he and I hadn't met," Bishop Jackson said. "My wife, even after meeting him, her whole attitude changed about him and many of the people who were there, their attitudes changed about him being on a one on one with him." The relationship between the two blossomed as they stayed in constant contact. "He called me and told me that he appreciates my Christian love and that he was grateful for that," Bishop Jackson said. "Then the next thing I know, I was asked to do the benediction at the Inauguration!"

Reverend Samuel Rodriguez became the first Hispanic evangelical leader to pray at a presidential inauguration. The energetic senior pastor at New Season Christian Worship Center in Sacramento, California, became someone Trump respected on issues related to immigration. Plus, Trump thinks he's great on TV! Rodriguez though was never shy about confronting Trump about some of the more rancorous language he used on the subject of immigration during the campaign. But Trump likes straight shooters, and if nothing else that's exactly what Pastor Rodriguez is.

"One of the greatest honors of my life took place on that day behind that podium to lift up the name of Jesus before the world," Rodriguez said. His prayer centered on Matthew Chapter 5, the Sermon on the Mount. "The impetus in my spirit was could I do anything to help this nation heal?" Rodriguez explained further. "Matthew Chapter 5. 'God will bless those that are persecuted for my name's sake. . . . When they lie about you and say so many evil things about you.' Many people suffered during the course of the campaign. Every individual has suffered at one moment in their personal lives, a moment of great darkness. My message was an olive branch, for lack of a better phrase. An olive branch, a reconciliatory message."

The one figure who got the most attention was Paula White. The pastor of New Destiny Christian Center in Apopka, Florida, and chairwoman of Trump's evangelical advisory board has received plenty of mentions in this book . . . and for good reason. Her close relationship with Donald Trump is based on a true abiding friendship, one that demands nothing of him and vice versa. She is a true spiritual companion for him and senses that Trump has been moving along on a journey toward becoming closer to God.

When she took the stage on that day in January, White became the first clergywoman to speak at a presidential inauguration. While her critics love to bring up her belief in the so-called prosperity gospel, what they truly don't understand is that her heart is for Jesus first, and then, of course, for this president. "The man that I know is a believer, a Christian and a man that's hungry for God," White said, even if "he doesn't know our 'Christianese' and perhaps our language that we know in the Christian world." As for the spiritual critics lined up at his door, White asked a very simple question: "If we just want to hold Mr. Trump to saying every day . . . he's going to be just spot on with God, well then I'd say, 'Are you?' No! None of us are. [The Apostle] Paul wasn't. The only one that was, was Jesus Christ." White understands a basic fact of life: we're all human; we all make mistakes, oodles of them. Jesus made this point in the Bible when the Pharisees accused the adulterous woman of disobeying the Mosaic Law. Jesus said simply, "He that is without sin among you, let him cast the first stone at her." That stopped the conversation cold.

With that biblical admonition in mind, we should all remember that nobody is perfect. But more crucially, Trump—and all of us—need to rely on God's wisdom for true success and peace. White's biblical prayer at the Inauguration hit squarely on this theme when she said, "In Proverbs 21:1, you instruct us that our leader's heart is in your hands. Gracious God, reveal unto our president the ability to know the will, your will, the confidence to lead us in justice and righteousness, and the compassion to yield to our better angels."

• • •

Later that evening at the ceremonial inaugural balls, the new President and the First Lady danced the night away. In typical Trump fashion, he would use the occasion of their first dance to poke a little fun at the mainstream media. The song chosen? "My Way" by Frank Sinatra.

While it played well for chuckles, it raised more pressing and serious questions: Would Trump's way be God's way? Would he rely on his own power or the Almighty power of God? Would he listen to James Robison's spiritual advice about exhibiting "biblical meekness" (not weakness)? Who would help him along the way in the infancy of his presidency? With the sport of a political campaign now over, it became time to govern. Was Trump ready to tackle his highest hurdle, and if so, where did God fit into the equation? "The presidency of the United States is the most powerful and awesome job perhaps in all the world," White House senior adviser Kellyanne Conway said. "But this President knows there's one above him who is even more awesome and more powerful. He's acutely aware of that."

27

Gorsuch a Time as This

The Bible is full of stories of how God uses the most unlikely people to accomplish His will. For most of his life, Donald Trump was not pro-life. In 1999, he even exclaimed, "I'm very pro-choice." But his view began to transform during the following decade. When I sat down with him for our very first interview in 2011, he explained why. "One of the reasons I changed—one of the primary reasons—a friend of mine's wife was pregnant, in this case, married. She was pregnant, and he didn't really want the baby. And he was telling me the story. He was crying as he was telling me the story. He ends up having the baby, and the baby is the apple of his eye. It's the greatest thing that's ever happened to him. Here's a baby that wasn't going to be let into life. And I heard this, and some other stories . . . they changed my view as to that."

Having a "conversion story" is great, but the proof is in the pudding. Would he deliver the goods now that he's president? An early clue of his resolve came during the third presidential debate in Las Vegas, Nevada, when the topic turned to late-term abortion. "I think it's terrible. If you go with what Hillary is saying, in the ninth month, you can take the baby and rip the baby out of the womb of the mother just prior to the birth of the baby. Now, you can say that that's OK and Hillary can say that that's OK. But it's not OK with me. . . ." Afterward, pro-life leaders fully realized something: They had finally found the person who had the guts to say what needed to be said in such stark terms. "That was a very pivotal moment," senior adviser Kellyanne Conway told me from her office in the West

Wing of the White House. "It took a Manhattan male billionaire who was pro-choice most of his adult life to give the most impassioned defense of life I had ever heard from a presidential debate podium . . . he basically looked at Hillary Clinton and said, 'You're the extreme one here' . . . he was willing to call it out."

With that memory in the forefront of their minds, it appeared conservative evangelicals were on the cusp of experiencing a different type of pro-life president. Others before Trump were authentically pro-life, but something seemed distinctive here. Trump's affinity for a rumble would work well when defending the unborn. Mike Huckabee remembers what it was like under the George W. Bush administration. "On the life question, President Bush was personally pretty good, but his own wife is really not pro-life. We didn't know this until later. There were a lot of senior people in his policy shop that, for them, it was just a political issue. They didn't care one way or the other. It was not a moral issue for them." So now, along comes Trump, who has no problem causing a ruckus. "He's going to go out on the field, and he's going to win the game," Huckabee said. "He'll stiff-arm everybody out there. He'll bite them in the pile. He will win."

Undeniably, President Trump's game of pro-life tackle football had begun. One of his very first acts was reinstating the pro-life "Mexico City Policy," requiring nongovernmental organizations to agree not to "perform nor actively promote abortion as a method of family planning in other nations." But in typical Trump fashion, he went bigger and bolder by significantly increasing the amount of global health assistance funds and government programs that would be covered under the policy. In another significant move, Trump signed a resolution into law that gives states the ability to withhold federal dollars from facilities that provide abortions. And it didn't go unnoticed that Trump chose Charmaine Yoest as assistant secretary of public affairs at HHS. For decades, she had been one of the top pro-life leaders and thinkers in the country. Jerry Johnson, president of the National Religious Broadcasters, said the impact will be profound: "You've got all this money now being used to promote adoption and pro-life initiatives."

While there was no doubt the pro-life policy machine was cranking away behind the scenes, we also know Donald Trump is a big fan of optics and making a splash. In the pro-life community, there's no better place to do it than the annual March for Life rally on the National Mall in Washington, DC. Hundreds of thousands show up from all over the country; many of them are students. That's not surprising considering recent polling shows a majority of millennials believe abortion should be illegal or only legal in cases of rape, incest, or to save the life of the mother.

The Trump administration was determined to make an early statement on the life issue. A president or vice president had never attended the rally in person before. Trump had a scheduling conflict that day, so instead the discussion turned to who else might be able to attend. It was suggested that Kellyanne Conway go. She would be the highest-ranking woman ever to appear from a White House administration. Trump loved the idea but had an even better one. Conway remembers the conversation with the President vividly. "Vice President Pence was standing there and I said, 'I'd be honored to go, sir.' He said, 'Please do. You'd be great. Give them my best. Tell them we're with them.' I did all of that. Then he [Trump] turned to Vice President Pence and said, 'Why don't you go, Mike?' The Vice President said, 'I'd be honored, sir. Are you sure?' He said, 'Yes.' "

Pence and Conway went on to make their notable appearances but beyond the historical aspect, the move sent a signal to Trump's base supporters: He would be faithful on the pro-life issue. With so many weekly Mass-attending Catholics in the crowd, it played perfectly. "I think they're highly approving of him," said Hugh Hewitt, the influential conservative Catholic radio talk-show host. "It's the Pope Benedict XVI, John Paul II wing. It's not the Pope Francis wing, it's not the liberation theology wing . . . but the traditional mass-attending weekly, confession-going Catholic who is part of that core Trump 35 percent."

There is plenty more to do on the abortion policy wish list: making the Hyde Amendment, which bans federal funding for most abortions in America, permanent rather than extending the provision yearly; passing a nationwide law that would ban abortions after twenty weeks of pregnancy; and of course the big one: eliminate all federal funding for Planned Parenthood. But there is no doubt that Trump has delivered for the pro-life community in just a short amount of time. Marjorie Dannenfelser, president of the pro-life Susan B. Anthony List, calls Trump and Pence "game changers for the pro-life movement." Yet leaving this discussion just as a "win" on policy for pro-lifers misses a more noteworthy point. Jerry Johnson sees the presidency as a "Romans 13 office." He explains it this way:

> It's very clear that the government minister is a minister of justice essentially, to protect us from evil and those who would do evil, essentially to protect the sanctity of innocent human life and that the government has the use of lethal force, the sword. That's in Romans 13. He's not to be a minister of the gospel. He's a minister of justice and of the sword. I think the confusion a lot of evangelicals have is they wanted a minister of the gospel, a minister of love, and a minister of missions. We love to see an "evangelical president." We love to see them talking our language. We love to see them with a long history of all of this, and it's wonderful when you have that, but the basic requirement

for a government official is someone who will protect us from evil, enemies foreign and domestic as the constitution would say or the oath would say. I think with Trump's pledge to protect us from Islamic terrorism, a strong stand on national security, and then his policy to protect the unborn . . . and so forth, he's honoring human life. He's protecting human life. That's really what the government is to be about. The church needs to do the work of the church and the mission and the gospel. We just want to live under a government that protects human life any way.

President Trump's pro-life efforts signaled the beginnings of a larger movement brewing inside this White House: access. He might as well have posted a sign on the front door of 1600 Pennsylvania Avenue: "Evangelicals Welcomed." The admittance would become so continuous that the Trump White House probably should have set up a shuttle bus with departures and arrivals on the hour! In one illustration, when I got word that a few evangelical leaders had made their way over to the White House, I emailed an influential evangelical leader about what he knows. The response: "There are leaders here, but there are almost always leaders here." I should have figured.

The faith of Donald Trump manifests in ways not always seen. His respect for the clergy and evangelical leaders is apparent. He not only values their prayers and spiritual counsel in private, but he also respects their public policy knowledge on the issues of the day as well. His evangelical advisory board is concrete evidence of that. Michele Bachmann, the former Minnesota congresswoman and 2012 presidential candidate, is part of that select group of evangelicals around the President who applaud how he is leaning into them. "For too long, Christians have been excluded from the table in decision-making in Washington, DC," Bachmann said. "They

[Trump and Pence] do not shy away, nor are they ashamed of being associated with evangelical Christians. In fact, they do take the advice; they listen to the advice of evangelical leaders." During the George W. Bush years, evangelicals would have access to the President and White House staffers, but the evangelical leaders we talk to today say the door is open even wider. "I've had a lot of talk with White House staffers and senior advisers about specifics, and I would say much more than I ever did under the Bush administration," said Bishop Harry Jackson, senior pastor of Hope Christian Church in Beltsville, Maryland.

Sometimes the visits aren't about policy. They're personal. Falwell speaks with Trump fairly regularly on the phone. When he visits the White House, the conversations are more lighthearted. "I commented to the President that he looked like he'd lost weight. We had the whole family there. He said, 'I don't know. They don't have any scales in the White House.' He said, 'But they only give me two meals a day, and they don't let me snack between meals, so yeah you're probably right, I'm probably losing weight.' " Falwell remembers another jovial moment inside the Oval Office. "He's got this red button on his desk. I said, 'What happens if you push that red button?' He reached over and pushed it. About thirty seconds later a butler walks in with a Coca-Cola, and sets it on the desk for him."

What do the stories illustrate? They give you a glimpse of a man who is comfortable in his own skin and relatable in private. "He's just a regular guy," Falwell said. "That's why I kept calling him a 'blue-collar billionaire' during the election. He's one of us." While his use of Twitter and his brash, in-your-face style rubs plenty of folks the wrong way (including some in his own party), Trump has a much softer side in private, a man who has no desire for all the games played in politics.

"My impression of him in a private setting is that he's often informal, he's at ease, and he's not obsessed with politics," Robert

Costa of the *Washington Post* said. "What makes President Trump different than so many politicians I've covered is how he doesn't really love to talk politics behind the scenes. So many other politicians I've covered love the game; who's up, who's down, where is the bill going on Capitol Hill, who's the key stakeholder, what's their backstory? With President Trump, he seems often more comfortable talking about golf or music. He's a big fan of Elton John, or talking about some great sports game from the 1950s or '60s, or just looking at the TV and ruminating on the news but not really looking at it through a truly partisan political lens."

I had my first White House interview with Trump within the first week of his presidency. Under the beautiful chandeliers and décor in the Blue Room of the White House, we met for just his third interview overall since being sworn into office. "Mr. President, thank you for inviting CBN News here into the White House," I said. "By the way, do you like Mr. President or Mr. Trump?" His forthcoming answer deserves a brief unpacking. "You can call me anything you want. You've known me for a long time." His response underscores the fact that evangelical access to him and this White House would be unparalleled. Dozens of mainstream media outlets were angling for an interview with him. CBN got it. Why? He values people who he sees treat him honestly. By extension, he sees the evangelical leaders who have come alongside him as honest brokers, not looking to pad their résumés and coffers but rather to advance Judeo-Christian principles that will, yes, here it comes: Make America Great Again.

During our CBN interview, a very important topic came up: the Supreme Court, specifically who he would nominate to the bench to replace Antonin Scalia. "I think evangelicals, Christians will love my pick and will be represented very fairly," Trump said to me that day. Enter Neil Gorsuch, stage right (emphasis on the word "right").

There's no need to regurgitate the entire Gorsuch confirmation process in this space, but suffice it to say this: Evangelicals and conservatives at large roundly applauded the pick, the process went off with relatively few glitches, and it became one of the crowning jewels of the Trump administration. From a more macro perspective, the Gorsuch pick gave Trump additional "evangelical street cred," considering how the federal judiciary has long been a constant source of frustration for conservative Christians. Hugh Hewitt believes the Gorsuch move showed his seriousness about how he viewed the intent of the framers of the US Constitution, saying, "I do believe he wants to be an originalist, American exceptionalist, and to be known as the guy who turned it around because we had eight horrible years. The friends of Obama, President Obama, do not want to hear that, but the fact is President Obama had a failed presidency, a terrible failure." Kellyanne Conway suggests there was a faith component to the pick as well. "He wanted this strict constructionist, an originalist, who also is pro-life. I think you see that as an example of his faith."

When assessing the faith of Donald Trump, the significance of the Neil Gorsuch nomination cannot be underestimated. Of course, the access evangelicals have had to this president is unprecedented and should not be overlooked. The push of the pro-life agenda was a major development as well in the first one hundred days of this administration. The confluence of all three in totality presents concrete evidence that Donald Trump is trying to live out his faith with deed. The Book of James states, "What good is it, my brothers and sisters, if someone claims to have faith but has no deeds?" While the Bible is clear that deeds or "works" don't grant you a ticket to heaven, it's still crucially important to live out your faith by the work you do to help others. Harkening back to Part One of this book, Trump knows hard work. That's what he does. That's how he was raised. It's in his blood. It's part of his faith tradition.

We do know, however, that no amount of human works or ingenuity will solve the world's problems. Sin nature blocks that from happening. The root of the problem is spiritual. The question for our purposes here is: Should that matter to an American president? And if so, will that person buy into the notion that our country needs serious prayer? Donald Trump seems to be demonstrating that he gets it and is unafraid to show it.

Look no further than the Oval Office where, at times, the regal room has been transformed into a glorified prayer closet! "I've never seen a President or a presidential candidate get prayed on as much as this guy did," Pastor Darrell Scott said. "Every time you turned around he was getting prayed on!" For sure, I can't recall a president of the United States bringing evangelical leaders into the Oval Office multiple times to pray with him and for our country, complete with the laying on of hands. We should have realized Trump would continue this prayerful theme once he became president, considering he prayed unashamedly in public and in private with numerous clergy members during the presidential campaign. Pastor Paula White, his close friend and one who counsels him often, has been right in the spiritual thick of it with him. "I could never even begin to imagine the weight that he's carrying," White said. "I know he has a full knowledge that he cannot carry that weight alone. That takes prayer, that takes God, that takes good counsel, that takes good people around him."

President Trump has followed the tradition of past presidents by attending the National Prayer Breakfast and issuing a National Day of Prayer proclamation. But in Trump's case, he took the National Day of Prayer ceremony in May to another level by holding it in the White House Rose Garden.

One of the more personal moments of his young presidency came after the utter devastation of Hurricane Harvey. Trump came up with the idea to have a National Day of Prayer on Sunday, September 3, 2017, after receiving word that Texas had issued one for their state. "When he heard about that, he just immediately said, 'Let's do it, great idea,' " Mike Pence recalled. "There happened to be a group of evangelical leaders, including Pastor Jeffress, on campus that day. They asked the president, 'Could we have a prayer at the end of the signing ceremony' and he just very readily said yes. You could tell he was very moved by the moment." Once again, evangelical leaders stood around the Oval Office desk, praying for our country as the cameras rolled for all to see. Cynics might see all of this as a man who loves the camera even more so when prayer is involved, but those who understand him best know otherwise. "If he wasn't happy with it or didn't feel like it was important in his life, he would never allow it to happen," his longtime friend Michael Cohen said. "Media pundits who claim that President Trump is doing this for a photo-op or for political expediency don't know the real Donald Trump." "Our President is a man that seeks prayer, that asks for prayer, that also prays," Paula White said. "It's not just a formality like 'here we go' through the motions. He genuinely respects, has the reverence for prayer and understands the power of prayer."

So why should anyone care about all this prayer gobbledygook? Praying to Jesus is vital for a number of reasons, but ultimately it's an act of obedience to God. He calls us to pray so we must do it. End of story. We submit to Him. Not the other way around. In Trump's case, his spiritual advisers say that it shows humility. "Here is the most powerful man in the world, yet he's not too proud to bow his head in the Oval Office and ask God for help," said Pastor Robert Jeffress, the man who led the prayer that day in the Oval Office.

Any honest assessment of Donald Trump's spiritual walk will show a man who has a reverence for God. Does he make mistakes?

Yes. Can he be a little "New Yawk" rough around the edges? You bet. But don't lose sight of the fact that a man with billions of dollars and more power than you can ever imagine could easily have no interest in a connection with God. Instead, he seeks out men and women of God. That's called submitting yourself to spiritual counsel. "He declares his faith in Jesus, he talks about praying," CBN's Pat Robertson said. "It's just simply astounding to see what he's done. That's why I think the anointing of the Lord is on him."

28

You've Got a Friend in Me

Edward Mote, an English pastor in the 1800s, penned the famous hymn "My Hope Is Built on Nothing Less" with lyrics that proclaim, "On Christ, the solid Rock, I stand; all other ground is sinking sand." If Donald Trump were to pen a hymn about the solid rock during his administration, there's no question who fits the bill: Mike Pence. In the world according to Donald Trump, his vice president has pulled off a trinity of sorts: crucial in helping him win over skeptical evangelicals in his run for the presidency; crucial in governing; and arguably most importantly, crucial in matters of faith. What blossomed over time was a true bond. "He and I have gotten to be very close," Vice President Pence said. "We're very good friends."

The first time they really got to know each other was over the Fourth of July weekend at Trump's National Golf Club in Bedminster, New Jersey. The soon-to-be presidential nominee was looking at choosing a running mate. Pence and his wife, Karen, were looking for something too. "I said for us to know whether we felt called to it, we'd need to know them as a family and need to spend time," Pence recalls. "The person who had contacted us called back the next day, and I said I'm not really being presumptuous, I totally understand if it can't work out because he's running for president . . . but we'd need to spend some substantial time with them as a family. The guy called me back the next day and said not only would they be willing to get together like that, they loved the idea, and they said bring your family to Bedminster, and their family will be there, and they'd love to spend time with you. They absolutely loved the approach. To know President Trump is to know a family. That was one of my first impressions."

Pence also got his first glimpse at a man who truly seemed to have a curiosity for things of God. "During the interview process over dinner at Bedminster with he and Melania, they had talked with us a lot about our faith and what it had meant in our lives," Pence remembers. "They were very tender, very warm conversations."

Having known and observed Trump for a number of years, what I've come to understand is that he deeply respects men and women of God who have such strong godly principles. He seems to feed off of that and take a genuine interest in the fact that they pursue God with such conviction. In Mike Pence, he sees a bountiful harvest.

As the weekend proceeded, Pence began to see a side of Donald Trump that, quite frankly, he had never really been privy to. What he witnessed was something fairly ordinary for Trump: a man who treated everyone around him with respect, no matter his or her title or job. "That weekend was my first glimpse at seeing him walking around Bedminster," Pence recalls. "He was just as comfortable with the guys taking care of the grounds as he was with members who were out there playing golf, with members of the staff. . . . He really treats everyone the same." Pence has a phrase for this type of camaraderie: "The ground is level around President Trump." He would end up seeing it time and time again in the months ahead. "On the campaign trail, he'd spend as much time talking to the guy that ran the freight elevator that brought us up the back of the building . . . or however long it would take before the plane would leave, he'd shake every one of the police officers' hands and take a picture. It didn't matter how long the day was. People get that. There's a genuineness there."

. . .

On the surface, these two men look like they couldn't be more different. And in certain ways they are: Trump is the brash New Yorker who lets it all hang out, complete with a rabble-rousing Twitter feed. Pence, on the other hand, is more like the human version of chamomile tea: calm, easy to digest, and good for settling the nerves. But a deeper look at the two men actually reveals a lot more in common than you might think. "Other than a whole lot of zeros, he and I have a lot in common," Pence said.

Both were actually Democrats for a period in their lives. Trump shuttled between parties in New York while Pence came from an Irish Catholic family of Democrats. At one point he was even the youth coordinator for the Bartholomew County Democrats in Indiana. From a faith perspective, they also have a bit in common: Pence first came in contact with evangelical Christian groups in his college days. It was all very new to him, especially the language about having a personal relationship with Jesus Christ. For Trump, that experience happened much later in his life, when Paula White and many of those Pentecostal preachers came into his world laying hands on him and praying in Jesus' name.

To a degree, their family histories are somewhat comparable too and Pence has taken note of it. "His [Trump's] grandfather emigrated to this country; my grandfather emigrated to this country. His father was a self-made man who built up a business with his own two hands; my father was a self-made man who built up a little gas station business. He [Trump] grew up, wanted to build on what he'd been given, he calls himself a kid from Queens, decided to go to Manhattan Island and build the big buildings. I felt a calling into public service. But it was grounded in the same principle of a passionate belief in the American dream that we both have, because we both have lived it. . . . I've always sensed that principle of giving back to the country that's given our family so much is also something that we share." That ethical code is found in the Bible (Luke 12:48) and Pence tells us that it turns out that both his father, Ed, and Trump's father, Fred, were apparently giving their boys the same biblical advice. "I was told by a family member that his father, Fred, often quoted the verse that 'to who much is given, much will be expected,' " the Vice President said. "It was interesting when I heard that, because that was one of the few verses my dad used to quote to me and my three brothers and two sisters most often."

Right from the beginning of the presidential transition process, Trump gave Pence significant responsibilities. He was responsible for the overall transition, a process that required a steady, knowledgeable person at the helm. But Trump was also relying on him for spiritual leadership.

Trump sees Pence as a "spiritual person," and that translates into a belief that it's good to be around people like that. This is something relatively new for Trump. You don't run into spirit-filled evangelical leaders on a regular basis in the high-stakes real estate circles of New York City. "I've been exposed to people that I would have never been exposed to," President Trump said. "Because I was on Fifth Avenue in Manhattan, you don't meet the same people that you meet when you're in Iowa, Ohio, and Pennsylvania and lots of other places that I like so much. So I was exposed to a lot of people, from a religious standpoint, that I would've never met before. And so it has had an impact on me."

Enter Mike Pence into that band of believers. He's right at the top. Throughout the course of his administration, Trump often calls on the Vice President to get things started with a prayer. "He'll nudge me and say, 'You want to say a prayer before the meal?' Or ask my wife to say a prayer. It's very natural. It's actually fairly routine. He's someone that invites faith into moments." But what's interesting is that Trump's Christianity, unlike other elements of his life and career, doesn't play out in a flashy way. His Mainline Protestant upbringing didn't come packaged that way. "One of the things about him is he's a very private person," Pence said. "His Presbyterian faith is genuine but he's interested in people. Genuinely interested." That's a main reason why he enjoys being around spiritual people. His critics will say he probably does that to "feel" more religious. But the real motivation for him is a desire to be around what he calls "good people." He sees them as a sincere group attempting to make the world a better place.

During the transition process, after a long day of interviewing prospective cabinet members in Bedminster, New Jersey, Trump had an idea. He wanted to go to church and in classic Trump fashion, he wanted a few "spiritual people" to accompany him. "It was the end of a really long day and we were grabbing a bite to eat upstairs in the clubhouse," Pence recalls. "Karen, my wife, is there and he just says, 'You guys want to go to church tomorrow?' It was a Saturday night and I said, 'Yeah. I think we'd like to but we don't really know the area.' He says, 'Where I go is this little Presbyterian Church here in Bedminster . . . you guys would like it.' And I said, 'Good, I'll have our guys check into it.' And he goes, 'No, we'll go.' I said, 'Okay. That'd be great.' He grabbed a couple of his guys and said, 'Find out when the church service is and tell them.' " That's how the backstory went. The next day cameras caught Trump and Pence walking into church together, but Pence reminds us, "That was one hundred percent him."

During his first term, we know that Trump has rarely attended church. And while we know that going to church regularly is good for the soul and for building community with other believers, we also acknowledge that ultimately God measures a man's heart, not his church attendance record. A lack of church attendance doesn't necessarily translate into a lack of spiritual significance. We know he is constantly surrounded by evangelical leaders who pray with him and for him on a consistent basis. Nobody except for God and Trump will know about the consistency of his prayer life, but in an interview I conducted with the President during his first week in office, he gave signs that he relies on a power much higher than his own. "I've always felt the need to pray," Trump told me. "So, I would say that the office is so powerful that you need God even more . . . there's almost not a decision that you make when you're sitting in this position that isn't a really life-altering position. So God comes into it even more so."

President Trump's first term in office has given him and his evangelical allies plenty of reasons to pray: North Korea, ISIS, Charlottesville, race relations, immigration, the Russia investigations, enemies in the media, enemies within his own party, and of course, the Democrats. Take your pick, there's plenty to choose from. History will judge this president on all those pressing issues, but one facet cannot be denied: Trump never stops working. "His work ethic is actually hard to describe," Mike Pence said. "His energy level is actually hard to describe. I heard once that President Teddy Roosevelt was described by a contemporary as pure energy, and I've often said that must come around every hundred years at the White House, because the President and I will generally talk early, we'll talk late, we talk through the day. It's amazing." As we've discovered in this book, this famous work ethic is a family trait, instilled within him by his Lutheran and Protestant faith roots. "He has an indefatigable capacity," Pence said. "Every day is a new day; we're back working on what we came here to do. I ultimately believe that springs from his faith and his upbringing, and a lifetime of building and overcoming."

When you're president, there is a need to balance two important concepts: law and grace. Just like in the Bible, God establishes the law/commandments/moral code and He affords grace to those at the same time. For God, it's not problematic. He's sovereign, so he has it covered. For us feeble humans, including presidents, it's trickier. On immigration, Trump's been clear about enforcing the laws of the land. At the same time, grace and compassion come into play when it comes to illegal immigrants who were brought here as children through no fault of their own. On allowing refugees from other countries into America, Trump has been clear that America will not be a gateway for the unknown. But America will still accept refugees. What's the proper balance?

Most Americans, whether they like Trump or not, understand that he calls it as he sees it, something the Vice President has seen play out extensively. "My experience with the President is what you see is what you get. He doesn't put on airs." We saw this play out during his big dispute with the NFL over players kneeling during the national anthem. While we won't litigate the merits of who's right or wrong in this space, it's important to point out that what may come across as insensitivity to issues of racial injustice is nothing of the kind in Trump's way of thinking. Remember, he's old school; think about good old-fashioned American patriotism and a time in America where the outward love of country expressed itself abundantly. Trump sees it through a traditional worldview of the America he remembers. So, is that mean-spirited? Hard to argue that it is. But one of Trump's main assets was also in play here: He has an uncanny knack for going with his gut instinct, which more often than not tends to either be outright correct or at least perfectly suited for how his base of supporters thinks. "He understands human nature," Vice President Pence said. "I've seen him in a lot of settings, whether it's recruiting people to the administration, whether it's the legislative process where we've got some things done. He just knows when to close, knows when the moment is."

Trump's view of America benefits evangelicals immensely. His traditional views translate into traditional policies more in line with a pre-1960s America that comports itself more in line with biblical Christianity than the watered-down cultural Christianity of today. "I think he has an enormous gratitude for the support of the evangelical community across the country," Pence explained. "And it's mutual. Here is a president who stood without apology for the sanctity of life. Here's a president that stood strong for Israel. He's followed through on what he said he would do, and I think people are grateful for that." Having Pence by his side gives evangelicals comfort that Trump will continue to receive good counsel. Evangelist James Robison said that's the key: to make sure Trump is surrounded with people who are preaching biblically sound advice to him. "If wisdom gets in the room with this man, and if truth is presented in unconditional love, my personal opinion is he will always receive the wisdom, and he will make the best decision." If that happens, evangelical leaders like Eric Metaxas see good things on the horizon for evangelicals who put their trust in this president. "I think Trump's going to be more than fine," Metaxas said. "I'm sure he'll be reelected. . . . I just think that he's going to do what God put him there to do."

Beyond the Neil Gorsuch Supreme Court victory and all the pro-life policies initiated by President Trump at the beginning of his first term, he has actually delivered on even more for evangelicals. His decision to ban transgenders from the military was a shot into the culture wars that few expected. The Trump Justice Department is now arguing aggressively in court on behalf of cake bakers who say their free speech rights will be violated if forced to bake a specialized cake for a gay wedding. And the attorney general's office is also contending that sexual orientation is not protected under civil rights discrimination laws. President Trump tells us he's not done. "I think you're going to see an upward track right now," the President said. "It's really right back on track right now. And we have much more to do."

Statements like that will provide liberals with even less sleep than they are probably already receiving since this administration started. But it shouldn't surprise anymore if Trump is right. He has been a man of his word when it comes to evangelical policy priorities, and it helps immensely to have "ole reliable Mike Pence" a few feet down from the Oval Office. On a spiritual provincial level, there's an expectation too. Michele Bachmann, an evangelical adviser to the Trump administration, sums it up pretty neatly. "It's the Most High God who lifts up who He will and takes down who He will. I have absolutely no doubt that the President of the United States is not there in his current position, together with the Vice President, by accident. They are there specifically by the design of the hand of God."

29

Riyadh, Jerusalem, and Rome

It's not every day that you run into Ivanka Trump as you board a commercial jetliner. I was a bit blurry-eyed after covering every moment of President Trump's "World Religion Tour" to Riyadh, Jerusalem, and Rome. I just wanted to sleep, even if I had the un-lucky seat assignment in the dreaded fortieth row next to the bath-room. Yet as I made my way on board the United Airlines plane in Rome on the way back to Washington, DC, even in my near zombie-like state, it was hard to miss her.

"Ivanka?" I inquired just to make sure this wasn't some sort of zombie dream. After all, why wasn't she in First Class? She was with the commoners! Or better yet, why wasn't she chartering some private plane? Surely her father could make those arrangements. But it wasn't a dream at all.

"David, oh my goodness! How are you?" Ivanka replied with a big smile. I quickly proceeded into her row, where I noticed a man sitting next to her looking down at a newspaper wearing a base-ball cap.

He looked up. "Hi David," he exclaimed in a jovial manner.

"Jared, how are you?" It was Jared Kushner, Ivanka's husband, or put another way: a pretty powerful player in the West Wing. Don't let the baseball cap fool you. He's not just the President's son-in-law. He's successful in his own right and has the President's ear in all matters, big and small.

In short, I had just had an encounter with "Javanka."

"David, what do you think of the trip so far?" Kushner said inquisitively, genuinely wanting to know my answer. On that plane that day, I gave him the thirty-second version, essentially explaining how it couldn't have gone any better for the President. But as the legendary radio icon Paul Harvey might interject: "Now, for the rest of the story."

The rest of this chapter of Donald Trump's story takes place on location: from the desert plateau of Riyadh, through the holy (and toxic) city of Jerusalem, and concluding amid the one hundred ten acres of sacred Vatican ground. You could say, in many ways, the faith of Donald Trump broke new ground here, in word and in deed. He was about to proclaim the name of God in public like no other modern American president before him, and he was about to experience a spiritual awakening in the Holy Land in front of a controversial wall, perfectly appropriate for Trump!

The fact that this President chose Riyadh, Saudi Arabia, as his first international stop came as a surprise to many in the media. They thought Trump would go the traditional route (why in the world would they think that?) by heading to Canada like President Obama before him or maybe Mexico like George W. Bush did in 2001. But in typical "Trumpian" fashion, he chose to go big.

God works in mysterious ways, and on that first overseas trip it didn't take a rocket scientist to figure out that God was up to something. Sure, he came to Riyadh to get the Saudis on board in the fight against terrorism and fortify strategic partnerships. Sure, he came to Jerusalem to begin "The Art of the Middle East Peace Deal." And yes, going to Rome to meet the Pope was an attempt to endear himself to the influential leader of Catholics worldwide. But spiritually speaking, it was hard to miss God during Trump's travels.

The moment President Trump landed in Riyadh, he was greeted by sweltering one-hundred-ten-degree-plus temperatures and a salute fit for a king. The red carpet was fully rolled out on the runway at King Khalid Airport, with seven attendants literally sweeping any lingering dust before the eagle (aka Air Force One) landed.

An official Saudi military salute ensued, complete with a red, white, and blue flyover and cannon fire. (They may want to rethink the cannon fire in any sort of Mideast fanfare. It can frighten a few Westerners who witness the festivities.) President Trump arrived to positive local headlines from the Saudis, honored to be host to this unconventional president and smitten with his reputation for boldness and fearlessness.

Driving through the streets of Riyadh, we saw immense signs over bridges proclaiming "Together We Prevail," with Trump's mug alongside that of Saudi King Salman. The only thing more striking may have been seeing a good old-fashioned American restaurant, Buffalo Wild Wings, on the way to the hotel from the airport arrival ceremony. But unlike the calorie-laden Buffalo Wild Wings, what Trump would offer would be low in calories yet high in spiritual wisdom.

One thing we know about Donald Trump is that the man will refuse to say anything he doesn't truly believe. It's well established that Trump is not your typical politician, so when Trump delivers a speech, he's going to lay it all on the table. Nobody—and I mean nobody—is going to put words in his mouth or tell him what to say. If he doesn't truly believe it, he won't say it. Or if he does, he'll qualify it if he must.

In that context, consider the following: On this five-day "World Religion Tour," Donald J. Trump would utter or invoke the name of God more than thirty times! We're not counting pithy ending lines in a speech like "God bless America." No, we're talking hardcore God speech. It was fire and brimstone language. Goodness gracious, when was the last time a president of the United States invoked the name of God in public remarks as often as Donald Trump did during that one week alone? Reagan? No. The evangelical George W. Bush? No. Trump stands alone. Just the way he likes it.

It seemed fitting that President Trump would give his signature speech to Gulf nations at the King Abdulaziz International Conference Centre. The center is stunning from an architectural standpoint, a truly regal setting fit for a big moment like this, situated in the upscale diplomatic zone. Locals understand it is here where major worldwide political and business leaders meet to do business and strike deals.

For Trump, it was an opportunity to shoot straight, not mince words, and throw God squarely in the center of all things. Try these statements on for size: "Terrorists do not worship God, they worship death," Trump exclaimed. "Every time a terrorist murders an innocent person, and falsely invokes the name of God, it should be an insult to every person of faith." And his warning to would-be terrorists had a bold message centered on the afterlife. "If you choose the path of terror, your life will be empty, your life will be brief, and your soul will be condemned!"

The mainstream media paid no attention to his faithful, evangelical-sounding words. But make no mistake: Evangelicals were paying attention. They remember President Obama's 2009 speech in Cairo, Egypt, where he labeled murderous terrorists as part of a "violent extremism" movement. Trump took that rhetoric to another, more realistic level, calling it "Islamist extremism."

Evangelicals also remember how President Obama glowingly gushed about the Quran multiple times during that 2009 speech. In the Age of Trump that was not going to happen—and it didn't. He had no words at all devoted to the Quran. That isn't surprising considering that during our first interview at Trump Tower back in 2011 he questioned what was being taught from the Quran, remarking, "There's something there that teaches some very negative vibe."

Speaking of negative vibes, what waited next for Trump was a land full of them, better known as Israel.

Fireworks lit up the night sky over the Old City in Jerusalem, a beautiful sight to behold indeed as our CBN crew watched nearby from a local rooftop. Those explosives in the sky were nothing compared to the emotionally explosive atmosphere that has gripped this ancient, holy city for, well, forever and a day. Israelis and Palestinians claim Jerusalem as their capital city. We'll leave that discussion for another time along with a seventeen-volume set of encyclopedias. The fireworks set off on this night in Jerusalem were to welcome Donald Trump to town, and for a man who creates plenty of fireworks himself, it seemed an appropriate welcome for him and for the volatile situation he came here to solve.

When Donald Trump took office in January 2017, there was great anticipation and excitement that he would move the United States embassy from Tel Aviv to Jerusalem. It would be a provocative move to clearly show the world that Jerusalem is indeed the capital of Israel, not Palestine. A year before this trip, on the campaign trail at Liberty University, Candidate Trump said to me that he was "for that one hundred percent." But during his first visit here to the Holy Land, he made no historic announcement. He would leave the embassy where it is . . . for now.

There's a different calculation as commander in chief when you're trying to negotiate the art of the deal between the Israelis and the Palestinians. The media was quick to call it a broken campaign promise but evangelicals knew better: They understood Trump wasn't betraying Israel or them. He was simply doing what he does best: negotiating. They didn't lose too much sleep over it, knowing full well that Trump will play that card when he has to.

It must be clearly understood that, from a public policy perspective, Trump's relationship with evangelicals hinges on top-tier issues like religious liberty, abortion, and, yes, a staunch protection and defense of Israel. Evangelicals stand with Israel, and they want to make sure Trump does too. They understand the biblical truth put forth in Genesis when God established the Abrahamic Covenant, saying to Abraham and all his descendants (read: the Jews), "I will bless those who bless you, and whoever curses you I will curse, and all peoples on earth will be blessed through you" (Genesis 12:3). Nobody is claiming Trump understands the theology and significance of all of this, but evangelicals believe fervently that this president authentically has Israel's back, the exact opposite of what they believed about President Obama before him.

Furthermore, it was here in the holiest of cities where Trump's spiritual walk seemed to take an upward turn. He felt something. It's not something you measure in a test tube, but God was moving. At Yad Vashem, Israel's Holocaust memorial, Trump took it all in: a concrete building shaped like a triangular prism, the nearly seven-hundred-foot-long skylight, and most notably the exhibition halls dedicated to the emotionally gripping stories of the millions of Jews who were brutally murdered. "It was the most savage crime against God and his children," Trump told the assembled crowd at the site. As he continued, he also felt something else here. "This is a land filled with beauty, wonder, and the spirit of God."

The spirit of God stayed with him at the Western Wall in Jerusalem, the historical and holy site where Jews and millions around the world from other faiths come to pray. President Trump made history by becoming the first sitting president of the United States to visit it. The others stayed away for fear of the controversy that would follow, considering the Palestinians see that area as the future site of their capital city. Regardless, Trump barreled forward, and evangelicals applaud him for it. He's fearless. Placing his hand gently on the wall with a traditional kippah adorning his head, Trump reflected. It was a solemn moment between Trump and God. Something transpired because, after all, it's hard to approach the imposing sixty-two-foot hallowed wall and not feel something. Indeed, a spiritual transaction occurred. "I was deeply moved by my visit today to the Western Wall," Trump said afterward. "Words fail to capture the experience. It will leave an impression on me forever." You can't quantify a moment like that. It just stays with you.

The spiritual hangover seemed to continue into the next day. His speech at the Israel Museum continued to hammer home this continual God-based theme that we had seen play out throughout this trip. He played to a packed house, so crammed, in fact, that reporters in the back of the room were standing on any chair they could find to get a clear view. What they witnessed, along with engrossed television-watching evangelicals back home, was an American president who didn't bring up the toxic issues of Palestinian statehood and a two-state solution. In this setting, Israelis didn't want to hear talk like that . . . and Trump delivered. Instead, what they got were consistent shout-outs to the Almighty. Among the gems included a spiritual tribute to Jerusalem: "This city, like no other place in the world, reveals the longing of the human heart—to know and worship God," Trump exclaimed.

Even in Bethlehem, one of his other stops where he met with Palestinian leader Mahmoud Abbas, Trump brought the godly message into the West Bank, a territory controlled by the Palestinians. "In this spirit of hope, we come to Bethlehem, asking God for a more peaceful, safe, and far more tolerant world for all of us." It should be noted that evangelicals didn't miss the fact that Trump and Abbas didn't shake hands in their traditional photo-op in front of the press. Moreover, sharp-eyed, faith-filled Christians noticed Trump's direct language when he spoke these words in front of Abbas: "Peace can never take root in an environment where violence is tolerated, funded, and even rewarded." Clearly, that was a strongly worded verbal jab at the Palestinian government's policy of providing payments for would-be terrorists who attack the state of Israel.

With his mission, for the time being at least, complete in Israel, it was time to turn his attention to a vastly different situation: mending fences with Pope Francis, the 266th pope of the Roman Catholic Church. Candidate Trump and the Pontiff had a bit of a spat during the presidential campaign when Francis questioned Trump's Christianity because of his fondness for building border walls around America. Trump didn't like the Pope's verbiage one bit and let him have it. Eventually, the controversy dissipated, but getting on the Pope's good side would have plenty of political upsides, considering the last time we checked this guy wields quite a bit of power with his Catholic flock. And plus, he has a cool car. Honestly, if Trump is ever going to hitch a ride in the Popemobile, he's got to play nice. And that's exactly what happened.

As our CBN crew ventured into the bright sunlight of the Vatican Courtyard in the early-morning hours, we waited with anticipation for President Trump's arrival. We looked around for a huge motorcade, but all we saw was an Uber-like old Ford Focus pull up. Surely, President Trump wasn't coming to the Vatican in a car like that! Yes, it's American, but that's not how he rolls. I was right. It wasn't Trump. "Oh my goodness," I said as I looked on in bewilderment. "That's the Pope." He arrived in humble fashion, but after looking at the car, the only thought running through my mind was "Does that thing even have air-conditioning?" Trump eventually made his way into the courtyard, greeted by a dozen or so dignitaries. The Pope was already inside getting ready for the historic meeting.

By all accounts, the meeting went very well. No major dust-ups, and in Trump Land that's always a good day. But something else happened that had nothing to do with such agenda items as climate change or immigration. Trump received a gift. A book called *Evangelii Gaudium*—"The Joy of the Gospel"—an exhortation written by the Pope about how the church needs to evangelize around the world. It contains plenty of social justice talking points, but more crucially it presents the gospel message in a compelling, personal way. Trump told the Pope he would be reading it. Take note of how the book starts out:

> The joy of the gospel fills the hearts and lives of all who encounter Jesus. Those who accept his offer of salvation are set free from sin, sorrow, inner emptiness and loneliness. With Christ joy is constantly born anew.
>
> The salvation which God offers us is the work of his mercy. No human efforts, however good they may be, can enable us to merit so great a gift.
>
> The Lord does not disappoint those who take this risk; whenever we take a step towards Jesus, we come to realize that he is already there, waiting for us with open arms. Now is the time to say to Jesus: "Lord, I have let myself be deceived; in a thousand ways I have shunned your love, yet here I am once more, to renew my covenant with you. I need you. Save me once again, Lord, take me once more into your redeeming embrace." How good it feels to come back to him whenever we are lost! Let me say this once more: God never tires of forgiving us; we are the ones who tire of seeking his mercy.

God definitely works in mysterious ways, but many times it's pretty obvious. This is one of those times. It's not happenstance that Donald Trump became president. The Apostle Paul wrote, "The authorities that exist have been established by God" (Romans 13:1). It's not a coincidence that Pope Francis is where he is at today. And it's not just simple "chance" that the two men intertwined on this day so Donald Trump could receive this specific book at this specific time in his life. Just like all of us, our spiritual walk is a journey: highs and lows; times of confidence; times of doubt; stretches of wandering and periods of profound closeness with the Almighty. Donald Trump's faith journey is no different. On this day, in this religious city, Trump received "The Joy of the Gospel." But after reading it and digesting it thoroughly, maybe he'll *experience* the joy too and receive the fullness of the gift that the Spirit intended.

In a way, in one week's time, Donald Trump's "World Religion Tour" morphed into "God's Holy Tour." Leave it to God to use Donald Trump, warts and all, and the bully pulpit of the American presidency to shout His name abundantly in three of the holiest cities around the globe. Egyptian president Abdel Fattah el-Sisi summed it up nicely when he told President Trump that "you have a unique personality that is capable of doing the impossible." That's true. But what's even more impressive is God doing the impossible. And Donald Trump's election to the highest office in the land is exhibit A.

30

Give Me Liberty

"I think evangelicals have found their dream president," Jerry Falwell told Jeanine Pirro, host of the Fox News program bearing her name. Falwell appeared on her show in late April 2017, to share his thoughts about the first one hundred days of the Trump administration. Falwell had choice words for Congressional Republicans who were failing to deliver on campaign promises from either ineptitude or chicanery: "These moderates just make my blood boil. Honestly, I have more respect for Democrats than I do moderate Republicans, because at least Democrats admit what they believe, and they say it up front, and you know what you're dealing with. These moderates pretend to be conservatives, they woo conservative voters, and then they're not conservative when they get in office."

Two weeks later, President Trump journeyed down to Lynchburg, Virginia, to deliver the commencement address at the 2017 graduation exercises at Falwell's Liberty University. Such an event at this location—the school that the founder of the Moral Majority built—makes a fit ending point for a book about "the faith of Donald J. Trump."

From the launch of Ted Cruz's campaign at Liberty University in March 2015 to Trump's May 2017 graduation speech, ten thousand news articles or opinion pieces have been written about "evangelicals and Trump." The campaign season produced a cottage industry of analysts giving their take on the question: "Who are evangelicals?"—or more precisely, "*In light of the 2016 election, who are evangelicals?*" The term has been fought over for almost seventy years now, since conservative Christians pioneered the movement as a response to what they deemed to be the isolationist and acerbic tendencies of Fundamentalists. Men like Billy Graham and Carl Henry saw the need to respond to both Liberalism and Fundamentalism, and Evangelicalism was the result—though they wouldn't want it to be said that they "created" it, because evangelicals would simply say that their belief and practice is simply biblical Christianity.

Falwell Sr. spent most of his ministry wearing the Fundamentalist label, as the Southern Baptist Convention was too liberal for him and fellow "Independent Baptists" at the time. Historically, Independents did not embrace the evangelical label—though, by any theological accounting, they were first cousins. Even so, when Cruz, Sanders, Carson, Trump (and many others) showed up to speak at a Liberty convocation, their appearance would always be described as "the candidate's outreach to evangelicals." Such is the nature of labels and group identification markers—they are malleable and change over time.

When Trump spoke to the Liberty graduation crowd of fifty thousand, one fact was unmistakably clear: Trump was with his people, and they were with him.

Trump: It's been a little over a year since I've spoken on your beautiful campus and so much has changed. Right here, the class of 2017, dressed in cap and gown, graduating to a totally brilliant future. And here I am standing before you as president of the United States. So I'm guessing there are some people here today who thought that either one of those things, either one, would really require major help from God. Do we agree? And we got it. . . .

Remember this, nothing worth doing ever, ever, ever came easy. Following your convictions means you must be willing to face criticism from those who lack the same courage to do what is right. And they know what is right, but they don't have the courage or the guts or the stamina to take it and to do it. It's called the road less traveled.

The crowd interrupted Trump dozens of times for applause, especially when he mentioned themes relating to God and love of country. "He got at least two standing ovations," Falwell recalled, "and he made the speech very personal to Liberty."

Trump: In just two days we will mark the tenth anniversary of Reverend Falwell's passing. And I used to love watching him on television, hearing him preach. He was a very special man.

Falwell said he worked with Trump's speechwriters a little in the days leading up to the speech, giving them some background information about the history of the university. "But he went way beyond that with his own," Falwell said. "You know how he likes to ad-lib— and those were the parts of the speech that people just absolutely loved. It was a wonderful speech by itself. It was one of the best commencement speeches I've ever heard. It's probably the best one."

Trump: America has always been the land of dreams because America is a nation of true believers. When the Pilgrims landed at Plymouth, they prayed. When the Founders wrote the Declaration of Independence, they invoked our creator four times, because in America we don't worship government, we worship God. That is why our elected officials put their hands on the Bible and say "so help me God" as they take the oath of office. It is why our currency proudly declares "in God we trust." And it's why we proudly proclaim that we are one nation under God, every time we say the Pledge of Allegiance.

"There's a tradition that goes back at least to Eisenhower, maybe earlier, that the new president would give his first commencement speech at Notre Dame," Jerry Falwell explained to us. "It meant a lot to us that the President came here first because we've always aspired to be for evangelical young people what Notre Dame is for Catholics. So, to have the United States president break that tradition and choose Liberty was sort of a 'coming of age' for us. It was a passing of the guard, in some respects, from Mainline and Roman Catholic faith to an evangelical Christian school. That's why I say it was the greatest day in Liberty's history."

> *Trump:* America is better when people put their faith into action. As long as I am your president, no one is ever going to stop you from practicing your faith or from preaching what's in your heart. We will always stand up for the right of all Americans to pray to God and to follow his teachings.

"So he just hit a home run out of the park," Falwell recalled. "I called him last night to make sure he knew how grateful we were and how much people loved him here."

Falwell said that he had gotten messages from well-known Southern Baptist pastors and other pastors around the country who were his dad's peers. They said that, from the speech, they can tell God's really working in Mr. Trump's life. "That was an observation they made from afar," Falwell said, adding, "I believe the same thing."

The Faith Advisory Committee continues to give counsel to Trump, meeting at the White House for daylong discussions that result in recommendations to the President about policy and messaging. All the members of the group are evangelical, though they come from different theological streams. The board's leadership is informal, though Paula White and Johnnie Moore are often seen or heard from in news stories about their gatherings. White has a special role since she has a very close spiritual bond with the President. "My purpose is to bring men and women of God to the President," White said. "To be a doorkeeper and to serve the President and his family and those that the Lord chooses in private counsel."

Samuel Rodriguez said the board offers "very straight talk" to the President. "I've never been in a conversation where the faith advisory board is silent. This is not a rubber-stamp board. It's a board that's committed to the centrality of Jesus and biblical truth."

Evangelist James Robison has been in a position to offer spiritual counsel to national leaders since the 1970s. It was Robison who gave then-candidate Ronald Reagan a line that was spoken to evangelicals at a big rally in 1980—a line that has been called one of "the most famous lines of the Age of Evangelicalism." Reagan said to the group of Christians: "I know this is nonpartisan so you can't endorse me. But I want you to know . . . I endorse you and what you're doing."

Robison, who never endorses a candidate, began meeting with Trump for spiritual counsel because of Ben Carson. After Carson dropped out of the race and was considering whom to endorse, he met with Trump and offered him an endorsement under one condition: that he meet at least once with this preacher named James Robison. "From that time on, we have been in ongoing communication," Robison recalled.

> I have never wavered; I have faithfully and in unconditional love presented the unadulterated Word of God as forcefully as I'm capable of. In fifty-five years of public ministry, meeting with people on all levels, I have never—I

repeat *never*—been received by anyone with greater appreciation, humility and focused interest in all the principles of freedom and biblical truths I have shared. I would say that Mr. Trump heard because of the prayers of concerned Christians for everything they longed for him to hear face-to-face. I have faithfully sown good seed. Only time will clearly reveal the soil on which it was sown. I personally do not think Donald Trump will ever be the same man. I think he is so concerned about correcting what is wrong and sees an over-reaching, out-of-control government along with policies that hurt the people, he will stand against those problems as long as he lives.

The Faith Advisory Board has not been without controversy, though the criticisms seem contrived and much ado about nothing. For example, after the Charlottesville, Virginia, tragedy, dozens of CEOs stepped down from their role on an economic advisory committee—citing President Trump's response to the alt-right. Immediately, a wave of critics demanded an explanation from the Faith Advisory Board as to why they did not disband and leave Trump to himself.

On the other hand, Christian author and radio host Eric Metaxas thinks "It's ridiculous. I think just about everybody on the Advisory Council is like, you've got to be kidding me. We're going to stand up for Trump a hundred times more. It's been unbelievably despicable the way he's been treated. And I think there's some kind of demonic deception. I mean I've never seen anything like it to begin to compare it to in my lifetime."

Also, in mid-July, the board members, who we should point out pay their own way to and from Washington, were at the White House for their meetings—not with the President, but simply with each other and with some administration officials who stopped by to discuss certain matters. Vice President Mike Pence stopped by and talked with them for a while. Later, Pence told the President about his meeting with the group, and Trump called for them to come and visit with him. They did so, and at the end, someone suggested praying for the President—hardly a shocking thing for any person of faith to do. While in prayer, someone snapped a picture and sent it out on Twitter—again, a pretty normal thing for people to do in the social media world that we live in.

Johnnie Moore said praying with the President was something that naturally flowed from the fact that the group consistently prays for him at their meetings. "I think we pray very specific things for him. We always pray the gospel, and we pray that God would protect and provide for him. That God would lead him as he leads us, would give him wisdom. We've even prayed that God would speak to him in the night. Lots of very, very specific things that we pray for him. We believe it makes a difference."

Michele Bachmann, who was in the Oval Office for that prayer with the President, became persuaded of something afterward. "I came away from that meeting in Washington, DC, more convinced than ever that the President of the United States, Donald J. Trump, truly is a real believer," Bachmann said. "He did not flinch when Paula White asked if we could lay our hands on the President and pray for him. For Christians, we know that it is very common standard practice to do this. Praying is not weird. Laying hands on someone isn't weird; because all it means is just that we are touching that person lightly and asking God to bless that person. And that's what we were doing, and the President was very, very familiar with being prayed for and very familiar with having people lay their hands on him to receive a blessing."

Nevertheless, cynical criticism erupted. William Barber, a North Carolina minister and political leader, said the Oval Office camaraderie and prayer amounted to "theological malpractice that borders on heresy." John Fea, a historian at an evangelical college and a consistent critic of Trump, wrote that "Trump has forced them [evangelicals] to embrace a pragmatism that could damage the gospel around the world, and force many Christians to rethink their religious identities and affiliations." Many speculated that the issue of "Russian involvement in the election" was pressing in on the President that week and that the picture-of-prayer seemed like a decoy to distract. Those who took part in the prayer, however, were left scratching their heads about that inference. They're pastors. They pray with parishioners—all the time and every day—and though praying in the Oval Office for the sitting president has a certain bit of uniqueness to it, he's just a man and they're still representing Christ as Christians and ministers. White House press secretary Sarah Huckabee Sanders said, "The idea that someone would pray only when they're in crisis is ridiculous."

This event served as another reminder that no good deed goes unpunished in our hyper-political and cynical world, where friendship and pastoral counsel with POTUS can be likened to "theological malpractice" and "heresy." Pastor Ronnie Floyd, former president of the Southern Baptist Convention and the head of the 2018 National Day of Prayer, said, "The Gospel is not being compromised. I believe firmly in the Gospel. I never one time compromised the Gospel of Jesus Christ."

The first Thursday of each May is the National Day of Prayer, an event that a sitting president observes with at least a proclamation encouraging US citizens to prayer. On May 3, the evening before Trump's first observance of the day, the President held a special dinner in the Blue Room of the White House for some of his evangelical advisers. The evening had the feeling of a reunion of sorts, as the leaders and Trump had battled together to win the White House the year before—something that had seemed to be a lost cause even on the morning of the election. But now they were all seated together, hearing a prayer by Franklin Graham before eating "a dinner of shrimp scampi with parsley butter, red wine braized short ribs, and wild ramp gnocchi."

Christian singer Steven Curtis Chapman sang two songs—"Be Still and Know" and "The Lord's Prayer." The Museum of the Bible, set to open in the fall of 2017, sent a special gift of a framed page from a 1611 KJV edition Bible. Paula White made the presentation of the gift, calling it "a Bible which as you know was commissioned by a political leader to the church." After the meal, the President even took several of the guests up to the residential quarters, a moment Pastor Robert Jeffress remembers vividly. "At the end of the dinner, he leaned over, and he said, 'Hey, would any of you be interested in going up and seeing the residence?' He said, 'You know the Secret Service says I'm not supposed to do that, but hey, I'm President, I can do what I want to.' So he took us up for another hour tour of the residence. It was unbelievable."

The next day in the Rose Garden, President Trump stood with religious leaders, including representatives from the Little Sisters of the Poor, and signed the Presidential Executive Order Promoting Free Speech and Religious Liberty—looking to kick-start the fulfillment of his campaign promise to put an end to the Johnson Amendment and to ensure religious freedom.

Fans of the Executive Order noted that it was only a start to a full-spectrum push-back against the assaults on religious liberty that have taken place in recent years. Franklin Graham said, of the executive order, that "Eighty percent is better than nothing." Pastor Jim Farlow, a leader of the Pulpit Freedom Sunday movement, which encourages pastors to ignore the threat of the IRS meddling with the content of a pastor's sermons, said that Trump's order was "a remarkable first step. Admittedly we need to be vigilant to see follow-up steps, but this was a great moment for the US Constitution, people of biblical values, people of any faith, and the future of the Republic." Ralph Reed said that it "removes a sword of Damocles that has hung over the faith community," but that it was "the first bite at the apple, not the last." And Tony Perkins called it "a clear reflection of his campaign promise to protect the religious freedoms of Americans."

Among other Evangelicals, however, criticism of the order was sharp. Rod Dreher said the order contains "nothing—zip, nada— to protect the religious liberty of people who dissent from LGBT rights dogmas."

Trump's heart is to bring peace to faith communities nervous about a clampdown on the free exercise of their religious freedom and speech—and not just the religion that takes place within worship or the four walls of a house of worship. "As long as I'm President, no one is going to stop you from practicing your faith or from preaching what is in your heart," Trump tells Christians. Did the executive order move mountains? No, but if it truly is a start, then that is a movement in the right direction that faith leaders will look back on with joy. Halt the brakes on the previous administration's direction, and start turning the public policy back around toward the protection of religion.

In my Oval Office interview with President Trump, he recognized that executive action on the Johnson Amendment is only the beginning. "Now we want to go through Congress also and make it permanent," Trump says. "But we've knocked it. And that was a horrible thing . . . they're not allowed to get involved, they're not allowed to have any say as to where the country has gone."

Tony Perkins recalled that the issue of religious liberty was something they began to center on through the recommendation of former congressman Frank Wolf—an international leader in the battle for religious liberty. "We had Wolf at our 2014 Summit, and when he and I were in the green room backstage, he told me, 'Tony, you need to make religious freedom the key issue in the 2016 presidential election.' And indeed, that became our focus—our number one issue. It is a tangible issue that people can feel and understand—and religious liberty is truly at risk here and around the world."

Though not yet forty, Johnnie Moore is a significant leader in telling the story of international threats to religious liberty. We asked him if he had lobbied President Trump about these issues. Was he interested in them because of Moore's passion? "No, I didn't have to raise the issues once—never sent a single email," Moore said. "He came up with the Johnson Amendment on his own, just through reading the newspaper and talking to people of faith. And in campaign speeches, Trump's constant talk about Christians being persecuted in the Middle East, that wasn't because some speechwriter was putting that in there. It's because he authentically and genuinely cared about it. He was speaking on those issues with integrity. Now, as it comes down to the nuances of policy since he became president, there have been a lot of conversations back and forth. But in terms of him coming at the issue from his own personal conviction, it was just that—his personal conviction."

One of the oft-repeated questions related to Donald Trump's relationship to evangelicals is "Who is using whom?" Yes, that's a cynical question, but given the reality of the lure of power that flows from the Oval Office, people have reason to be leery of anyone who wants to get into that room—either as president or as counsel to the president. Even in our lifetimes, men of great integrity, like Billy Graham, wrestled with the question of how much access to the president is too much. When does friendship with the man called POTUS begin to blind one to his faults? Is the relationship between a president and the Christian pulpit or pew little more than a "you scratch my back and I'll scratch yours" give and take?

Moore said that, from the beginning, the group told the President they weren't going to bring him "problems without solutions." They wanted to only bring the President problems that were coupled with solutions—and even to bring about the solution themselves through the broader faith community. "There's all kinds of things that we've done for him, that he's probably not even aware of," Moore said. "That's about the authenticity of the relationship. You don't want it to be transactional. You want it to be real."

That note of maintaining authenticity and integrity was often heard among the evangelicals we talked to—that they would maintain their Christian identity, even as they didn't expect the President to suddenly be someone who walked in evangelical shoes for the past seventy years. As Moore explains, "He didn't become something for us. We found who we were looking for, for a long time. He came disguised as a New York businessman in a golden tower, and he was somehow a kind of knight in shining armor I think for the evangelical community. I think for those of us who take the Bible seriously, it wasn't a surprise to us that God had for whatever reason picked the person we wouldn't have expected to be our champion. I mean he's done that a lot in history."

So, even while understanding that Trump did not "come from us," the way explicitly evangelical candidates like Mike Huckabee or Ben Carson did, leaders like Jeffress can state, "We thank God every day that he gave us a leader like Donald Trump. And Donald Trump returns the love with his own public affirmation: 'You fought hard for me, and now I'm fighting hard for all of you.'"

Now, such language causes some evangelicals concern; Rob Schenck wrote that "Evangelicals are a tool of Donald Trump. This could be the undoing of American evangelicalism. We could just become a political operation in the guise of a church." And John Fea wrote that "Trump threatens to change the course of American Christianity."

That seems a bit over the top to say the least. Grassroots evangelicals are happy to know that the people who run our nation hear wisdom from evangelicals. If there is no counsel being given to a president by men and women of faith, then the leader of the free world will still get counsel from somewhere. So, rather than leave POTUS without any spiritual counsel or friendship from faith leaders, it seems the wiser approach to have seasoned and prudent faith leaders enter the Oval Office with both joy and trepidation. As Proverbs 23:1–3 says, "When you sit down to eat with a ruler, observe carefully what is before you, and put a knife to your throat if you are given to appetite. Do not desire his delicacies, for they are deceptive food." The delicacies the author is talking about are more than food. In the Oval Office, the "deceptive food" is power and prestige. As for everyday people of faith who will never visit the White House, it is their calling to pray both for the president and for his counselors.

Robison, no amateur when it comes to giving counsel within the halls of power, addressed the issue of manipulation head on with none other than Trump himself. "In the first meeting, I told Mr. Trump he had lived as an intimidator and manipulator, and that must change to inspiration and motivation. I still believe this." Robison told Trump "he must get to know wise people who know how to effectively address every legitimate concern, and they are not wrapped up in themselves. . . . A thoroughbred racehorse can only win if a thousand pounds of power is submitted totally into the hands of a less-than-a-one-hundred-pound jockey. If you learn that lesson, you might win the Triple Crown and help America out of the ditch and see the blessings of freedom preserved."

In the end, what are we to make of a non-evangelical who received the majority of votes from evangelicals? Here are three lessons gleaned from evangelical leaders who think deeply about these issues.

First, as long as the Democratic Party is unreservedly pro-choice, then there's nothing to be ashamed of when Bible-reading, Jesus-loving Christians vote for the Republican candidate in every election. Such voting is not a matter of being co-opted by the GOP. Rather, it comes from a reflexive commitment to a biblical worldview. As Russell Moore wrote a decade ago, about Southern Baptists—but the same thing applies to all who are biblically orthodox:

> When confronted with American sexual libertarianism and public-square secularization, Southern Baptists committed to biblical orthodoxy have spoken reflexively from intuitions rooted in a biblically informed worldview. They were not pushing a "religious right" political program. They just didn't know what else to say. . . . Southern Baptists were not co-opted by Republican politicians or professional culture warriors. As they reflected on their deeply held commitments to a biblical worldview and Evangelical conversionism, they found allies in others who understood that the culture wars were about more than just "culture" in the abstract but about issues directly related to Christian worship and submission to biblical authority.

Second, if it is the case that the United States is slipping further into a "post-Christian" secularist culture like that of Europe, then the church needs to mature quickly and learn better methods for maintaining the unity of the body of Christ during elections when neither party's candidate can be embraced easily by Christians. Elections are a messy business, but 2016 brought out an unprecedented level of Christian-on-Christian vitriol. As James Robison wrote:

> The greater problem we see today in our nation is the church—not just people who claim a religious affiliation,

but people who actually have a personal relationship with Christ and have experienced an encounter that impacted their life in a very positive, undeniable fashion. We are watching these Bible-people seeking to destroy one another, to accuse one another. They have joined with "the accuser of the brethren," and they are firing at one another and questioning everything another person may do. If you happen to be seen with the wrong person, praying with the wrong person, caring about the wrong person, then you are a target of their disapproval. They are actually judging the heart, not just the actions because they don't know what may be happening behind the scenes. Imagine what the media today would say about Jesus going in the house of a Pharisee sitting on his sofa with a prostitute at his feet.

Third, we need to be realistic about the "religious right"—or whatever you want to call it—and just admit that it's not really going anywhere anytime soon. The electorate in the United States contains a big lump of clay called "Christians"—and from one generation to the next, leaders will cast a vision for how these people are to be involved in politics.

We asked Ralph Reed, who has been involved in Christian political action since the 1980s, what he thought the future of "the Religious Right" looked like:

> If you look at the electorate, the people who self-identify as born-again or evangelical Christians—who frequently attend church, who regularly pray and read the Bible— have outward behaviors that are evidence of an internal faith commitment. Depending on the election, the vote from those people as a share of the electorate is never less

than one out of every five voters, and on some election days it's as high as one out of every three voters. If you look at 2016, the evangelical number in our poll that we (Faith and Freedom) commissioned with Public Opinion Strategies showed that 27 percent of the electorate was evangelical, and when you asked them if they were conservative Christians, it actually rose to 32 percent of the electorate. Well, there is no way to have a constituency that big—larger than the African-American, gay, feminist, and Hispanic vote combined—and not have a market for their views, their values, and their issues.

As Christians, let's give each other the liberty to have different political opinions, and not be so quick to exercise strategies that serve only to divide.

In conclusion, we offer a few final thoughts about the faith of Donald Trump. First, this book was not titled "The Lamb's Book of Life." That's a separate nonfiction book written exclusively by Jesus Christ. Critics or supporters of Trump sometimes like to adopt the role of final spiritual arbiter, but remember: God will have that final say, not supportive evangelical leaders, not the Never Trumpers, not Republicans, Democrats, Independents—and not even we in the media (shocking, I know). God's word is the only one that matters. However, we will guarantee this: When believers in Jesus Christ enter heaven, they're going to be surprised by who they see and who they don't see. We'll leave it at that.

We also offer this thought to peruse: Donald Trump has two qualities that give one encouragement as one negotiates what to make of his faith: respect for the God of the Universe, and a desire to draw closer to Him. As our research clearly lays out, the yearning plays out in this President's regular tendency to seek prayer and spiritual guidance. That should not be discounted. It leads to this second area of respect for God.

Far too many individuals on earth choose selfishness over pursuing a relationship with God. In other words, one of the main reasons many don't choose God is because they choose themselves. They figure they don't need help from God, they can do it themselves just fine. While Donald Trump has a healthy ego, buckets of self-confidence, and a belief that he can get the job done, he doesn't leave God out of the equation. He knows God is bigger and better than him. How do we know? He has said it with his own lips, declaring to me on his California golf course that "God is the ultimate! I mean God created this and here's the Pacific Ocean right behind us . . . there's nothing like God." Does he state it like a thirty-year veteran of evangelical Christianity would? No, not even close. But getting hung up on the verbiage misses the point: Trump understands a simple but dramatically important concept: God created the universe. He is the ultimate builder.

Finally, Donald Trump relishes the role of culture warrior—and evangelicals have become the beneficiaries. While we know good works don't get you into heaven, his Mainline Protestant faith, along with his family upbringing, taught him that work and service go hand in hand. Chronicled throughout this book are policies and guidelines implemented by President Trump that show him to be someone evangelicals believe is standing up for traditional Judeo-Christian principles. Given that the Republican Party has let evangelicals down in the past, they were looking for someone different to come along. And different is what they got!

It's no secret that white, evangelical Christians, while still dominant politically, see their culture slipping away. They're not the majority they once were and they've been looking for that fierce protector. And along came Donald Trump, warts and all. But while the mainstream media was focusing on past blemishes that they thought would derail Trump with evangelicals, what they missed was the cultural link they had with the past: a connection of worldviews that encompassed patriotism, respect for God and Country, a disdain for political correctness, and a restoration of good old-fashioned Judeo-Christian values. The combination struck political gold for Trump and for evangelicals. But it was never fake. It was a solid union made possible by two willing participants: a mega-billionaire who was yearning for the great America he remembered, and evangelicals hoping to rekindle the culture they once knew.

While Donald Trump may have been the unlikeliest vessel, God works in mysterious ways. The same can be said about Trump's Faith Journey. From his Protestant confirmation in Jamaica, Queens, through the wild ride of the seventies, eighties, and nineties, and concluding with the laying on of hands in the Oval Office, we see that God can take any lump of clay and fashion it for His own purposes and glory. That's something Donald Trump and evangelicals can both be eternally grateful for.

Soli Deo Gloria—to God be all the glory.

Acknowledgments

David would like to thank:

Jesus . . . plus nothing. Ultimately, I owe all the credit to my Lord and Savior Jesus Christ so I begin with Him. I'm so thankful that I serve a God who loves me even when I fail . . . and that happens pretty regularly! He gave me the strength to partake in this venture and the serenity to see it through!

To my wife Lisette, thank you for putting up with lost weekends and late nights. When I look up the word "sacrificial" in the dictionary, your picture is front and center.

To my children, Drew, Lance, and Arielle, your constant encouragement means the world to me and the fact that you followed this endeavor along the way has been so meaningful.

Thank you to my CBN family: Rob Allman and Dana Brown Ritter, who, right from the very beginning, gave me the flexibility to do this project. A big "bless your heart" to Jennifer Wishon, who has been a big fan of this book from the very beginning; to my joyful CBN Faith Nation co-host and friend Jenna Browder, a dedicated prayer warrior who encouraged me throughout this process; and thank you to Amber C. Strong, Ben Kennedy, and John Jessup, who all lifted me up and took great interest throughout the development of this venture.

Finally, a big thank you to my co-author, Scott Lamb. Call him whatever you want: assiduous, faithful, indefatigable. The list of adjectives goes on and on. All I know is that beyond being one of the smartest guys I know, he's genuinely one of the nicest too. Thank you, Scott, for this partnership but even more importantly, thank you for a friendship that will last a lifetime.

Scott would like to thank:

To my wife Pearl, thank you for walking so faithfully through life with me and our children. Because of you, "Enjoy life with the wife whom you love" (Ecclesiastes 9:9) is a delightful verse.

To my five sons and daughter—Josiah, Nathanael, Isaac, Benjamin, Savannah, and Aaron—each of you are a grace from the Lord, a daily remembrance to me that the Lord is good and faithful. Love Jesus with all your heart, soul, mind, and strength—and the rest of life will flow from that affection.

To David Brody, I am grateful for your friendship and your jumping into this project when your plate of commitments was already full beyond measure. Long before we met, your godly reputation among our mutual friends preceded you. And now, having worked long hours together on this book, I can say that every bit of those accolades is true. And in addition to that, you exemplify Proverbs 22:29: "Do you see someone skilled in their work? They will serve before kings; they will not serve before officials of low rank."

David and Scott would like to thank:

A heartfelt thank you to Hope Hicks, Marc Lotter, and Jarrod Agen, who were instrumental in making two very important interviews happen. And while we're on the subject of interviews, thanks to the dozens of newsmakers, pastors, and political commentators who took the time to talk with us about this very important subject. This book is immensely better because of your efforts.

To the team at Broadside Books: Eric Nelson and Eric Meyers—thanks for believing in this book and making it sing!

Notes

Introduction

xiii *"Here you go":* Donald Trump interview with David Brody, April 2011.

xvii *eight of ten baby boomers:* "Religious Landscape Study." Pew Research Center's Religion & Public Life Project, May 11, 2015. http://www.pewforum.org/religious-landscape-study/generational-cohort/baby-boomer/.

xviii *He was born into the Mainline church:* Ibid. For an opposing view, see Ted A. Campbell, "Glory days? The myth of the mainline," *Christian Century,* July 2, 2014, https://www.christiancentury.org/article/2014–06/glory-days.

xviii *neither hot nor cold:* A paraphrase of Revelation 3:15–16.

xviii *"Jesus talked about removing the log:* A paraphrase of a portion of Matthew 7:1–5.

xviii *"Voters don't just send a candidate":* D. Michael Lindsay, *Faith in the Halls of Power: How Evangelicals Joined the American Elite* (New York: Oxford University Press, 2009).

xviii *Since eight of ten white evangelicals:* Kate Shellnutt, "Trump Elected President, Thanks to 4 in 5 White Evangelicals," *Christianity Today,* November 9, 2016. For a contrarian view see Joe Carter, "No, the Majority of American Evangelicals Did Not Vote for Trump," *The Gospel Coalition,* November 15, 2016. https://www.thegospelcoalition.org/article/no-the-majority-of-american-evangelicals-did-not-vote-for-trump.

1. Luck and Pluck

3 *"My dad, Fred Trump, was the smartest":* "Donald Trump's Republican National Convention speech, in full," *The Telegraph,* July 22, 2016. http://www.telegraph.co.uk/news/2016/07/21/donald-trumps-leaked-republican-national-convention-speech-in-fu/.

3 *"When I think about the visionary founder":* "Donald Trump's Liberty University Commencement Speech," *TIME,* May 13, 2017. http://time.com/4778240/donald-trump-liberty-university-speech-transcript/.

4 *Frederick Trump, Donald Trump's grandfather:* A wonderful source of biographical information is Gwenda Blair's *The Trumps: Three Generations of Builders and a Presidential Candidate* (New York: Simon & Schuster Paperbacks, 2001). This is the closest thing to a "definitive biography" that has been written to date.

5 *President Harry Truman and King George VI of England:* "John Trump Dies; ENGINEER WAS 78," *New York Times,* February 25, 1985.

http://www.nytimes.com/1985/02/26/us/john-trump-dies-engineer-was
-78.html.

6 *"Just like that," Fred recalled later:* Blair, *The Trumps,* 116–117.

6 *When he died at the age of ninety-three:* Tracie Rozhon, "Fred C. Trump,
Postwar Master Builder of Housing for Middle Class, Dies at 93," *New York
Times,* June 26, 1999. http://www.nytimes.com/1999/06/26/nyregion/fred
-c-trump-postwar-master-builder-of-housing-for-middle-class-dies-at-93
.html?mcubz=0.

2. Making Augsburg Great Again

8 *Ever since the Protestant Reformation began five hundred:* See Roland
Bainton, *Here I Stand: A Life of Martin Luther* (Peabody, MA: Hendrickson
Publishers Marketing, 2016), and Eric Metaxas, *Martin Luther: The Man
Who Rediscovered God and Changed the World* (New York: Penguin
Publishing Group, 2017).

8 *The meeting was held at the immense new home:* Source material about
Fugger in this section comes from Greg Steinmetz's *The Richest Man
Who Ever Lived: The Life and Times of Jacob Fugger* (New York:
Simon & Schuster Paperbacks, 2016). You don't want to miss reading
this fascinating biography.

9 *"the most influential businessman of all time":* Ibid., xiv.

9 *"He had character flaws like anyone else":* Ibid., xv–xvii.

9 *"Second to none in the acquisition":* Ibid., xvi.

9 *"As soon as the coin in the coffer rings":* William R. Estep, *Renaissance
and Reformation* (Grand Rapids, MI: W.B. Eerdmans Publishing Company,
1986), 119.

9 *"An Open Letter to the Christian Nobility":* Martin Luther, *Three Treatises*
(Philadelphia: Fortress Press, 1960).

11 *"how to read a blueprint, frame a building":* Gwenda Blair, *The Trumps:
Three Generations of Builders and a Presidential Candidate* (New York:
Simon & Schuster Paperbacks, 2001), 457.

11 *"Truly, this evil, shameful time":* Martin Luther, *What Luther Says: An
Anthology,* comp. Ewald M. Plass (St. Louis: Concordia Publishing House,
1959), 1110.

11 *"The Gospel does not overthrow civil authority":* Theodore G. Tappert,
The Book of Concord: The Confessions of the Evangelical Lutheran Church
(Philadelphia: Fortress Press, 1959), 38.

11 *"It's because of him that I learned":* "Donald Trump's Republican National
Convention speech, in full," *The Telegraph,* July 22, 2016.

12 *"He never thought about anything":* Blair, *The Trumps,* 226.

12 *"What else would he do on":* Ibid.

12 *"I don't consider it work":* Gerald S. Snyder, "One-Time 'Horse's Helper'
Made Fortune in Building," *The Morning Call* (Allentown, Pennsylvania),
July 26, 1964.

12 *"What do you do for a vacation?":* Donald Trump interview with David
Brody, 4/ 2011.

13 *"Look at the work ethic"*: Matt Bevin interview with the author(s), June 2017.

13 *"The world is so tough and competitive"*: Seth McLaughlin, "Trump says straight-edged lifestyle more likely to lead to happiness, success," *Washington Times*, December 1, 2015. http://www.washingtontimes .com/news/2015/dec/1/donald-trump-touts-lifestyle-without-alcohol -drugs/.

14 *"You must like what you do"*: Marc Fisher and Michael Kranish, "The Trump we saw: Populist, frustrating, naive, wise, forever on the make," *Washington Post*, August 12, 2016.

14 *"It was the home of a man"*: Blair, *The Trumps,* 226.

14 *"It took a long time to sell me the idea"*: Gerald S. Snyder, "Builder Turns Slum Areas Into Profitable Apartments," *The Town Talk* (Alexandria, Louisiana), July 21, 1964.

14 *"he wasn't flashy"*: Blair, *The Trumps,* 158.

15 *"turning off lights and getting up"*: Ibid., 160.

16 *75 percent of all Americans:* Brad Wheeler, "God Helps Those Who Help Themselves?" 9 Marks, February 25, 2010. https://www.9marks.org/article /god-helps-those-who-help-themselves/.

16 Sola bootstrapsis *is not in the Bible:* Ibid.

16 "do all to the glory of God" 1 Corinthians 10:31; Colossians 3:23–24.

17 *"Many very successful fathers, self-made men"*: Blair, *The Trumps,* 262.

18 *"When asked about his own career"*: Ibid., 441.

3. Mother Mary Comes to Queens

20 *This is the land of John Knox:* See John Knox, *History of the Reformation in Scotland* (London: Nelson, 1949).

21 *"Lord, open the King of England's eyes"*: David Daniell, *William Tyndale: A Biography* (New Haven: Yale University Press, 2001), 383.

21 *he also pamphleteered:* James A. Oliver, *The Pamphleteers: The Birth of Journalism, Emergence of the Press & the Fourth Estate* (London: Information Architects, 2010), 22.

21 *"Give me Scotland, or I die"*: Burk Parsons, "Give Me Scotland, or I Die," Ligonier Ministries, March 1, 2014. http://www.ligonier.org/learn/articles /give-me-scotland-or-i-die/.

21 *"I fear the prayers of John Knox"*: Ibid.

21 *"If their princes exceed their bounds"*: William C. Placher, *Readings in the History of Christian Theology*, Vol. 2, *From the Reformation to the Present* (Louisville, KY: Westminster John Knox Press, 2017), 56.

21 *"The theory of the justification of revolution"*: Francis Schaeffer, *A Christian Manifesto* (Wheaton, IL: Crossway Books, 2005), 97.

22 *"There is an expression you hear"*: Nic Robertson and Antonia Mortensen, "Donald Trump's Scottish roots," CNN, November 3, 2016. http://www .cnn.com/2016/11/02/politics/donald-trump-ancestry-scotland/index.html.

22 *"As for 'Lewis straight talking' "*: Comment from online discussion at

Reddit. https://www.reddit.com/r/EnoughTrumpSpam/comments/5asbg4
/it_may_surprise_many_to_learn_that_donald_trump/.

22 *gas stations are closed on Sunday:* Steven Brocklehurst, "Does the Sabbath
still exist on the isle of Lewis?," BBC News, October 24, 2014. http://www
.bbc.com/news/uk-scotland-29708202.

23 *"God wants us to have a break":* Ibid.

23 *Lutherans believed they had Christian freedom:* Thanks to historian Kyle
Roberts, who granted us an interview and pointed out this basic fact of
how first-generation Lutherans would have differed in their piety from that
of Christians in the Calvinistic traditions. See his *Evangelical Gotham:
Religion and the Making of New York City, 1783–1860* (Chicago: University
of Chicago Press, 2016).

24 *family worship and active participation:* See "The Directory for Family
Worship" published in 1647 and available online.

24 *"It's not that he has made it big":* Peter Geoghegan, "The island roots
of Donald Trump," *The Herald* (Scotland), May 21, 2016. http://www
.heraldscotland.com/news/14508751.The_island_roots_of_Donald_Trump/.

24 *"People here are modest in terms":* Peter Geoghegan, "Few rooting for
Donald Trump on his mother's Scottish island," *Irish Times*, May 27, 2016.
https://www.irishtimes.com/news/world/us/few-rooting-for-donald-trump
-on-his-mother-s-scottish-island-1.2663636.

25 *"supports the Bible":* Ibid.

25 *"Among the Puritans which came to":* From a transcript we made of a video
of Graham addressing ministers in a pre-Crusade meeting.

25 *"Rebellion to tyrants is obedience to God":* Witherspoon was not alone
among the Founders, explicitly Christian and otherwise, who embraced
this as a guiding motto.

25 *"There is not a single instance in history":* Joe Carter, "10 Quotes for
Religious Freedom Day," Gleaned from Acton Institute PowerBlog,
January 15, 2017. http://blog.acton.org/archives/91175–10-quotes-for
-religious-freedom-day-2.html.

25 *"Call this war by whatever name":* Donald Fortson, "Scotland and
the Birth of the United States," Ligonier Ministries, March 1, 2014.
http://www.ligonier.org/learn/articles/scotland-and-birth-united-states/.

25 *"Witherspoon had taught his students":* Ibid.

26 *The book sold 300,000 copies:* Ryan Lizza, "A Christian Manifesto's
Call to Arms," *The New Yorker*, June 20, 2017. http://www.newyorker
.com/news/news-desk/a-christian-manifestos-call-to-arms.

27 *"It follows from Rutherford's thesis":* From Schaeffer's *A Christian
Manifesto*, but also used in the Ryan Lizza piece in *The New Yorker.*

27 *"a unique window open in the United States":* From Schaeffer's *A Christian
Manifesto*, 132.

27 *"It is also an indisputable fact":* https://www.c-span.org/video/?430774-2
/president-trump-tribute-veterans-kennedy-center. https://www.dailykos
.com/stories/2017/7/3/1677574/-Singing-Make-America-Great-Again
-Evangelicals-say-Trump-is-God-giving-us-another-chance.

28 *"And so, I believe that had Hillary gotten":* Bob McEwen interview with the author(s), July 2017.

29 *"sported a yellow-and-black patterned scarf":* Robertson and Mortensen, "Donald Trump's Scottish roots."

29 *"I like it. I feel very comfortable here":* Severin Carrell, " 'I feel Scottish,' says Donald Trump on flying visit to mother's cottage," *The Guardian*, June 9, 2008. https://www.theguardian.com/world/2008/jun/09/donal dtrump.scotland.

29 *"She never, ever forgot her roots":* Reverend Calum MacLeod interview with author(s), August 2017.

29 *"She was a philanthropist with a genuine interest":* Geoghegan, "The island roots of Donald Trump."

30 *"You who are listening throughout many parts":* Transcription we made from video of sermon clips from the 1957 Crusade.

31 *"Go into your pulpits and preach a gospel message":* Gayle Ritchie, "Preacher's crusade after Glasgow was branded most unholy place in UK," *Daily Record*, July 1, 2012. http://www.dailyrecord.co.uk/news/uk-world -news/preachers-crusade-after-glasgow-was-branded-1057113.

4. Back to the Future Presbyterians

33 *two very famous clergy married the young couple:* "Miss Carnegie is Married to Roswell Miller," *New York Tribune* (New York City), April 23, 1919.

33 *Coffin, himself an heir to a fortune:* See Morgan Phelps Noyes, *Henry Sloane Coffin: The Man and His Ministry* (New York: Scribner, 1964).

33 *As America prepared to turn the page:* See Gary Dorrien's three-volume history, *The Making of American Liberal Theology* (Louisville, KY: Westminster John Knox Press, 2001, 2003, and 2006).

34 *Presbyterian laity wanted accountability:* D. G. Hart and John R. Muether, *Seeking a Better Country: 300 Years of American Presbyterianism* (Phillipsburg, NJ: P&R Publishing, 2007).

34 *"Doctrinal Deliverance of 1910":* PCA Historical Center: Doctrinal Deliverance of 1910 [PCUSA]. http://www.pcahistory.org/documents /deliverance.html.

35 *The Fundamentals:* R. A. Torrey, A. C. Dixon, and Louis Meyer, *The Fundamentals: A Testimony to the Truth* (Chicago: Testimony Publishing Company, 1910).

35 *Some Christian Convictions:* Henry Sloane Coffin, *Some Christian Convictions* (New Haven: Yale University Press, 1915).

35 *J. Gresham Machen:* See D.G. Hart, *Defending the Faith: J. Gresham Machen and the Crisis of Conservative Protestantism in Modern America* (Phillipsburg, NJ: P&R Publishing, 2003); Ned Bernard Stonehouse, *J. Gresham Machen: A Biographical Memoir* (Willow Grove, PA: Committee for the Historian of the Orthodox Presbyterian Church, 2004).

35 *"Liberalism or Christianity?":* John Gresham Machen, *Christianity and*

Liberalism (Grand Rapids, MI: W.B. Eerdmans Publishing Company, 2009).

36 *"Shall the Fundamentalists Win?"*: DeWitte Talmadge Holland, Hubert Vance Taylor, and Jess Yoder, *Sermons in American History: Selected Issues in the American Pulpit, 1630–1967* (Nashville, TN: Abingdon Press, 1971).

36 *"The question is not whether"*: Mark Galli and Ted Olsen, *131 Christians Everyone Should Know* (Nashville, TN: Broadman & Holman, 2000), 105.

36 *"you are too wealthy"*: Ron Chernow, *Titan: The Life of John D. Rockefeller, Sr.* (New York: Vintage Books, 2013), 640.

36 *Rockefeller biographer Ron Chernow:* Ibid.

37 TIME *magazine celebrated:* "Henry Sloane Coffin," *TIME*, November 13, 1926. http://content.time.com/time/subscriber/article/0,33009,72272 2-1,00.html.

38 *"It is impossible to use electrical light"*: As quoted in C. Stephen Evans, *The Historical Christ and the Jesus of Faith: The Incarnational Narrative as History* (Oxford: Oxford University Press, 1996), 64.

38 *Lyman Beecher Lectures on Preaching in 1931:* "Bibliography of the Lyman Beecher Lectureship on Preaching," Yale University Divinity School Library, http://www.library.yale.edu/div/beecher.html.

38 *private correspondence with President Roosevelt:* A. Polk, " 'Unnecessary and Artificial Divisions': Franklin Roosevelt's Quest for Religious and National Unity Leading Up to the Second World War," *Church History* 82, no. 3 (2013): 667–677.

38 *At century's end,* Preaching *magazine editor:* Michael Duduit, "The Ten Greatest Preachers of the Twentieth Century," *Preaching*, June 30, 2017. https://www.preaching.com/articles/the-ten-greatest-preachers-of-the -twentieth-century/.

5. City on a Jamaican Hill

44 *"tied to a stake and received thirty-six stripes"*: George Winans, *First Presbyterian Church of Jamaica, New York 1662–1942* (Jamaica, NY: The Church, 1943). Except where noted, the quotations and background material within this chapter that relates to First Presbyterian Church of Jamaica comes from this volume, published by the church. Also see their earlier work from the 200th anniversary: James M. Macdonald, *Two Centuries in the History of the Presbyterian Church, Jamaica, L.I.* (New York: Robert Carter & Brothers, 1862).

45 *"We shall find that the God of Israel is among us"*: William C. Placher, *Readings in the History of Christian Theology*, vol. 2, *From the Reformation to the Present* (Louisville, KY: Westminster John Knox Press, 2017), 93. For a contrary position see Richard M. Gamble, *In Search of the City on a Hill: The Making and Unmaking of an American Myth* (New York: Bloomsbury Academic, 2012).

45 *Scots-Presbyterian Peter Marshall Jr.'s:* Peter Marshall, *The Light and the Glory* (Old Tappan, NJ: Revell, 1977).

45 *"I have been guided by the standard":* "John F. Kennedy's 'City Upon a Hill' speech," YouTube, https://www.youtube.com/watch?v=uaXt7GE 0aUo.

46 *"And that's about all I have to say tonight":* "Transcript of Reagan's Farewell Address to the American People," *New York Times*, January 11, 1989. http://www.nytimes.com/1989/01/12/news/transcript-of-reagan -s-farewell-address-to-american-people.html?pagewanted=all& mcubz=0.

47 *"all other liberties will not be worth the naming":* This comes from the 1646 London Baptist Confession of Faith.

48 *During the Second Awakening:* For Asahel Nettleton, see the following two works: John F. Thornbury, *God Sent Revival: The Story of Asahel Nettleton and the Second Great Awakening* (Durham, Eng.: Evangelical Press, 1988), and Bennet Tyler and Andrew A. Bonar, *The Life and Labours of Asahel Nettleton* (Edinburgh: Banner of Truth Trust, 1975).

50 *"We make men without chests:* Joe Carter, "C.S. Lewis on Men Without Chests (And What That Means)," Acton Institute PowerBlog, May 31, 2016. http://blog.acton.org/archives/87047-c-s-lewis-on-men-without-chests-and -what-that-means.html.

51 *"prayed every morning from eleven to noon":* James Dobson, "Praying for Future Generations." http://drjamesdobson.org/blogs/dr-dobson-blog/dr -dobson-blog/2016/06/23/praying-for-future-generations.

51 *"No, it isn't silly to pray":* Billy Graham, "Pray For Future Generations," Billy Graham Evangelistic Association, October 17, 2014. https:// billygraham.org/answer/prayer-is-powerful-even-for-those-not-yet-born/.

6. Hindenburg

53 *The pastor of the church at the time, Andrew Magill:* The Magill quotes come from Winans' 1943 history of FPC.

53 *In the history of Presbyterian schisms in America:* See D. G. Hart and John R. Muether, *Seeking a Better Country: 300 Years of American Presbyterianism* (Phillipsburg, NJ: P&R Publishing, 2007); Mark A. Noll, *The Princeton Theology, 1812–1921: Scripture, Science, and Theological Method from Archibald Alexander to Benjamin Breckinridge Warfield* (Grand Rapids, MI: Baker Academic, 2001); James H. Moorhead, *Princeton Seminary in American Religion and Culture* (Grand Rapids, MI: Eerdmans, 2012); and David B. Calhoun, *Princeton Seminary*, 2 volumes (Edinburgh: Banner of Truth Trust, 1996).

54 *This made front-page news:* "Possibility of Presbyterian Rift is seen," *Cincinnati Enquirer* (May 22, 1935).

55 *"Elder Frank Donaldson of Hollis":* From page 6 of the June 2, 1936, edition of *Brooklyn Eagle*. Donaldson would go on to receive "Holy Orders" from FPC in 1938 and moved into a lifetime of pastoral ministry. He also attended Biblical Seminary of New York, graduating in 1938. This

seminary closed in 1969, but not before graduating a young senator's son named Pat Robertson and the prolific evangelical author Eugene Peterson. But what is most fascinating is that this is the seminary that the late evangelical Christian apologist Francis Schaeffer had wanted to attend, but his wife was entirely taken with Machen's message, and so Schaeffer started his seminary program at Westminster. At that time in Schaeffer's life, he considered himself to be a Fundamentalist first and a Presbyterian second. Had Schaeffer gone to Biblical Seminary, he would have been a classmate of Donaldson—who, to complete the circle, was a fellow member at FPC with the Trumps.

55 *"Elder Frank Donaldson, who attended":* From page 2 of the June 6, 1936, edition of *Brooklyn Eagle.*

56 *"Lewis Lampman was more than an efficient pastor":* From the Winans' 1943 history of FPC, pages 164–165.

56 *"Too often has the insistence on subscription":* From the Winans' 1943 history of FPC, page 165.

7. We Have Confirmation

64 *"represented all Protestant denominations":* "History of Jamaica Hospital—Jamaica Hospital Medical Center." https://jamaicahospital.org /general-info/history-of-jamaica/.

64 *Trump Pavilion:* "Welcome," Trump Pavilion. http://trumppavilion.org/.

64 *June 14, 1946:* Certificate of Birth for Donald Trump. http://www.foxnews .com/projects/pdf/20110328125536753.pdf.

65 *sell at an antique bookstore:* Dan Gilgoff, "The Story Behind the Lincoln Bible at Obama's Inauguration," *U.S. News & World Report,* December 23, 2008. https://www.usnews.com/news/blogs/god-and-country/2008 /12/23/the-story-behind-the-lincoln-bible-at-obamas-inauguration.

65 *Revised Standard Version (RSV):* Published by Thomas Nelson & Sons, now an imprint owned by HarperCollins, the publisher of this book.

66 *Yale Divinity School scholar named Luther Weigle:* See Peter Johannes Thuesen, *In Discordance with the Scriptures: American Protestant Battles Over Translating the Bible* (New York: Oxford University Press, 2002).

66 *"[N]o state law or school board may require":* "Abington School Dist. v. Schempp," Findlaw. http://caselaw.findlaw.com/us-supreme-court/374 /203.html.

67 *"if religious exercises are held to be":* Ibid.

67 *This is not dusty history:* Ironically enough, it was Mr. Weigle (the head of the RSV committee) who had been called in as an expert witness when the Schempp case went before the US District Court in 1958. Weigle wrote words that could be cut and pasted onto the website of the Heritage Foundation or the Alliance Defending Freedom: "The First Amendment to the Constitution has two clauses dealing with religion. . . . Most of the discussion in these recent years has centered about the first of these clauses, quaintly disguised as the erection of a wall. It is time to center our thought

and action about the second clause; it is time for believers in God to claim and to justify their full religious freedom." Weigle, the Modernist Bible translator, and his defense of Bible reading in public schools is a fascinating example of the fluctuations in political and theological alliances that have taken place during the lifetime of Donald Trump.

69 *"for admission to the Lord's Supper":* For an excellent discussion of how the catechism and confirmation process has changed over the years, see Richard Robert Osmer, *Confirmation: Presbyterian Practices in Ecumenical Perspective* (Louisville, KY: Geneva Press, 1996). For the words of the service, see *The Book of Common Worship: Approved by the General Assembly of the Presbyterian Church in the United States of America* (Philadelphia: General Division of Publication of the Board of Christian Education of the United Presbyterian Church in the United States of America, 1946).

8. The Church for Spock Babies

71 *a boomer infant came:* For a quick overview see Richard Croker, *The Boomer Century 1946–2046* (New York: Springboard Press, 2007).

72 *and 50 million copies so far:* Eric Pace, "Benjamin Spock, World's Pediatrician, Dies at 94," *New York Times*, March 16, 1998. http://www .nytimes.com/1998/03/17/us/benjamin-spock-world-s-pediatrician-dies-at -94.html?mcubz=0.

72 *"It counseled indulgence":* Croker, *The Boomer Century,* 16–17.

73 *"I was brought up in a family with stern morals":* Clarence E. Olson, "Dr. Spock and His Conscience," *St. Louis Post-Dispatch*, January 18, 1970.

74 *"What I really, really like about him":* Michele Bachmann interview with David Brody, June 2016.

76 *"It was blisteringly hot":* Gwenda Blair, *The Trumps: Three Generations That Built an Empire* (New York: Simon & Schuster, 2000), 339.

77 *As the story goes, Donald had been hopping:* Michael D'Antonio, *Never Enough: Donald Trump and the Pursuit of Success* (New York: Thomas Dunne Books, St. Martin's Press, 2015), 40–41.

77 *he wanted to instill in his boys;* Ibid., 43.

77 *"I coached baseball and football":* Ibid., 41.

77 *"really tough on the kid";* Ibid., 43.

77 *"He felt comfortable in uniform":* Ibid., 45.

9. The Power of Positive Thinking

79 *"the man who may well be the":* Jonathan Yardley, "The Power of Positive Preaching," *Washington Post*, December 27, 1992. https://www .washingtonpost.com/archive/entertainment/books/1992/12/27/the-power -of-positive-preaching/6fff0380–89ff-4f0c-88dd-15b8b2208912/?utm _term=.e571f3217cf0.

80 *When* Church History: "Survey Results: What Do You Think?" *Christian

History, Issue 65 (Vol. XIX, No. 1), 2000. http://www.christianitytoday
.com/history/issues/issue-65/survey-results-what-do-you-think.html.

80 *"How one evaluates Peale":* Tim Stafford, "Half-full Christianity,"
Christianity Today, June 21, 1993, 35.

80 *"the patriarch of the twentieth-century self-help movement":* Randy
Frame, "Self-help patriarch Peale dies," *Christianity Today,* February 7,
1994, 56.

80 *"the first American clergyman":* George Vecsey, "Norman Vincent
Peale, Preacher of Gospel Optimism, Dies at 95," *New York Times,*
December 25, 1993. http://www.nytimes.com/1993/12/26/obituaries/
norman-vincent-peale-preacher-of-gospel-optimism-dies-at-95
.html?pagewanted=2.

81 *he "winces when Trump":* Paul Schwartzman, "How Trump got religion—
and why his legendary minister's son now rejects him," *Washington Post,*
January 21, 2016. https://www.washingtonpost.com/lifestyle/how-trump
-got-religion—and-why-his-legendary-ministers-son-now-rejects-him
/2016/01/21/37bae16e-bb02–11e5–829c-26ffb874a18d_story.html?utm
_term=.0f66b1bdd2ac.

81 *"the greatest building of our time":* Ibid.

81 *"his greatest student of all time":* Ibid.

82 *"Well, when I fill an arena":* Donald Trump interview with David Brody,
September 2015.

83 *The first thing to note about Peale:* The definitive biography of Peale and
the main source in this chapter is Carol V. R. George, *God's Salesman:
Norman Vincent Peale & the Power of Positive Thinking* (Bridgewater, NJ:
Replica Books, 2000).

83 *intertwined with a patriotic love for country:* Many describe Peale as a
"Christian nationalist"—using the term pejoratively.

83 *absorbed American originals:* For good reason, Carol George's biography
opens every chapter with a quote from Emerson.

83 *Dutch Reformed congregation:* Peale led his first pastorate to strong
growth, attracting the attention of larger and more prominent churches.
As one scholar wrote: "A diligent work ethic, provocative advertising
strategies, admirable rhetorical skills, and a simple, practical message made
him a success at King's Highway Church. He served as its minister from
1924 until 1927 and watched it grow from 40 weekly attendees to more than
900 member families. The success of the church drew interest from many
suitor churches." Daniel James Walsh, "Positive-Thinking and Post-War
Prosperity: An Analysis of the Life and Writing of Norman Vincent Peale,"
Master's thesis, Gordon-Conwell Theological Seminary, 2012. https://
theologypilgrim.files.wordpress.com/2009/03/positive-thinking-postwar
-prosperity-to-share.pdf

84 *"It was a place to see and be seen":* Michael D'Antonio, *Never Enough:
Donald Trump and the Pursuit of Success* (New York: Thomas Dunne
Books, St. Martin's Press, 2015), 52–54. Of course, every small town or
city in America—even in the Bible Belt—has churches where businessmen

went to church even if they didn't want to go to church. The "It's good for business" motivation for church attendance used to account for a certain percentage of "white collar" people in American pews. After all, can you really trust someone to be your banker, lawyer, judge, or accountant if they don't even go to church? These churches typically were on the town square, or close to it, and were built in brick. On the outskirts and poorer sections of town or in the rural communities, however, was where you found the folks who got "enthusiastic" with their religion: most Baptists south of the Mason Dixon line, certain Methodists, and in the twentieth century, Pentecostals.

84 *Peale considered Beecher a model:* George, *God's Salesman,* 57–58.

84 *At the time of Peale's coming to Marble Collegiate:* Emory Ward, *Faith of Our Fathers Living Still: The Story of Marble Collegiate Church* (New York: The Church, 1978); Blanche Tessaro Cleaver, *The Marble Collegiate Church* (New York: Scribners, 1954).

85 *"At a Thanksgiving Day service in the Marble Collegiate Church":* A notice of current religious happenings. J. Henry Carpenter, *The Christian Century,* 65 no. 50, December 15, 1948, 1379.

85 *One can hardly imagine:* A perennial evangelical debate each January is whether churches that normally hold Sunday-evening worship should cancel on Super Bowl Sunday.

85 *"It is obvious to every thoughtful person":* From a newspaper column by Peale titled "The Church Pew Is an Institution" and published on or around July 4, 1946. For example, page 4 of the *Fort Lauderdale News,* July 3, 1946.

87 *foisted on America by Roosevelt:* "Read what Norman Vincent Peale says in an open letter to the clergy," *Emporia Gazette* (Emporia, Kansas), October 30, 1940, 3.

87 *"the most strategic center in the world":* "Crusade City Spotlight: New York, NY," Billy Graham Library, July 17, 2015. https://billygrahamlibrary .org/crusade-city-spotlight-new-york-ny/.

88 *"I had the new birth experience before Billy Graham was born":* George, *God's Salesman,* 146–149.

89 *"The book, for all its success":* Tim Stafford, "Half-full Christianity," *Christianity Today,* 6/21/93, Vol. 37, Issue 7, p35. 3p. 4.

90 *"I find [Saint] Paul appealing":* Vecsey, "Norman Vincent Peale, Preacher of Gospel Optimism, Dies at 95." Apparently, there was no love lost between these two men, as Peale had voiced opposition to Stevenson, saying his status as a divorced man made him unfit to be president.

90 *Wayne Oates, a Southern Baptist:* Wayne Edward Oates, "The Power of Positive Thinking," *Review & Expositor* 51, no. 2, April 1954, 280–281.

90 *A Lutheran critic:* William Lee Miller, "Gospel of Norman Vincent Peale," *Union Seminary Quarterly Review* 10, no. 2, January 1955, 15–22.

90 *"Mr. Sunday School":* Gaines S. Dobbins, "A guide to confident living," *Review & Expositor* 45, no. 3, July 1948, 365–366.

90 *"I'm a conservative, and I will tell you":* George, *God's Salesman,* 153.

91 *"Looking back, Dr. Peale concedes":* Kenneth A. Briggs, "Dr. Norman Vincent Peale Still an Apostle of Cheer," *New York Times*, January 2, 1978. http://www.nytimes.com/1978/01/02/archives/dr-norman-vincent -peale-still-an-apostle-of-cheer-a-compelling.html?_r=0. We first discovered this quote in the Vecsey obituary of Peale.

91 *"I've got plenty of worst qualities":* Quoted in Randy Frame's 1993 obituary in *Christianity Today*, Vol. 38, Issue 2, February 7, 1994, p. 56.

92 *"Political similarities rather than theological affinity":* George, *God's Salesman,* 149.

93 *"for his contributions to the field of theology":* National Archives and Records Administration, March 26, 1984. https://www.reaganlibrary. archives.gov/archives/speeches/1984/32684a.htm. Also in 1984, when Peale's periodicals needed a new editor, they hired a young man out of Graham's alma mater, the evangelical stalwart Wheaton College. And before serving Peale, the man had been a director of *Moody Monthly*— a magazine with rock-solid evangelical bona fides.

94 *something unique and new:* Those words—"unique" and "new"—when put in the hands of a theologian, do not always produce orthodox teaching. But the question of Peale's orthodoxy is left to be answered by others. Ours is mostly to observe, and from what we have seen we agree with the scholar who wrote that "Peale's ministry flowed from the confluence of three streams: liberal Protestantism, popular conservative evangelicalism, and ancient folk spirituality and mind-cure philosophy" (Gerald Sittser, *Church History*, March 1996). Or as Tim Stafford wrote in the previously cited article for *Christianity Today*, Peale "belonged to both and neither party [fundamentalist and modernist] because he represented something genuinely new: the first example of non-denominational, entrepreneurial, communications-savvy, pragmatic, populist religion that rose out of the fundamentalist-modernist split."

94 *"In 1990, after splurging on a third casino":* Gwenda Blair, "How Norman Vincent Peale Taught Donald Trump to Worship Himself," *POLITICO*, October 6, 2015. http://www.politico.com/magazine/story/2015/10/donald -trump-2016-norman-vincent-peale-213220.

95 *"citing his father's friendship with Peale":* Ibid.

96 *Of that, we can be positive:* For further study about Peale, including a deeper dive into the intellectual relationship between Peale and "New Thought" theology, see the following: Christopher Lane, *Surge of Piety: Norman Vincent Peale and the Remaking of American Religious Life* (New Haven: Yale University Press, 2016); Richard Weiss, *The American Myth of Success: From Horatio Alger to Norman Vincent Peale* (Urbana: University of Illinois Press, 1988); Donald B. Meyer, *The Positive Thinkers: Religion as Pop Psychology, from Mary Baker Eddy to Oral Roberts* (New York: Pantheon Books, 1980); and Mitch Horowitz, *One Simple Idea: How the Lessons of Positive Thinking Can Transform Your Life* (New York: Skyhorse Publishing, 2016).

10. Manhattan, Malaise, and Morning in America

97 *Two of Donald Trump's great-aunts:* Gwenda Blair, *The Trumps: Three Generations that Built an Empire* (New York: Simon & Schuster, 2000), 122–123.

97 *"Will you forsake all and follow Me":* Joyce Lee and Glenn Gohr, "Women in the Pentecostal Movement," *Enrichment Journal.* http://enrichmentjournal.ag.org/199904/060_women.cfm, Fall 1999. This issue was titled "A Century of Pentecostal Vision."

98 *"purge the city of some of its sin":* These quotes come from the *New York Times,* which gave daily coverage to Aimee Semple McPherson's time in New York City and her preaching at Glad Tidings. As quoted in Edith Waldvogel Blumhofer's *Aimee Semple McPherson: Everybody's Sister* (Grand Rapids, MI: W.B. Eerdmans Publishing Company, 2000), 301–303. Also see Matthew Avery Sutton, *Aimee Semple McPherson and the Resurrection of Christian America* (Cambridge, MA: Harvard University Press, 2009).

99 *an Assembly of God pastor in rural Pennsylvania:* Wilkerson obituaries provide a quick overview of his life: Margalit Fox, "Rev. David Wilkerson Dies at 79; Started Times Square Church," *New York Times,* April 28, 2011, http://www.nytimes.com/2011/04/29/nyregion/rev-david-wilkerson -79-evangelist-dies-in-crash.html; Robert Crosby, "Remembering David Wilkerson," *Christianity Today,* April 29, 2011, http://www.christianity today.com/ct/2011/aprilweb-only/rememberingdavidwilkerson.html. Also see Gary Wilkerson, *David Wilkerson: The Cross, the Switchblade, and the Man Who Believed* (Grand Rapids, MI: Zondervan, 2014).

99 *According to Robertson's autobiography:* Pat Robertson and Jamie Buckingham, *Shout It from the Housetops* (Virginia Beach, VA: Christian Broadcasting Network, 1986). Chapter 6 contains the events related here.

100 *more than 50 million copies of this book:* "The Top 50 Books That Have Shaped Evangelicals," *Christianity Today,* accessed October 6, 2006. http://www.christianitytoday.com/ct/2006/october/23.51.html?start=2.

100 *A few months later in October 1970:* This anecdote is recorded in Bob Slosser's 1984 book about the faith of Ronald Reagan, published by Word Books—which is now an imprint of HarperCollins (like Broadside, the publisher of this book). This anecdote that Slosser tells about Reagan and "the prophecy" would go on to be retold by dozens of authors who sought to better understand the faith of President Reagan. Read Lou Cannon's "Reagan & God," wherein he discusses the faith of Reagan in light of Slosser's book, *Washington Post,* April 16, 1984, 2017. https://www .washingtonpost.com/archive/politics/1984/04/16/reagan-38/019d9165 -a3d8–4f73–8396-d2bd529f2bbc/?utm_term=.1398addb9ce7.

101 *"I worried about the future":* Donald Trump and Tony Schwartz, *Trump: The Art of the Deal* (New York: Ballantine Books, 2017), 102.

102 *"Moving into that apartment was probably":* Blair, *The Trumps,* 250.

103 *Peale stood by his disgraced parishioner:* John Omicinski, "Positive thinking about Nixon—after Peale sermon," *Democrat and Chronicle* (Rochester, New York), March 24, 1974, 2.

103 *"You can be whatever you want to be":* "Art Fleming of NBC: A Show Business Apostle," *Daily Independent Journal* (San Rafael, California), August 12, 1974, 29.

105 *"There is a fear that our best years are behind us":* " 'Our Nation's Past and Future': Address Accepting the Presidential Nomination at the Democratic National Convention in New York City," July 15, 1976, The American Presidency Project. http://www.presidency.ucsb.edu/ws/index .php?pid=25953.

106 *"The Year of the Evangelical":* There are dozens of excellent historical treatments on the rise of the Christian Right. See these two for a start: Steven P. Miller, *The Age of Evangelicalism: America's Born-Again Years* (Oxford: Oxford University Press, 2014), and William C. Martin, *With God on Our Side: The Rise of the Religious Right in America* (New York: Broadway Books, 1996).

106 *"It had begun brewing in me":* Norman Lear, *Even This I Get to Experience* (New York: Penguin Books, 2014).

107 *have only intensified:* In August 2017, the *New York Times* reported that Norman Lear will snub the White House reception at the end of the year when he receives a Kennedy Center Honor. Using shades of Hillary Clinton's "Deplorables" line, the *Times* wrote, "Plenty of viewers in the 1970s laughed with, not at, Archie's political incorrectness. In 2016, plenty of their modern-day counterparts voted for Donald J. Trump's." And in September 2017—nearly a year after the election—Rob Reiner ("Meathead" on *All in the Family*) formed a group called the Committee to Investigate Russia to "protect democracy" from what he believes was Russian cyber-manipulation of the 2016 election—a stealing of the election from Hillary Clinton.

107 *In August 1976, Tom Wolfe penned a lengthy essay:* Tom Wolfe, "The 'Me' Decade and the Third Great Awakening," *New York Magazine,* August 23, 1976. http://nymag.com/news/features/45938/.

108 *"The contemporary climate is therapeutic":* Christopher Lasch, *The Culture of Narcissism* (New York: W. W. Norton & Company, 1978), 7.

108 *Jimmy Carter called Lasch:* Robert Schlesinger, *White House Ghosts: Presidents and Their Speechwriters* (New York: Simon & Schuster, 2009), 301–305.

108 *"The threat is nearly invisible":* Jimmy Carter, "Address to the Nation on Energy and National Goals," The American Presidency Project, July 15, 1979. http://www.presidency.ucsb.edu/ws/?pid=32596.

108 *"warm, luxurious, and even exhilarating":* "How Donald Trump transformed New York without any regard for design quality," *Architects Newspaper,* March 20, 2017. https://archpaper.com/2016/06/donald-trump -architecture/.

109 *"Half a lifetime after Trump built it":* Thomas De Monchaux, "Seeing

Trump in Trump Tower," *The New Yorker*, June 19, 2017. https://www
.newyorker.com/culture/cultural-comment/seeing-trump-in-trump-tower.

11. The Man Who Has Everything

110 *Guthrie signed a lease with Fred Trump:* For Fred's building of Beach
Haven, see Blair, *The Trumps: Three Generations That Built an Empire*
(New York: Simon & Schuster, 2000), 169–174. For the Woody Guthrie
anecdote, see Will Kaufman, "Woody Guthrie, 'Old Man Trump' and a real
estate empire's racist foundations," *The Conversation,* January 21, 2016.
https://theconversation.com/woody-guthrie-old-man-trump-and-a-real
-estate-empires-racist-foundations-53026.

110 *in accordance with the federal policies in place:* Charles Lane, "The New
Deal as raw deal for blacks in segregated communities," *Washington Post*,
May 25, 2017. https://www.washingtonpost.com/opinions/the-new-deal
-as-raw-deal-for-blacks-in-segregated-communities/2017/05/25/07416bba
-080a-11e7-a15f-a58d4a988474_story.html?utm_term=.6bf2073781cb.

110 *This was more than a decade before:* Blair, *The Trumps,* 144–145.

111 *Hillary Clinton brought up the lawsuit:* Aaron Blake, "The first Trump-
Clinton presidential debate transcript, annotated," *Washington Post*,
September 26, 2016. https://www.washingtonpost.com/news/the-fix
/wp/2016/09/26/the-first-trump-clinton-presidential-debate-transcript
-annotated/?utm_term=.75f9f8a56e52.

112 *Reagan had tasked Lee Iacocca:* "Two of our country's proudest
landmarks," Lee Iacocca—The Statue of Liberty–Ellis Island Foundation.
http://leeiacocca.net/what-i-believe-in/statue-of-liberty.html.

112 *"Perhaps, indeed, these vessels embody":* Ronald Reagan, "Remarks
During Operation Sail in New York, New York," National Archives and
Records Administration, July 4, 1986. https://www.reaganlibrary.archives
.gov/archives/speeches/1986/70406a.htm.

113 *"It was their last gift to us":* Ronald Reagan, "Address to the Nation on
Independence Day," National Archives and Records Administration,
July 4, 1986. https://www.reaganlibrary.archives.gov/archives/speeches
/1986/70486c.htm.

113 *"Trump even had a hand in making":* "Refugee Girl Is Guest For Liberty
Weekend," *New York Times*, May 28, 1986. http://www.nytimes.com
/1986/05/29/nyregion/refugee-girl-is-guest-for-liberty-weekend.html
?mcubz=0.

114 *That October, on the true one hundredth anniversary:* "80 Named as
Recipients of Ellis Island Awards," *New York Times*, October 15, 1986,
http://www.nytimes.com/1986/10/16/nyregion/80-named-as-recipients
-of-ellis-island-awards.html; Paula Span, "The Real Centennial,"
Washington Post, October 29, 1986, https://www.washingtonpost.com
/archive/lifestyle/1986/10/29/the-real-centennial/c4fa1a5b-7540–4848
–8dd4–509f65240f55/?utm_term=.53ec22fb75dc.

114 *"systematic and continuous abuse":* Span, "The Real Centennial."

114 *"This bill that we will sign today is not":* Lyndon B. Johnson, "1965 Immigration Act," LBJ Presidential Library, October 3, 1965. http://www.lbjlibrary.org/lyndon-baines-johnson/timeline/lbj-on-immigration.

115 *"In the decades since, America's founding":* Tom Gjelten, *Nation of Nations: A Great American Immigration Story* (New York: Simon & Schuster Paperbacks, 2016).

115 *"White Christian America":* See Robert P. Jones, *The End of White Christian America* (New York: Simon & Schuster Paperbacks, 2016).

115 *from 12 million people to 156 million:* "Pentecostalism in Latin America," Pew Research Center's Religion & Public Life Project, October 4, 2006. http://www.pewforum.org/2006/10/05/overview-pentecostalism-in-latin-america/.

116 *two of the leading Pentecostal denominations:* Michael Lipka, "The most and least racially diverse U.S. religious groups," Pew Research Center, July 27, 2015. http://www.pewresearch.org/fact-tank/2015/07/27/the-most-and-least-racially-diverse-u-s-religious-groups/.

117 *"I'm not here today because":* Harry Hurt, *The Lost Tycoon: The Rise and Demise of Donald J. Trump* (New York: W.W. Norton, 1993), 191.

117 *In November, he released his book:* Ibid., 189–197; Blair, *The Trumps,* 380–381.

117 *The book held the #1 rank:* Hurt, *The Lost Tycoon,* 190–197, and Blair, *The Trumps,* 380–381.

117 *"What do you feel like when":* Hurt, *The Lost Tycoon,* 191–192.

118 *overpaying by $100 million:* Ibid., 208.

118 *"I haven't purchased a building":* Dan Alexander, "Vintage Trump Ads Say a Lot About the President," *Forbes,* September 19, 2017. https://www.forbes.com/sites/danalexander/2017/09/19/trump-vintage-old-ads-advertisement-forbes-president-donald/#aa03d6d5100b.

118 *including O. J. Simpson, Howard Stern, Rosie O'Donnell, and Robin Leach:* Georgia Dullea, "It's a Wedding Blitz for Trump and Maples," *New York Times,* December 21, 1993. http://www.nytimes.com/1993/12/21/nyregion/vows-it-s-a-wedding-blitz-for-trump-and-maples.html.

121 *"I still prefer to believe":* Glenn Stanton, "C.S. Lewis and G.K. Chesterton Quotes," *The Gospel Coalition,* April 14, 2013. https://www.thegospelcoalition.org/article/factchecker-c-s-lewis-and-g-k-chesterton-quotes.

12 Prospereality

122 *"He's a wonderful promoter":* This is from an interview with Ben Berzin, vice president of Midlantic National Bank, taken from "The Choice 2016." Transcript: http://www.pbs.org/wgbh/frontline/film/the-choice-2016/transcript/, and Video: http://www.pbs.org/wgbh/frontline/film/the-choice-2016/.

123 *"Our biggest advice in our lives came from* Playboy*":* This is from an interview with Sandy McIntosh, a younger cadet at NYMA, from the *Frontline* (PBS) documentary.

123 *"Ladies' Man":* Ibid.

123 *"tap dancing in Donald's mind"*: This quote comes from an interview with Trump biographer Timothy O'Brien, from the *Frontline* documentary.

123 *"My life was so great in so many ways"*: ABC News, "Donald Trump: 'Putting a Wife to Work Is a Very Dangerous Thing,' " YouTube, https:// www.youtube.com/watch?v=zfMqgdOA5PM.

124 *Trump met Melania while on a date:* Larry King, "Donald and Melania Trump's 2005 interview as newlyweds," YouTube, https://www.youtube .com/watch?v=q4XfyYFa9yo.

124 *"The era of fear"*: "Giuliani Says Fighting Crime His Top Priority," *Christian Science Monitor*, January 4, 1994. https://www.csmonitor.com /1994/0104/04082.html.

124 *hovered around two thousand per year:* http://www.nyc.gov/html/nypd /downloads/pdf/crime_statistics/cs-en-us-city.pdf.

125 *"Bring Back the Death Penalty!"*: See "New York Crime Rates 1960–2016" at http://www.disastercenter.com/crime/nycrime.htm.

125 *When Trump discovered the hero in danger:* "Trump makes the holiday brighter for New Yorker who rescued his mother," *Jet*, December 30, 1991–January 6, 1992, 8. The man's name was Lawrence Herbert.

125 *"broken windows"*: George L. Kelling and James Q. Wilson, "Broken Windows," *The Atlantic*, February 19, 2014. https://www.theatlantic.com /magazine/archive/1982/03/broken-windows/304465/.

125 *"stop and frisk"*: William J. Bratton and Peter Knobler, *Turnaround: How America's Top Cop Reversed the Crime Epidemic* (New York: Random House, 1998).

125 *The murder rate is now as low:* Jen Kirby, "New York City Had Record-Low Crime Rate in 2016," *New York Magazine*, January 14, 2017. http:// nymag.com/daily/intelligencer/2017/01/new-york-city-had-record-low -crime-rate-in-2016.html.

126 *about 120 of the roughly 200 evangelical churches in Manhattan:* I wrote about this using the data gleaned from the journalists mentioned in the next paragraph. Scott Lamb, "Sixty percent of Manhattan's evangelical churches have startedsince 1978," *Washington Times*, September 6, 2017. http://www.washingtontimes.com/news/2017/sep/6/sixty-percent-of -manhattans-evangelical-churches-h/.

126 *"In sum, no other city's ups and downs"*: If you want to learn more about this evangelical renaissance in Manhattan, the first place to go is the incredible website *A Journey Through NYC Religions* (http://www .nycreligion.info). In particular, read their twelve-part series "The Making of the Post-Secular City"—beginning with the first part: "The Manhattan Evangelicals" at http://www.nycreligion.info/making-postsecular-city -manhattan-evangelicals-part-1/. The block quote from Carnes comes from the final installment in the series.

127 *I committed my life to Christ:* I recently told this testimony in more detail in "5 Minutes With . . . David Brody," *Newsmax*, August 16, 2017. https://www.newsmax.com/Newsfront/david-brody-cbn-profile-brody -file/2017/08/16/id/807904/.

128 *"to find out if Christianity":* Taffy Brodesser-Akner, "Inside Hillsong, the Church of Choice for Justin Bieber and Kevin Durant," *GQ*, December 17, 2015. https://www.gq.com/story/inside-hillsong-church-of-justin-bieber -kevin-durant.

128 *he favorably quoted Warhol twice*: Donald Trump and Meredith McIver, *Think Like a Champion* (New York: Vanguard, 2009), 56 and 119. Trump did, however, have something to say about modern artists in general: "I've always felt that a lot of modern art is a con, and that the most successful painters are often better salesmen and promoters than they are artists."— From Donald J. Trump and Tony Schwartz, *The Art of the Deal* (New York: Ballantine, 2015), 34.

129 *"Deals are my art form":* Donald Trump and Tony Schwartz, *Trump: The Art of the Deal* (New York: Ballantine, 2015), 1.

129 *"I've always thought that Louis B. Mayer":* From the 1990 *Playboy* article. No, we haven't seen it, but Peter O'Brien uses this quote as his epigram for chapter 7 of his *TrumpNation: The Art of Being The Donald* (New York: Grand Central Publishing, 2016).

130 *"It's crazy, but I could build a $300 million":* Quoted in *The Orlando Sentinel*, March 8, 1984.

130 *"Oprah. I love Oprah":* "Donald Trump's Advocate Interview Where He Defends Gays, Mexicans," *The Advocate*, September 28, 2015. https://www .advocate.com/election/2015/9/28/read-donald-trumps-advocate-interview -where-he-defends-gays-mexicans.

130 *"Like an awful lot of people":* David French interview with the author(s), June 2016.

131 *"I concluded that I'd have to present Bible truths":* From Schuller's autobiography, as quoted here: Elizabeth Eisenstadt-Evans, "Farm Boy Makes Good," *Christianity Today*, Vol. 46, Issue 9, August 5, 2002, p. 57.

131 *"Someday is today":* Video of Schuller giving the invocation at the 1988 Republican National Convention in New Oreans found here: "Nomination VicePres Speeches, August 18, 1988," C-SPAN. https://www.c-span.org /video/?3846–1%2Fnomination-vice-pres-speeches.

132 *"Well, I think I'd have a very good chance":* "Donald Trump at the 1988 Republican Convention," YouTube. https://www.youtube.com/watch?v =acpmInqcuH4.

133 *"You can go anywhere from nowhere":* Eisenstadt-Evans, "Farm Boy Makes Good."

133 *"I know that so many people have gotten to know":* Paula White quotes are from interview with the author(s), September 2017.

134 *"In Paula, he met a girl who had missed the mark":* James Robison interview with the author(s), July 2017.

136 *After yet another evangelical theologian:* Michael Horton, "Evangelicals should be deeply troubled by Donald Trump's attempt to mainstream heresy," *Washington Post*, January 3, 2017. https://www.washingtonpost .com/news/acts-of-faith/wp/2017/01/03/evangelicals-should-be-deeply

-troubled-by-donald-trumps-attempt-to-mainstream-heresy/?utm
_term=.1b6bd14ad90b.

13. The Escalator

141 *"His voice is perfect and haunting":* Andy Greene, "Neil Young's Biggest
Fan Speaks: 'His Voice Is Haunting,' Says Donald Trump," *Rolling
Stone*, December 18, 2008. http://www.rollingstone.com/music/news
/neil-youngs-biggest-fan-speaks-his-voice-is-haunting-says-donald
-trump-20081218.

141 *"F—you, Donald Trump":* Sarah Grant, "Neil Young Onstage: 'F—k
You, Donald Trump,' " *Rolling Stone*, June 11, 2016. http://www
.rollingstone.com/music/news/neil-young-onstage-f—ck-you-donald
-trump-20160611.

141 *"Didn't love it":* Sophie Tatum, "Donald Trump responds to Neil Young's
diss," CNN, June 25, 2015. http://www.cnn.com/2015/06/24/politics
/trump-responds-to-neil-young-on-twitter/index.html.

142 *"They sweated like dogs":* For all quotes from the speech, see "Donald
Trump's Presidential Announcement Speech," *TIME*, June 16, 2015.
Accessed September 28, 2017, at http://time.com/3923128/donald-trump
-announcement-speech/.

142 *"the worst campaign rollout of the year":* Naomi Shavin, "Lincoln Chafee
Had the Worst Campaign Rollout of the Year," *New Republic*, June 4, 2015.
Accessed September 2017, at https://newrepublic.com/article/121962
/lincoln-chafee-had-worst-campaign-rollout-year.

143 *deported to Mexico five times:* Pamela Brown, "Suspect in San Francisco
woman's death deported 5 times," CNN, July 4, 2015. http://www.cnn
.com /2015/07/03/us/san-francisco-killing-suspect-immigrant-deported
/index.html.

144 *"who are trustworthy and hate a bribe":* See also "He commanded
the judges: 'You shall take no bribe, for a bribe blinds the clear-sighted
and subverts the cause of those who are in the right' " (Exodus 23:8).
God serves as the ultimate example of such integrity: "For the LORD
your God is God of gods and Lord of lords, the great, the mighty, and
the awesome God, who is not partial and takes no bribe" (Deuteronomy
10:17).

144 *The Bible condemns bribery:* See also "A bribe corrupts the heart"
(Ecclesiastes 7:7); "The wicked accepts a bribe in secret to pervert the
ways of justice" (Proverbs 17:23); "Your princes are rebels and companions
of thieves. Everyone loves a bribe and runs after gifts. They do not bring
justice to the fatherless, and the widow's cause does not come to them"
(Isaiah 1:23).

14. What Is Your Relationship with God?

146 *Iowa ranks first in the nation:* See "Iowa Agriculture Quick Facts," Iowa Agriculture Department, http://www.iowaagriculture.gov/quickFacts .asp; and Joni Ernst, "6 Amazing Facts About Iowa Agriculture That the Rest of the Country Should Know," https://www.ernst.senate.gov/public/index .cfm/press-releases?ID=6A36B684–7C8F-4B9C-83BD-7459C8640D27.

146 *"Full Grassley":* Niels Lesniewski, "2016 Prospects Encouraged to Do the 'Full Grassley' in Iowa," *Roll Call*, June 10, 2015. http://www.rollcall.com /news/policy/2016-iowa-republican-candidates-grassley.

147 *with nearly 80 percent of Iowans:* "Religious Landscape Study," Pew Research Center's Religion & Public Life Project, May 11, 2015. http:// www.pewforum.org/religious-landscape-study/state/iowa/.

147 *"Common core has to be ended":* For all quotes from the discussion between Frank Luntz and Donald Trump, see "Presidential Candidate Donald Trump Family Leadership Summit," C-SPAN, July 2015. https:// www.c-span.org/video/?327045–5%2Fpresidential-candidate-donald -trump-family-leadership-summit.

148 *"he fired up the crazies":* Ryan Lizza, "John McCain Has a Few Things to Say About Donald Trump," *The New Yorker*, June 6, 2015. https:// www.newyorker.com/news/news-desk/john-mccain-has-a-few-thing -to-say-about-donald-trump?intcid=mod-latest.

150 *"He cannot survive this":* Mike Huckabee interview with the author(s), June 2017.

152 *"Maybe I was getting a little bit cute":* Donald Trump interview with the author(s), September 2015.

152 *"The audience, which was largely evangelical":* Ibid.

153 *by Jake Tapper and Cal Thomas:* Jake Tapper, "Trump has a 'great relationship' with God," CNN's *State of the Union,* January 17, 2016; and Cal Thomas, "Donald Trump Interview with Cal Thomas: The Transcript," June 8, 2016, http://calthomas.com/node/985.

154 *"it's pretty evident by the things that he said":* Mike Huckabee interview with the author(s), June 2017.

154 *In late August, Trump traveled to Mobile:* For all quotes from the Mobile rally, see "Donald Trump Campaign Rally Mobile Alabama, August 21, 2015," C-SPAN. https://www.c-span.org/video/?327751–1%2Fdonald -trump-campaign-rally-mobile-alabama.

155 *"He's a cutie!":* The Shuford story is told by Michelle Matthews, "Meet the Mobile mom holding baby in viral photo from Donald Trump rally," AL.com, August 27, 2015. http://www.al.com/news/mobile/index .ssf/2015/08/meet_the_mobile_mom_in_viral_p.html.

155 *"A source of Mr. Trump's strength":* Peggy Noonan, "A Campaign Full of Surprises," *Wall Street Journal*, August 20, 2015. http://www.wsj.com /articles/a-campaign-full-of-surprises-1440111271.

15. The B-I-B-L-E. Yes, That's the Book for Me

157 *Mark Halperin and John Heilemann interviewed:* "Donald Trump: The
Full 'With All Due Respect' Interview," Bloomberg.com, August 26, 2015.
https://www.bloomberg.com/news/videos/2015–08–26/donald-trump-the
-full-with-all-due-respect-interview.

158 *While walking down the hallway of our CBN office:* Phone call and
email exchange between Donald Trump and David Brody, September
2015.

160 *"He had seen me on Fox News":* Robert Jeffress interview with the
author(s), June 2017.

161 *five hundred days later:* Technically, 495 days later.

162 *"There's so many things that you can learn from it":* Donald Trump
interview with David Brody, September 2015.

163 *"Proverbs 24 teaches that envy":* David Brody, "Donald Trump's Email
on Proverbs 24," *The Brody File,* September 17, 2015. http://blogs.cbn
.com/thebrodyfile/archive/2015/09/17.aspx?mobile=false.

164 *"The word Christmas: I love Christmas":* David Brody covered this
event for CBN. See also Tom LoBianco, "Trump brings personal bible
for religious appeal," CNN, September 26, 2015. http://www.cnn
.com/2015/09/25/politics/donald-trump-bible-values-voter/index.html.

165 *a survey of evangelical leaders:* J. C. Derrick, "Rubio, Fiorina, and Cruz
up among evangelical insiders," *WORLD,* September 24, 2015. https://
world.wng.org/2015/09/rubio_fiorina_and_cruz_up_among_evangelical
_insiders.

16. Pentecostals, Prayer, and Dinner at the Polo

166 *a tall man with orange-blond hair:* "Donald Trump Meets with Religious
Leaders, Including Robert Jeffress," YouTube, September 30, 2015. https://
www.youtube.com/watch?v=Uk4c2uoOF3o.

167 *"He has a very high regard":* Darrell Scott interview with the author(s),
June 2017.

167 *"I think you've gotten weak":* Lance Wallnau interview the author(s), June
2017. See also Lance Wallnau, "Our Meeting With Trump!," October 5,
2015. https://lancewallnau.com/our-meeting-with-trump/.

167 *"People had a lot to say to him":* Eric Bradner, "Trump meets with
Christian, Jewish leaders," CNN, September 28, 2015. http://www.cnn.com
/2015/09/28/politics/donald-trump-religious-leaders-meeting/index.html.

167 *"bring into his life a strong African-American":* "David Jeremiah,
Charismatics, Rabbi Anoint Donald Trump," YouTube, September 30, 2015.
https://www.youtube.com/watch?v=t973azt5trU.

167 *"give this man Your wisdom":* Ibid.

168 *When you have dinner with Donald Trump:* This story is a firsthand account
of a dinner at a New York restaurant that Donald and Melania Trump
invited my wife and me to, September 2015.

17. Mr. Cyrus Meets Wrecking Ball

171 *"Nothing evokes a stronger image":* Lance Wallnau interview with the author(s), August 2017. Also see www.LanceWallnau.com and Wallnau's book, *God's Chaos Candidate: Donald J. Trump and the American Unraveling* (Keller, TX: Killer Sheep Media, Inc., 2016).

173 *what the late Chuck Colson taught:* For example: Jordan J. Ballor, "Colson on Common Grace," Acton Institute PowerBlog, April 25, 2012. http:// blog.acton.org/archives/31839-colson-on-common-grace.html.

18. 3 Wings, 2 Corinthians, and February 1

178 *the Rubio campaign launched an email and video:* "Marco Rubio Says in New Ad, 'The Purpose of Our Life is to Cooperate With God's Plan,' " YouTube, January 7, 2016. https://www.youtube.com/ watch?v=ZOmnOsOjkkI. Also see Rubio's discussion with Iowa pastors: David Brody, "Marco Rubio's Sermon to Iowa Pastors Blows Them Away," CBN.com, November 30, 2015. http://www1.cbn.com/thebrody file/archive/2015/11/30/only-on-the-brody-file-marco-rubios-gospel -presentation-to.

179 *The Moore-Teetsel-Rubio email seemed to backfire:* Joseph Farah, "Marco Rubio fumbles, again," *WND*, January 1, 2016. http://www.wnd .com/2016/01/marco-rubio-fumbles-again/.

179 *Columnist Doug Wead wrote:* Doug Wead, "Rubio's Blunder Helps Trump," *Newsmax*, February 1, 2016. http://www.newsmax.com/DougWead/rubio -trump-president-election/2016/02/01/id/712119/.

179 *"I don't think we want to divide Christianity":* Samuel Smith, "Rubio Not Only Candidate With 'Billy Graham' Evangelicals, Cruz Campaign Says," *Christian Post*, January 1, 2016. http://www.christianpost.com /news/rubio-billy-graham-evangelicals-cruz-campaign-russell-moore -155844/.

179 *"Politics is about addition and multiplication":* David Lane, "Virtue and Righteousness Are Key Components of Freedom," *Charisma News*, January 19, 2016. https://www.charismanews.com/opinion/renewing -america/54540-virtue-and-righteousness-are-key-components-of -freedom.

180 *Bernie Sanders spoke the previous September:* Nick Corasaniti, "Bernie Sanders Makes Rare Appeal to Evangelicals at Liberty University," *New York Times*, September 14, 2015. https://www.nytimes.com/politics/first -draft/2015 /09/14/bernie-sanders-makes-rare-appeal-to-evangelicals-at -liberty-university/.

180 *Falwell took the stage and introduced Trump:* "Jerry Falwell Jr. Introduces Trump at Liberty University," C-SPAN, January 18, 2016. https://www .c-span.org/video/?c4577810%2Fjerry-falwell-jr-introduces-trump-liberty -university.

181 *Sarah Pulliam Bailey:* "Why Donald Trump didn't REALLY mess up when he said 'Two Corinthians' instead of 'Second Corinthians,' " GetReligion,

January 19, 2016. https://www.getreligion.org/getreligion/2016/1/18/donald
-trump-two-corinthians-at-liberty-university.

181 *"Tony Perkins wrote that out for me":* Eric Bradner, "Trump blames
Tony Perkins for '2 Corinthians,' " CNN, January 21, 2016. http://www
.cnn.com /2016/01/20/politics/donald-trump-tony-perkins-sarah-palin
/index.html.

181 *Perkins told us that he had gone:* Tony Perkins interview with the author(s),
June 2017.

183 *"Today we come to thank you":* Leonardo Blair, "Robert Jeffress Thanks
God for Trump's Selfless Desire to Be President," *Christian Post*, January
26, 2016. http://www.christianpost.com/news/robert-jeffress-thanks-god
-trump-selfless-president-155966/.

183 *"Wow, I want to thank the pastor":* Ibid.

184 *"Jimmy Carter is a great Sunday School teacher":* Jerry Falwell, "Here's
the backstory of why I endorsed Donald Trump," *Washington Post*,
January 27, 2016. https://www.washingtonpost.com/news/acts-of-faith
/wp/2016/01/27/jerry-falwell-jr-heres-the-backstory-of-why-i-endorsed
-donald-trump/?utm_term=.09d4c1310da8.

184 *"Dad was a political pragmatist":* Jerry Falwell Jr. interview with the
author(s), June 2017.

185 *"We finished second":* Gregory Krieg, "Ted Cruz triumphant, Donald
Trump gracious in defeat," CNN, February 2, 2016. http://www.cnn
.com/2016/02/01/politics/iowa-caucuses-republican-speeches/index.html.

186 *"The truth is, the evangelical vote is always splintered":* Mike Huckabee,
interviews with the author(s), June 2017.

19. Pat, the Pope, and the Palmetto State Primary

187 *Trump won New Hampshire:* CNN, February 10, 2016. http://www.cnn
.com/2016/02/09/politics/new-hampshire-primary-highlights/index
.html.

187 *"I think they should put it in the museum":* Jacqueline Alemany, "Donald
Trump tees off on the Confederate flag," CBS News, June 23, 2015.
https://www.cbsnews.com/news/donald-trump-tees-off-on-the-confederate
-flag/.

187 *TV Land removed* The Dukes of Hazzard: Julie Miller, *"The Dukes of
Hazzard* Pulled Off TV Following Confederate Flag Controversy," *Vanity
Fair*, July 2, 2015. https://www.vanityfair.com/hollywood/2015/07/dukes
-of-hazzard-confederate-flag.

188 *In my interview that day:* Donald Trump interview with David Brody,
February 2016.

189 *$60,000 per hour—every hour of every day:* Joe Carter, "Why Didn't
the Planned Parenthood Videos Change the Abortion Debate?" The
Gospel Coalition, July 15, 2017. https://www.thegospelcoalition.org
/article/why-didnt-the-planned-parenthood-videos-change-the-abortion
-debate.

191 *"Ted's been caught in a lot of lies":* Donald Trump interview with David Brody, February 2016.

191 *"A person who thinks only about":* Jim Yardley, "Pope Francis Suggests Donald Trump Is 'Not Christian,' " *New York Times*, February 18, 2016. https://www.nytimes.com/2016/02/19/world/americas/pope-francis-donald -trump-christian.html.

192 *"If and when the Vatican is attacked":* "Donald J. Trump Facebook—In response to the Pope: If and when . . . ," February 18, 2016. https://www .facebook.com/DonaldTrump/posts/10156658168535725.

194 *"You inspire us all":* Brody was the moderator at the event. Also, see the video of the event: "Donald Trump at Regent University," CBN.com, February 24, 2016. http://www1.cbn.com/content/donald-trump-regent -university.

20. #NeverTrump

195 *"Why I Will Never Vote for Donald Trump":* Peter Wehner, "Why I Will Never Vote for Donald Trump," *New York Times*, January 14, 2016. https:// www.nytimes.com/2016/01/14/opinion/campaign-stops/why-i-will-never -vote-for-donald-trump.html?mcubz=0.

196 *"the saddest political situation in my life":* Tom Strode, "Trump promises change; Baptists remain divided," *Baptist Press*, July 22, 2016. http: //www.bpnews.net/47273/trump-promises-change-baptists-remain -divided.

196 *"Mr. Trump and Secretary Clinton: An Evangelical Assessment":* Bruce Ashford, "Mr. Trump and Secretary Clinton: An Evangelical Assessment," BruceAshford.net, November 1, 2016. http://bruceashford.net/2016/mr -trump-and-secretary-clinton-an-evangelical-assessment/.

197 *"Christians Called to Resist Trump's Bigotry":* Called to Resist Bigotry— A Statement of Faithful Obedience. http://www.calledtoresist.org/.

197 *"We're responsible for what values":* Brian Kaylor interview with the author(s), June 2015.

197 *Indiana handed Trump another victory:* Stephanie Wang, "How Trump won big in Indiana," *Indianapolis Star*, November 9, 2016. http://www .indystar.com/story/news/politics/2016/11/09/how-trump-won-big -indiana/93548586/.

198 *"launched numerous vitriolic attacks":* "Donald Trump Attacks Evangelical Leader Russell Moore," *TIME*, May 9, 2016. http://time .com/4323009/donald-trump-southern-baptist-russell-moore-evangelicals -christianity/.

198 *"My first choice was Marco Rubio":* Richard Land interview with the author(s), June 2016.

199 *"No, that was foolish":* Tony Perkins interview with the author(s), June 2016.

200 *"Not someone in a certain model":* Ralph Reed interview with the author(s), June 2016.

200 *"I honestly believe that a President Trump"*: Jonah Goldberg, "Sorry, I Still Won't Ever Vote for Trump," *National Review*, May 21, 2016. http://www.nationalreview.com/article/435686/donald-trump-republican -nomination-i-still-wont-vote-him.

21. Coalesce or Two Evils?

201 *"restore faith to its proper mantle"*: Brody covered this event for CBN. Or see "Trump takes aim at Clinton in appeal to evangelicals," *USA Today*, June 10, 2016. https://www.usatoday.com/story/news/politics/elections/2016/06/10 /donald-trump-faith-freedom-coalition-hillary-clinton/85691020/#.

201 *"That's the way it is—and it's been"*: Donald Trump interview with the author(s), June 2016.

201 *"the Christian conservative confab's shameless"*: Jennifer Rubin, "The Christian conservative confab's shameless Trump cheerleading," *Washington Post*, June 13, 2016. https://www.washingtonpost.com/blogs /right-turn/wp/2016/06/13/the-christian-conservative-confabs-shameless -trump-cheerleading/?utm_term=.28bd82ebd0f3.

202 *"I had an advantage over other"*: All of the Ralph Reed quotations come from his interview with the author(s), June 2017.

205 *"I was really concerned about the decline"*: Johnnie Moore interview with the author(s), August 2017.

206 *"I always say don't let people take advantage"*: "Donald Trump at Liberty University Convocation," YouTube, September 25, 2012. https://www .youtube.com/watch?v=Gvl2y34puhY.

206 *"Of course, as a Bible-believing evangelical"*: Johnnie Moore, "It's true, Christians should be tough—like Jesus," Fox News, October 7, 2012. http:// www.foxnews.com/opinion/2012/10/07/donald-trump-right-christians -should-be-tough-like-jesus.html.

207 *"All of a sudden it turned out"*: Tony Perkins interview with the author(s), June 2017.

207 *"Up until that point, there were several"*: Mike Huckabee interview with the author(s), June 2017.

208 *"All the factors say go, but my heart"*: Frank James, "Mike Huckabee: 'All The Factors Say Go, But My Heart Says No,' " NPR, May 14, 2011. http:// www.npr.org/sections/itsallpolitics/2011/05/14/136318484/mike-huckabee -all-the-factors-say-go-but-my-heart-says-no.

208 *"I'm Donald Trump and this is a special announcement"*: "Donald Trump says Mike Huckabee would be a terrific President," YouTube, November 17, 2016. https://www.youtube.com/watch?v=S42sOKMjocM.

209 *"has a God consciousness about him that's real."*: Mike Huckabee interview with the author(s), June 2017.

209 *"Trump is not the guy you're going to see"*: Michael Cohen interview with the author(s), August 2017.

210 *"God's man to lead our great nation"*: Sarah Posner, "How Donald Trump Divided and Conquered Evangelicals," *Rolling Stone*, July 21, 2016. http://

www.rollingstone.com/politics/features/how-donald-trump-divided-and
-conquered-evangelicals-w430119.

210 *"Sir, if you are elected president":* Bob Eschliman, "Dr. James
Dobson: What Really Happened In My Meeting With Donald Trump,"
Charisma News, August 5, 2016. https://www.charismanews.com
/politics/events/59073-dr-james-dobson-describes-his-meeting-with
-donald-trump.

211 *"No, in my understanding":* Samuel Rodriguez interview with the
author(s), June 2016.

22. Cleveland Rocks . . . and Prays

221 *"I would like to thank the evangelical community":* "Donald Trump's
speech at the Republican convention, as prepared for delivery," CNN,
July 22, 2016. http://www.cnn.com/2016/07/22/politics/donald-trump
-rnc-speech-text/index.html.

23. Pastors and Pews

223 *Omar Mateen called Orlando's 911:* Gal Tziperman Lotan, Rene Stutzman,
and David Harris, "Audio of Omar Mateen's 911 calls during Pulse
massacre released," *Orlando Sentinel*, October 31, 2016. http://www
.orlandosentinel.com/news/pulse-orlando-nightclub-shooting/os-omar
-mateen-pulse-911-calls-20161031-story.html.

223 *CNN's Anderson Cooper and the* New York Times*:* Jeremy Peters and
Lizette Alvarez, "After Orlando, a Political Divide on Gay Rights Still
Stands," *New York Times*, June 15, 2016; and "Anderson Cooper grills
Bondi on LGBT support," YouTube, June 14, 2016. https://www.youtube
.com/watch?time_continue=1&v=BkSUE7esjG8.

223 *Trump tweeted:* Rebecca Savransky, "Trump thanks supporters for praise
about 'being right' after Orlando shooting," *The Hill,* June 12, 2016. http://
thehill.com/blogs/ballot-box/presidential-races/283193-trump-thanks
-supporters-for-congratulating-him-on-being.

223 *"some of the most hateful anti-LGBT persons":* Alex Leary, "Rubio defends
appearance at religious conference critics say is antigay," *Tampa Bay Times*,
August 4, 2016. http://www.tampabay.com/blogs/the-buzz-florida-politics
/rubio-defends-appearance-at-religious-conference-critics-say-is-anti-gay
/2288181.

224 *"There's no way you can give that speech":* Mike Huckabee interview with
the author(s), June 2017.

224 *"I've explained it in more detail":* "Donald Trump Addresses Evangelical
Leaders Orlando Florida," C-SPAN, August 11, 2016. https://www
.c-span.org/video/?413877–1/donald-trump-addresses-evangelical-leaders
-orlando-florida.

224 *"We all knew he was saying it in jest":* Johnnie Moore interview with the
author(s), August 2017.

224 *"I just spoke up quite boldly":* James Robison interview with the author(s), August 2017.

225 *"Mr. Trump said, 'Thank you' ":* Richard Land interview with the author(s), July 2017.

225 *"good first step":* Jennifer Jacobs, "Trump Goes Traditional With Florida Meeting of Evangelical Leaders," Bloomberg, August 9, 2016. https://www .bloomberg.com/news/articles/2016–08–09/trump-to-meet-privately-with -700-evangelical-leaders-in-florida-this-week.

225 *"didn't make himself out":* David Lane interview with the author(s), June 2016.

225 *Lane received an email:* All quotes in this anecdote come from our interview with David Lane, June 2016.

228 *"Unless politicians see scalps":* Gary Miller, "8 things pastors need to know if we are to save America," American Renewal Project, July 21, 2015. http://theamericanrenewalproject.org/2013/09/seven-things-pastors-can -learn-from-david-lane/.

229 *"How White Evangelicals Won the 2016 Election":* Doug Wead, "How White Evangelicals Won the 2016 Election," Doug Wead The Blog, February 25, 2017. https://dougwead.wordpress.com/2017/02/25/how -white-evangelicals-won-the-2016-election/.

230 *"we've been blowing this":* Chad Connelly interview with the author(s), June 2016.

24. What the Hell Do You Have to Lose?

232 *"Paul, I'm going to have to get back":* Tony Perkins interview with the author(s), June 2016.

234 *"The first thing he thought of":* Various Michael Cohen interviews with David Brody.

234 *"But: Trump got to Louisiana before Obama or Clinton":* Rod Dreher, "Populism And The Great Flood," *American Conservative*, August 19, 2016. http://www.theamericanconservative.com/dreher/trump-populism -flood/.

235 *"If Donald Trump wins this election":* Chris Gacek, "Trump Visit to Louisiana May Be Seen as the Turning Point in the 2016 Presidential Election," FRC Action, April 24, 2016. https://blog.frcaction.org/2016/08 /trump-visit-louisiana-may-be-seen-turning-point-2016-presidential-election/.

235 *"What did you lose":* "Flood Survivor Gets Tearful as Trump Visits Louisiana," ABC News, August 2016. http://abcnews.go.com/Politics /video/flood-survivor-tearful-trump-visits-louisiana-41515647.

236 *"Tonight, I'm asking for the vote":* Our transcription of "Donald Trump in Dimondale Michigan FULL Speech," YouTube, August 19, 2016. https:// www.youtube.com/watch?v=XYSpjMlH2tE&list=PLzAjR5gW2zMrWsZX BCLUXAM_YCVCsrewl&index=2.

237 *"When he got out of the SUV":* Bishop Wayne Jackson interview with the author(s), August 2017.

237 *"amazing experience"*: "Donald Trump Speaks African-American Church Detroit, September 3, 2016," C-SPAN, September 3, 2016. https://www.c -span.org/video/?414743–1%2Fdonald-trump-speaks-africanamerican -church-detroit&start=470.

238 *"For centuries, the African-American church"*: "Donald Trump addresses African-American congregation in Detroit," *POLITICO*, September 3, 2016. http://www.politico.com/story/2016/09/donald-trump-detroit -transcript-227713.

239 *"I love my people"*: Niraj Warikoo, "Detroit bishop who hosted Trump will join his swearing-in ceremony," *USA Today*, December 29, 2016. https:// www.usatoday.com/story/news/local/michigan/detroit/2016/12/28/detroit -bishop-take-part-trumps-swearing—ceremony/95933138/.

240 *"I love his movies"*: "Donald Trump Addresses Values Voter Summit," C-SPAN, September 9, 2016. https://www.c-span.org/video/?415005–101 /donald-trump-addresses-values-voter-summit.

240 *"It's the power to make all of us"*: Ibid., as well as the remainder of the DJT speech in this section.

242 *"truly great American patriot"*: Rebecca Morin, "Trump honors 'true patriot' Phyllis Schlafly at her funeral," *POLITICO*, September 10, 2016. http://www.politico.com/story/2016/09/donald-trump-phyllis-schlafly -funeral-227994.

242 *"You know, to just be grossly generalistic"*: "Hillary Clinton Transcript: 'Basket of Deplorables' Comment," *TIME*, September 10, 2016. http://time .com/4486502/hillary-clinton-basket-of-deplorables-transcript/.

242 *"bitterly cling to their guns and God"*: Ben Smith, "Obama on small-town Pa.: Clinging to religion, guns, xenophobia," *POLITICO*, April 11, 2008. http://www.politico.com/blogs/ben-smith/2008/04/obama-on-small-town -pa-clinging-to-religion-guns-xenophobia-007737.

243 *"I believe in providence"*: Mike Pence interview with David Brody, August 2016.

243 *"I believe you're going to be the next president"*: Robert Jeffress interview with the authors, June 2016.

25. What Happens in Vegas

245 *"They all were saying about Trump"*: Samuel Rodriguez interview with the author(s), June 2016.

246 *"Are you sure you want me to sit there"*: Pasqual Urrabazo interview with the author(s), July 2017. All Urrabazo quotes are derived from interview(s) and/or personal correspondence with the author(s).

248 *"Listen, we'd love for him to come see our school"*: Paul Goulet interview with the author(s), June 2016. All Goulet quotes are derived from interview(s) and/or personal correspondence with the author(s).

250 *"About twenty seconds after the* Access Hollywood *tape"*: Richard Land interview with the author(s), July 2017.

250 *"decided that he was going to judge the one area"*: Lance Wallnau interview with the author(s), August 2017.

250 *"We did not invite any campaign people":* Johnnie Moore interview with the author(s), August 2017.

251 *"We all believed he was a different person":* Johnnie Moore interview with the author(s), July 2017.

251 *"mediate a meeting between then candidate Trump":* Robert Jeffress interview with the author(s), June 2017.

251 *"Never Trump is our best chance":* Voddie Baucham, "NEVER TRUMP is our best chance to actually make America great again," *The Gospel Applied,* October 24, 2016. http://www.gospelapplied.com/never-trump-movement/.

251 *"Donald Trump has created an excruciating moment":* R. Albert Mohler Jr., "Donald Trump has created an excruciating moment for evangelicals," *Washington Post,* October 9, 2016. https://www.washingtonpost.com/news/acts-of-faith/wp/2016/10/09/donald-trump-has-created-an-excruciating-moment-for-evangelicals/.

251 *"It was a pretty unforgettable weekend":* Ralph Reed interview with the author(s), June 2017.

253 *"That's exactly what Donald Trump said":* Bradford Richardson, "Recordings back Trump assertions on late-term abortions," *Washington Times,* June 20, 2017. http://m.washingtontimes.com/news/2017/jun/20/planned-parenthood-late-term-abortion-assertions-b/.

254 *"I promised Pat, and I'm gonna do it":* Pat Robertson interview with the author(s), July 2016.

256 *"Have you lost a little weight":* Donald Trump interview with David Brody, October 2016.

256 *"Donald Trump wants to come to church tomorrow":* Paul Goulet interview with the author(s), June 2016.

257 *"worshipping God, just like a normal person":* Pasqual Urrabazo interview with the author(s), July 2017.

26. The Art of the Unreal

259 *"I don't know, Jerry, these exit polls look":* Jerry Falwell interview with the author(s), June 2017.

259 *"I think it was a very important victory":* Donald Trump interview with David Brody, August 2017.

260 *"President Trump represented to the evangelical community":* Robert Costa interview with the author(s), August 2017.

260 *"Don't use religious talk":* James Robison interview with the author(s), July 2017. Except where noted, the Robison quotes in this chapter come from our interview with him.

261 *"He asked me to help him check":* Ibid.

261 *"It's the best Bible study":* Jennifer Wishon, "Bible Studies at the White House: Who's Inside This Spiritual Awakening?" CBN, July 31, 2017. http://www1.cbn.com/cbnnews/politics/2017/july/bible-studies-at-the-white-house-whos-at-the-heart-of-this-spiritual-awakening.

263 *"The first time you and I talked":* James Robison, "My Message and Prayer

for the President," The Stream, January 29, 2017. https://stream.org/my
-prayer-for-the-president/.

265 *"a Southern Baptist pastor who has history"*: Sarah Pulliam Bailey, " 'God
is not against building walls!' The sermon Trump heard from Robert
Jeffress before his inauguration," *Washington Post*, January 20, 2017.
https://www.washingtonpost.com/news/acts-of-faith/wp/2017/01/20/god
-is-not-against-building-walls-the-sermon-donald-trump-heard-before-his
-inauguration/?utm_term=.b50aba13c47d.

265 *"You know, many administrations would have"*: Robert Jeffress interview
with the author(s), June 2017.

265 *"I thought there was just some"*: Ibid. Also see transcript of "When God
Chooses a Leader—Inauguration Day Message," First Baptist Dallas,
January 22, 2017. http://www.firstdallas.org/blog/when-god-chooses-a
-leader-dr-jeffress-inauguration-day-message/.

266 *"He's a great guy and is very much"*: Donald Trump interview with David
Brody, August 2017.

266 *"praying and fasting and Bible-believing church"*: Wayne Jackson
interview with the author(s), August 2017.

267 *"One of the greatest honors of my life"*: Samuel Rodriguez interview with
the author(s), June 2017.

268 *"In Proverbs 21:1, you instruct us"*: "Invocation by Pastor Paula White,"
CNN, January 20, 2017. http://www.cnn.com/2017/01/20/politics/donald
-trump-inauguration-paula-white/index.html.

27. Gorsuch a Time as This

270 *"One of the reasons I changed"*: Donald Trump interview with David
Brody, April 2011.

270 *"That was a very pivotal moment"*: Kellyanne Conway interview with
David Brody, August 2017.

271 *"On the life question"*: Mike Huckabee interview with the author(s), June
2017.

271 *"reinstating the pro-life 'Mexico City Policy' "*: Kimberly Leonard,
"Trump administration broadens 'Mexico City' policy against abortion,"
Washington Examiner, May 15, 2017. http://www.washingtonexaminer
.com/trump-administration-broadens-mexico-city-policy-against-abortion
/article/2623143.

272 *"You've got all this money"*: Jerry Johnson interview with the author(s),
June 2017.

272 *"Vice President Pence was standing"*: Kellyanne Conway interview with
David Brody, August 2017.

273 *"I think they're highly approving of him"*: Hugh Hewitt interview with
David Brody, July 2017.

273 *"game changers for the pro-life movement"*: Paul Strand, "100 Days
of Unexpected Victories: How Trump's Been a Game Changer for Pro-
Life Movement," CBN, April 29, 2017. http://www1.cbn.com/cbnnews/

politics/2017/april/100-days-of-unexpected-victories-how-trumps-been-a
-game-changer-for-pro-life-movement.

273 *"It's very clear that the government minister"*: Jerry Johnson interview
with the author(s), June 2016.

274 *"For too long, Christians have been excluded"*: Michele Bachmann
interview with the author(s), July 2017.

275 *"I've had a lot of talk"*: Harry Jackson interview with the author(s), June
2016.

275 *"I commented to the President"*: Jerry Falwell interview with the author(s),
June 2016.

275 *"My impression of him in a private setting"*: Robert Costa interview with
the author(s), August 2017.

276 *"You can call me anything you want"*: Donald Trump interview with the
author(s), February 2017.

277 *"I do believe he wants to be"*: Hugh Hewitt interview with the author(s),
August 2017.

277 *"He wanted this strict constructionist"*: Kellyanne Conway interview with
David Brody, August 2017.

278 *"I've never seen a President or a presidential"*: Darrell Scott interview
with the author(s), June 2017.

278 *"I could never even begin to imagine"*: Paula White interview with the
author(s), August 2017.

279 *"When he heard about that"*: Mike Pence interview with the author(s),
September 2017.

279 *"Here is the most powerful man"*: Robert Jeffress interview with the
author(s), June 2017.

280 *"He declares his faith in Jesus"*: Pat Robertson interview with the
author(s), July 2017.

28. You've Got a Friend in Me

281 *"My Hope Is Built"*: Edward Mote, "My Hope Is Built on Nothing Less."
http://www.lutheran-hymnal.com/lyrics/tlh370.htm.

281 *"He and I have gotten to be very close"*: All Mike Pence quotes in this
chapter are from the interviews with the author(s), September 2017.

284 *"Trump sees Pence as a 'spiritual person' "*: Oval Office interview with
Donald Trump by the author(s), September 2017.

286 *"I've always felt the need to pray"*: David Brody, "Brody File Exclusive
Interview: President Trump Relying on God Now More Than Ever," CBN,
January 30, 2017. http://www1.cbn.com/thebrodyfile/archive/2017/01/27
/brody-file-exclusive-interview-president-trump-relying-on-god-now-more
-than-ever.

288 *"If wisdom gets in the room"*: James Robison interview with the author(s),
August 2017.

288 *"I think Trump's going to be"*: Eric Metaxas interview with the author(s),
August 2017.

289 *"It's the Most High God":* Michele Bachmann interview with the author(s), August 2016.

29. Riyadh, Jerusalem, and Rome

290 *"David, oh my goodness! How are you?":* Discussion between Ivanka and Jared Kushner and David Brody, May 2017.

293 *"If you choose the path of terror":* "President Trump's Speech to the Arab Islamic American Summit," The White House, May 21, 2017. https://www .whitehouse.gov/the-press-office/2017/05/21/president-trumps-speech-arab -islamic-american-summit.

293 *"There's something there that teaches":* Donald Trump interview with David Brody, April 2011.

295 *"It was the most savage crime":* "Visit of President Donald J. Trump to Yad Vashem," Yad Vashem, May 23, 2017. http://www.yadvashem.org/yv/trump /index.asp.

296 *"I was deeply moved by my visit":* "Remarks by President Trump and Prime Minister Netanyahu in Joint Statement," The White House, May 22, 2017. https://www.whitehouse.gov/the-press-office/2017/05/22/remarks-president -trump-and-prime-minister-netanyahu-joint-statement.

296 *"This city, like no other place":* "Remarks by President Trump at the Israel Museum," The White House, May 23, 2017. https://www.whitehouse.gov /the-press-office/2017/05/23/remarks-president-trump-israel-museum.

296 *"In this spirit of hope":* "Remarks by President Trump and President Abbas of the Palestinian Authority in Joint Statements," The White House, May 23, 2017. https://www.whitehouse.gov/the-press-office /2017/05/23/remarks-president-trump-and-president-abbas-palestinian -authority-joint.

298 *"The joy of the gospel fills the hearts":* Pope Francis, *The Joy of the Gospel: Evangelii Gaudium* (United States Conference of Catholic Bishops, 2013), 9.

299 *"you have a unique personality":* David Rutz, "Egyptian President Tells Trump He's 'Capable of the Impossible,' " *Washington Free Beacon*, May 21, 2017. http://freebeacon.com/national-security/egyptian-president -trump-is-capable-of-the-impossible/.

30. Give Me Liberty

300 *"I think evangelicals have found":* Ed Mazza, "Christian Leader: Trump Is 'Dream President' for Evangelicals," *Huffington Post*, April 30, 2017. http:// www.huffingtonpost.com/entry/jerry-falwell-jr-dream-president-trump_us _5906950fe4b05c3976807a08.

301 *"It's been a little over a year":* "President Trump Delivers Liberty University Commencement Address," C-SPAN, May 13, 2017. https:// www.c-span.org/video/?428429–1%2Fpresident-trump-delivers-liberty -university-commencement-address.

302 *"He got at least two standing":* Jerry Falwell interview with the author(s), June 2017.

303 *"There's a tradition that goes back":* Jerry Falwell Jr. interview with the author(s), June 2017.

304 *"My purpose is to bring men":* Paula White interview with the author(s), August 2017.

304 *"very straight talk":* Heather Sells, "Inaugural Pastor Blasts Critics of President's Evangelical Advisory Board," CBN News, August 29, 2017. https://www1.cbn.com/cbnnews/us/2017/august/inaugural-pastor-blasts -critics-of-presidents-evangelical-advisory-board.

304 *"the most famous lines":* Steven P. Miller, *The Age of Evangelicalism: America's Born-Again Years* (Oxford: Oxford University Press, 2016), 62. See also Scott Lamb, *Huckabee: The Authorized Biography* (Nashville, TN: Thomas Nelson, 2015), 142.

304 *"I know this is nonpartisan":* Ibid.

304 *"From that time on":* James Robison interview with the author(s), August 2017. The block quote comes from James Robison and Michael Brown, "The Church, The Nation, Donald Trump and the Future of Freedom," The Stream, November 2, 2016, https://stream.org/the-church-the-nation -trump/.

305 *"It's ridiculous":* Eric Metaxas interview with the author(s), August 2017.

306 *"I think we pray very specific":* Johnnie Moore interview with the author(s), August 2017.

306 *"I came away from that meeting":* Michele Bachmann interview with the author(s), July 2017.

306 *"theological malpractice that borders on heresy":* Abbie Bennett, "Praying for Trump 'borders on heresy,' says prominent pastor," *Miami Herald,* June 17, 2017. http://www.miamiherald.com/news/nation-world/national /article161778348.html.

307 *"Trump has forced them":* John Fea, "Trump threatens to change the course of American Christianity," *Washington Post,* July 17, 2017. https://www .washingtonpost.com/news/acts-of-faith/wp/2017/07/17/trump-threatens-to -change-the-course-of-american-christianity/.

307 *"The idea that someone would pray":* Daniel Burke, "Why Trump puts his faith in evangelicals," CNN, July 13, 2017. http://www.cnn.com/2017/07/13 /politics/trump-evangelicals/index.html.

307 *"The Gospel is not being compromised":* Samuel Smith, "Evangelical Leaders Aren't Selling Themselves to Trump, Ronnie Floyd Says," *Christian Post,* July 21, 2017. http://www.christianpost.com/news /evangelical-leaders-arent-selling-themselves-to-trump-ronnie-floyd -says-192714/.

308 *"a dinner of shrimp scampi":* Elizabeth Dias, "National Day of Prayer: Donald Trump White House Dinner," *TIME,* May 3, 2017. http://time .com/4766485/national-day-prayer-white-house-dinner/.

308 *"At the end of the dinner":* Robert Jeffress interview with the author(s), June 2017.

308 *"Presidential Executive Order":* For text see "Presidential Executive Order Promoting Free Speech and Religious Liberty," The White House,

May 4, 2017. https://www.whitehouse.gov/the-press-office/2017/05 /04/presidential-executive-order-promoting-free-speech-and-religious -liberty.

308 *"Eighty percent is better than":* Sarah Pulliam Bailey, "Many religious freedom advocates are actually disappointed with Trump's executive order," *Washington Post*, May 5, 2017. https://www.washingtonpost.com /news/acts-of-faith/wp/2017/05/05/many-religious-freedom-advocates-are -disappointed-with-trumps-executive-order/.

308 *"a remarkable first step":* Jim Garlow, "Some God-fearing, Bible-believing people," Facebook, May 6, 2017. https://www.facebook.com/jimgarlow /posts/10212684594887063.

309 *"removes a sword of Damocles":* Emma Green, "Why Trump's Executive Order on Religious Liberty Left Many Conservatives Dissatisfied," *The Atlantic*, May 4, 2017. https://www.theatlantic.com/politics/archive /2017/05/religious-freedom-executive-order/525354/.

309 *"nothing—zip, nada":* Rod Dreher, "Trump's Phony Religious Liberty EO," *The American Conservative,* May 4, 2017. http://www .theamericanconservative.com/dreher/trumps-phony-religious-liberty-eo/.

309 *"As long as I'm President":* Donald Trump, "Remarks by President Trump at the Faith and Freedom Coalition's Road to Majority Conference," The White House, June 9, 2017. https://www.whitehouse.gov/the-press-office /2017/06/08/remarks-president-trump-faith-and-freedom-coalitions-road -majority.

309 *"Now we want to go through Congress":* Donald Trump interview with David Brody, August 2017.

309 *"We had Wolf at our 2014 Summit":* Tony Perkins interview with the author(s), June 2017.

310 *"No, I didn't have to raise the issues once":* Johnnie Moore interview with the author(s), June 2017.

311 *"There's all kinds of things":* Ibid.

311 *"We thank God every day":* Robert Jeffress, "President Trump Tribute Veterans Kennedy Center, July 1, 2017," C-SPAN, July 1, 2017. https:// www.c-span.org/video/?430774–2%2Fpresident-trump-tribute-veterans -kennedy-center.

311 *"You fought hard for me":* Donald Trump, "Remarks by President Trump at the Faith and Freedom Coalition's Road to Majority Conference," The White House, June 9, 2017. https://www.whitehouse.gov/the-press -office/2017/06/08/remarks-president-trump-faith-and-freedom-coalitions -road-majority.

311 *"Evangelicals are a tool":* Sarah Posner, "Amazing Disgrace," *New Republic*, March 20, 2017. https://newrepublic.com/article/140961/amazing -disgrace-donald-trump-hijacked-religious-right.

311 *"Trump threatens to change the course":* John Fea, "Trump threatens to change the course of American Christianity," *Washington Post*, July 17, 2017. https://www.washingtonpost.com/news/acts-of-faith/wp/2017/07/17 /trump-threatens-to-change-the-course-of-american-christianity/.

312 *"In the first meeting, I told Mr. Trump":* James Robison and Michael Brown, "The Church, The Nation, Donald Trump and the Future of Freedom," The Stream, November 2, 2016. https://stream.org/the-church -the-nation-trump/.

313 *"When confronted with American sexual libertarianism":* Russell Moore, "The Baptist Headway," *Touchstone: A Journal of Mere Christianity,* April 2006. http://www.touchstonemag.com/archives/article.php?id=19 –03–033-f.

313 *"The greater problem we see today":* Robison and Brown, "The Church, The Nation, Donald Trump and the Future of Freedom."

314 *"If you look at the electorate":* Ralph Reed interview with the author(s), June 2017.

Index

About the Authors

DAVID BRODY is an Emmy Award–winning, thirty-year veteran news journalist who is currently the chief political correspondent for CBN News, host of the show *Faith Nation*, and the author of *The Brody File*, a respected national blog featuring top newsmakers that explores key issues relating to faith and politics. He is also a political analyst for Fox News, CNN, and MSNBC, and has appeared frequently as a roundtable panelist on NBC's *Meet the Press*.

SCOTT LAMB is a vice president of Liberty University, a Baptist minister, and a columnist for the *Washington Times*. He has authored three biographies with HarperCollins, including *Pujols: More Than the Game* and *Huckabee: The Authorized Biography*.